THE
FALLING
SEASON

INSIDE THE LIFE AND DEATH DRAMA OF
ASPEN'S MOUNTAIN RESCUE TEAM

HAL CLIFFORD

**THE
MOUNTAINEERS**

Published by
The Mountaineers
1001 SW Klickitat Way, Suite 201
Seattle, WA 98134

First edition 1995 by Cloud Cap. Second edition by The Mountaineers
Books: first printing 1998, second printing 2000, third printing 2004.

Cover design by Jennifer Shontz

Cover photographs (front): *Colorado Rockies* © John Russell/
    Network Aspen; (back): *Lifting patient up over the edge, high angle
    rescue* © Hal Clifford

Manufactured in the United States

Library of Congress Cataloging-in-Publication Data Available

ISBN 0-89886-633-2

INTRODUCTION

ON JULY 28, 1992, I sat down at a storefront lunch shop in Basalt, Colorado, with Chris Myers, who was then the president of Mountain Rescue-Aspen. We ate sandwiches under an umbrella by a small parking lot while I explained why I wanted to write this book. It was a hot day. He listened carefully and watched intently as I tried to describe what I hoped to accomplish, how I wanted to explore Mountain Rescue-Aspen and write an honest account of what I discovered. This would be a book, I said, that I hoped would appeal to anyone intrigued by the human condition and our relationships to one another. I talked until he finished his sandwich.

In order for me to accomplish what I set out to do, Chris saw that I would have to join the rescue team. It was not possible, either legally or technically, for me to observe everything the team does without being a participant. The fly-on-the-wall option was out. Since that summer lunch with Chris I have become a full member of Mountain Rescue-Aspen and I remain actively involved with the team and its work. I count team members and sheriff's office officials as my friends, some as good friends. For me to pretend that I have been an unbiased observer would be false; I have enormous respect, admiration, and fondness for many of the people who are in these pages.

Yet, from the time I first walked into Mountain Rescue-Aspen at 630 West Main Street, I have been a writer working on a book. I freely acknowledge my biases, but I have tried to remain true to my original goals. The members of Mountain Rescue-Aspen trusted me to tell their story as honestly and forthrightly as I know how. I hope I have succeeded in accomplishing that, if only in a small way.

—*Hal Clifford*
Aspen, Colorado

ACKNOWLEDGMENTS

MANY PEOPLE MADE this book possible. First and foremost were the members of Mountain Rescue-Aspen. They had no reason to allow me to write this book, and at times I wonder why they did. All of them deserve my thanks. Many sat for long interviews, some five or six times. All of these people deserve my gratitude: Marion Berg, Ron Bracken, Jon Gibans, Lori Hart, Debbie Kelly, Van Kyzar, Josh Landis, Dave Lofland, Tom McCabe, Scott Messina, Jace Michael, Chris Myers, Ray Peritz, David Swersky, John Zell, and Bob Zook.

Others who were equally gracious in fulfilling my requests for interviews include Dick Arnold, Steve Crockett, Bob Braudis, Katie Gartner (now Meyers), Julie Mace, Kristina Mace, Jim Ward, and Mariela Zell.

Additional assistance was provided by Suzanne Martens of High Country Critical Incident Stress Management Team; Killeen Russell, Aspen Skiing Company; Darren Greve; and the staff at the Aspen Historical Society.

A handful of the names in this book were changed; most were not.

I was ably assisted in the text by Carol Mann, Shirley Christine, Lisa Zuniga Carlsen, and Keating Coffey. Most significantly, without the inspiration, unremitting support, encouragement, and countless rereadings provided by Debbie Ayers and Marty Carlock, this book would never have come to be.

PHOTOGRAPHS

CONTENTS

THE FALLING SEASON

WE WERE getting banged around a lot. The [rescue] litter was flying around. And since Colin was exhausted, he couldn't hold the litter anymore. We went up a little further, and I saw Ray Peritz on the second line. We were coming up toward the second line. I was like, "Ray, we need your help. Colin is shot." So he's trying to maneuver around. Then we started going up toward the scree. They were uphauling fast and I had my radio in a pouch. I'm trying to pull the litter out, but a big root gets her in the side, and she starts screaming. We see it, but they keep pulling, and it's impaling her in the side. I can't get to my radio fast enough because I'm trying to pull her out, so I'm screaming for it to stop. I finally get to my radio and I say, "We're going to need help down here." Colin can't hold it anymore, I'm getting exhausted from trying to maneuver the whole thing myself, so we ask for Ray's help. He's trying to maneuver and

move rocks and everything else, rocks are dropping on her, we're trying to cover her up, we're getting pelted with rocks.
—*John Zell*

Gwen Garcelon and Craig Wheeless hike up the East Snowmass Creek Trail into the Snowmass-Maroon Bells Wilderness on
June 6, 1993, looking for a picnic spot. But the snowpack still
lies heavy and the high valley remains in winter. Unable to proceed more than a few miles, they turn around and are headed
back to their car when they spot a beautiful thirty-foot waterfall
in a small gorge below the trail. Seeking a place for lunch, Gwen,
twenty-eight years old and a recent arrival to Aspen, starts toward it down a steep slope dusted with loose scree and a few
low bushes. Suddenly she slips and begins cartwheeling down
the pitch toward a cliff. She launches off the precipice and falls
forty feet through the air, landing in the shallow waters of the
creek, a translucent and frigid brook brimming with snowmelt.
Craig, rushing down another route, finds Gwen facedown in the
stream near the base of the waterfall. He pulls her out and, by
slapping and shaking her, gets her to start breathing again.

Craig begins climbing frantically out of the gorge back toward
the trail, scrambling on all fours. Halfway up, a handhold comes
loose, sending him tumbling dozens of feet backward into the
creek. His forehead is badly gashed and he is bruised. As he
staggers upright in the stream he sees that Gwen has rolled back
into the watercourse and is facedown. Craig drags her out and
starts her breathing yet again, struggles up to the trail, and, unable to run due to his own injuries, hobbles a mile to the trailhead and his car.

David Swersky, a forty-six-year-old dentist and former silver-
smith, is driving down the Roaring Fork Valley from Aspen, almost at his Woody Creek home, when his Mountain Rescue
pager squeals. For these two weeks it is his turn to run rescues.
The brief message from the sheriff's office dispatcher on the
pager tells him enough; he abandons his groceries in the kitchen
and orders an all-call page to the team. Across Colorado's Roaring Fork Valley, as an overcast sky drifts in and the afternoon air
begins to cool, forty-five people pause and listen.

"All Mountain Rescue members, call the cabin for a high-angle rescue in Snowmass Creek."

I drop the hose at our communal vegetable garden and bolt three blocks home on my mountain bike. John Zell answers the phone in the Mountain Rescue cabin, a beige, split-level Panabode at the west end of Aspen's cottonwood-lined Main Street. He is breathless and his voice tight. "Can you get here right away?"

"Five minutes," I say and slam the phone. No time to change into rescue gear; I go in shorts. I grab my thirty-pound rescue pack and lumber down the steps to the Subaru. The cabin is only about a mile and a half away across the onetime silver-mining town, but summer tourist traffic is thick, and it is a full five minutes before I brake hard at the curb. The red Rescue 1 truck idles in the alley. "High angle, let's go," John yells. I yank a radio from the charger rack, then throw my pack in the rear compartment and myself into the backseat of the six-passenger Chevy truck. In less than two minutes we are on the road.

John, a thirty-five-year-old bartender and part-time mountain guide, drives. Debbie Kelly, thirty-six, a compact, powerful ski guide and landscaper, sits in front. Lithe, blond, forty-five-year-old Linda Koones, a landscaper and graphic artist, has fallen in the backseat with me, along with Ray Peritz, an athletic, balding, forty-six-year-old hotel broker. Traffic out of town is heavy and we have fourteen miles to go, first down the valley's two-lane highway, then up a side canyon to the creek behind the Snowmass ski area.

The Chevy's cab is full of noise. Linda passes around water. The radio squawks with urgent voices as volunteers converging from several directions grind gears, squeal around corners, and try to discern what is happening. John, pounding on the steering wheel in frustration, forces a half-dozen cars off the highway as he hammers the big Chevy and its thousand pounds of rescue equipment down Colorado State Highway 82 at seventy miles an hour.

Up above to the west, Gwen Garcelon lies in the spray of a beautiful waterfall.

Nobody in Rescue 1 knows Gwen's name. Most won't until the next day, when they read it in the papers. In the adrenaline

and rush of a developing situation, rescuers gather their knowledge in snippets. The team does much of its operating in the
dark during the incipient stages of an emergency. The imperative
now is to move. Moving is easier on the psyche than waiting.

Volunteer firefighters from the Snowmass Village ski resort respond first because they are closest. One hikes directly up the
creek bed until he finds Gwen; two others rappel down ropes
from the point on the trail where she fell. A radio report comes
back from their paramedic: Gwen is alive. "Shaky, but alive,"
David Swersky says. Grinding up toward the Snowmass ski area
in Rescue 1, we listen on the radio to the first, shouted medical
assessment: "possible flail chest." That means multiple broken
ribs on one side and could mean a lot more: fluid in the lung, a
punctured lung, even pneumothorax, where air seeping into the
chest cavity presses on the heart and can stop it.

John thumps and rattles the truck down a twisting dirt road
on the west side of the Snowmass ski area, nearly running a couple of unwary mountain bikers off the side. David Swersky and a
pair of Pitkin County deputies wait at the trailhead to brief us.
The Snowmass firefighters, David says, are dressed in heat-
draining, water-absorbent cotton and are carrying only basic
medical gear and a ratty wire Stokes litter. They are far out of
their element. It will be up to us to get Gwen to the ambulance
idling at the trailhead.

We throw open the rescue truck's seven gear doors and load
up: fifty-foot anchor ropes, three-hundred-foot haul rope, two-
hundred-foot belay rope, spider for the litter, uphaul bag, extra
webbing bag, brake bag, and, lastly, "the wheel," a cumbersome
contraption of steel and rubber that clamps onto the bottom of a
litter and allows us to roll a victim down a trail. Together with
my personal pack, I carry close to sixty pounds. Ray, Debbie,
John, and I set off as fast as we can, climbing an old, switch-
backing jeep trail through the dark timber of subalpine fir. Everybody is tired: Debbie had hiked and skied the high ridges of
Independence Pass that morning; John and Ray rode their mountain bikes up the back side of the Aspen Mountain ski area. We
hike with heads down, hands on hips, eyes on the legs in front,
steaming up this lung-searing, sweat-pumping climb.

There isn't much talking. Ray leads with the litter wheel perched on his pack, bent over like a coolie. After a few minutes he asks John if he wants to pass. "No, I'm dying," John gasps. "Debbie, you go ahead."

"I'm going as fast as I can," she replies, sweat running off the straight ridge of her nose.

I am last in line, and don't wait to be asked. "I'm dying back here," I croak. Up front, Ray barks a short laugh.

"Okay," John sums up brightly, "we're all dying."

We make the waterfall overlook, a mile up the trail, in ten minutes. Several volunteer firefighters stand off to one side in shorts and T-shirts and incongruous firefighter's helmets. Some of them bear potbellies. Two Mountain Rescue volunteers—Dave Brown, a cement contractor, and Chris Myers, a lighting consultant—had arrived at the trailhead from a different road and are minutes ahead of us. Chris has buckled on his climbing harness and rappelled over the edge to see what is happening; Dave sits on the trail, minding the rope attached to Chris.

We dump our loads to the side, wipe the sweat from our faces, and try to get organized. Each rescuer wears a hard plastic climbing helmet and a climbing harness clinking with hardware. The gear bags pulled from Rescue 1 will, with a little ingenuity, allow the team to build whatever technical rescue system a situation demands. The river fills the gorge; carrying Gwen downstream is impossible, so our job is to devise a system to bring a rescue load—a litter, victim, and a pair of litter attendants—150 feet up the slope. Gwen will have to come up the way she went down.

Debbie stands on a jutting boulder and pauses in the middle of the communal adrenaline cloud, trying to think.

The team faces a one-hundred-foot, fifty-degree scree slope, then the cliff to the creek. From our vantage we can't see the watercourse, the victim, or the rescuers. The firefighters, once they found Gwen, had sent two men down from here. Chris, trying to get as quick a handle as possible on the situation, chose to rappel over the side on the firefighters' ropes, which are old, a little frayed, and so short that two have been rigged in succession to reach the gorge's bottom. Halfway down, a climber has to stop and switch to another rope—a dicey situation. Chris, first on the scene, had rigged a figure-eight rappel ring onto his harness. The top rope is tied to a weak anchor, a small aspen sapling. With his rescue pack and a radio, he started backing down the hill on the first rope anyway, using the friction of the figure-eight to control his descent.

> One of the first things I noticed when I went down was the fire department had not tied a knot in the end of their rope, so anybody who was too adrenaline crazed could have gone *zinnggg* right off the end of it. So I stopped and tied a knot, and transferred over to the other rope, which they had tied down at the bottom to allow them more direct access.
>
> We just had a big, narrow-walled canyon, a hole where waterfalls just pound out the rock year after year. The waterfall was probably seventy-five feet away, thirty feet tall, something like that, making a lot of noise. It was virtually raining down there because of the mist, and I went down in a T-shirt and shorts. In my pack I had my Mountain Rescue raincoat. I did not have my windpants, to my chagrin. I had a poncho, a huge poncho. I had a chamois shirt, long-sleeved, [and a] space blanket; and as soon as I got there, each one of those pieces of gear was used up. The poncho was used to protect her from the spray, keep her from getting more hypothermic. The space blanket was also used for her. My raincoat went to one of the firemen. At that point, I was trying to survey what was the best route out.
>
> —*Chris Myers*

The two firefighters, Phil Caffey and Marshall Weitz, and paramedic Colin Brome (these names have been changed) pull large garbage bags that were in Chris's pack over their torsos, punching holes for their heads and arms. They empty the pack and use it to try to shelter Gwen. The noise and the spray pound relentlessly on Chris, the three other rescuers, and Gwen; everyone is soaked. Gwen is incoherent, babbling as she lapses in and out of consciousness. It is twenty degrees colder down in the hole than up on the trail, and a storm is blowing in. For the people in the hole, even thinking is difficult.

"We need to build an uphaul," Debbie declares up on the trail after talking on the radio with Chris. John takes the litter and backs over the side. He is lowered by Dave Brown, a friendly, quiet six-footer in his early forties whose boyish look is accentuated by the blond hair hanging slackly across his head. Dave mans a friction brake tied to an aspen tree, slowly paying out the rope attached to John.

Brown-eyed and handsome, with a lantern jaw and a quick smile, John moved to Colorado from New York City in the late 1980s and now manages the bar at Aspen's Hard Rock Cafe. Nearly six feet tall but weighing only 150 pounds, John is always on the lookout for the next meal. An Emergency Medical Technician with tremendous empathy for people he has never met, he is often one of the first people to reach a victim.

Ray follows John, rappelling down one of the firefighters' ropes. More rescue team members scramble up the trail. Soon fifteen people are milling around. Some tie anchor ropes to trees, while others build the pulley system that will give the team a mechanical advantage to raise the main haul line, with its rescue load of a litter and rescuers, up to the trail.

A safety rope is rigged along the ground beside the edge of the trail, both ends tied to solid anchors; anybody stepping over it has to have his or her harness clipped into it. Debbie, out on the edge of the boulder, clips in with a fifteen-foot piece of red webbing. If she falls, she'll go a ways—but not all the way. Designated as "edge man," I clip in at the lip of the slope where the main rope and a backup belay line go over together into the gorge and to the litter. In twenty minutes we have the system rigged and ready to go. We wait on the team in the hole.

The biggest problem facing the litter team appears to be the risk of a "pendulum." The litter is several yards downstream from the point where the rope comes over the cliff; once it is elevated by the uphaulers, the rescue load could swing violently upstream if it isn't controlled by a "tag line," another rope belayed by a man below. The litter is attached to a "spider," a half-inch aluminum plate roughly shaped like a piece of pie that hangs by its tip from the end of the uphaul rope. Four short ropes radiate down from carabiners that are clipped into holes drilled along the bottom "crust" edge of the pie slice. These ropes lead to the four corners of the litter.

The litter and two attendants—one medical person, one desig-nated climber—all clip into these carabiners and dangle from the spider. The attendants place their feet on the cliff wall and lean out, almost horizontal, like sailors hiking out over a sailboat's windward gunwale. The litter dangles from the spider just above their laps; they maneuver it with their arms. The climber, through a radio pack on his chest, directs the raising or lowering of the load; as the uphaul rope is raised, the attendants walk up the wall, holding the litter clear of obstructions.

Colin [Brome, the Snowmass fire department paramedic working on Gwen], I don't think he had much experience with doing any of this before. I said, "Colin, I need five minutes of your time to explain ex-actly what's going to happen here; where you're going to be clipped in, what's going to happen, how we put our feet underneath the lit-ter and try to balance it around the rock and keep her off the rock, and everything that is going to happen." And I thought he was really with me, really understanding. I said, "If you need anything from me for the patient, you just tell me, because I'm going to move around. You're going to stay at the head in one spot, and I'm going to be jumping around, trying to get her off the rocks, but I can't do it by myself; we have to do it together." So I thought he totally understood that. I was looking at him in the face; he seemed like he was totally with me.
            —*John Zell*

Chris Myers attaches a short tag line and the uphaul team starts raising the litter.

We started to head out. It was really difficult getting up and around. First we were moving [upstream], kind of climbing this little slope of rocks. We were getting soaked, slipping all over, and when it started to get to the overhang they had a tag line on us, which wasn't long enough. Maybe thirty feet long. So we're making progress with the tag line, which was really holding us [Chris was belaying it]. But once the tag line ran out, we went flying around the corner, out of control. We slammed hard. Our feet were way behind us getting dragged, we were like Superman flying around. The litter hit first. She screamed. She was screaming a lot. It was a really rough ride.
            —*John Zell*

Chris knows he should rig a longer tag line, but doesn't want to take the time.

You're like, "Oh, man, she's in really bad shape, we've got to move on this." We could have rigged some sort of system so we could have avoided that pendulum. In the interest of expediency you sort of weigh "Well, we've got to move, we've got to do it quickly, but what are the consequences?"

From where she was, probably the best thing to do was get her out of there. It was not an easy environment in which to operate. You could barely hear [because of the waterfall]. I mean, five feet away I'd be screaming at you, which heightens the tension in the atmosphere. When you're yelling things at somebody and they can't hear you, you almost want to throw a rock and hit them so they'll turn around and talk to you. It wasn't a conducive environment for care.

 —*Chris Myers*

After that point Colin and I tried to get it together. I said "Okay, we've really got to watch the rocks, you've got to balance this way, I've got to balance that way." At that point Colin tells me, "I can't hold it." I'm like, "Wh-wh-wh-what do you mean?" He says, "I'm exhausted, I have no strength left." I go, "Oh, that's not good, that's not good at all."

So I'm getting really nervous. I said, "We've got a really tough part to go up." We're still getting wet. We keep going, and he's having trouble. He's cold and he has no strength left. I didn't realize he was just totally shot. And I tried to look for that when I was down there talking to him. I looked in his eyes and all that. I thought he was fine, but he wasn't. He's almost useless at this point. He couldn't really do anything for the patient anyway, she's strapped in, but he's just telling her, "Hang in there, we're going to get you out of there soon."

 —*John Zell*

Up at the trail, the uphaul team is working almost blind. No one can see what is happening to the litter, and the noise of the waterfall makes it nearly impossible to understand what John and Chris are saying on their radios. The uphaul system is clamped to the main rope, and on Debbie's command a half-dozen people grab and pull. Through a series of pulleys, they gain a six-to-one advantage, so for every six feet they pull, the rope attached to the litter—carrying about six hundred pounds—moves up a foot. They can move the litter up about ten feet at a time. Then they pause and "take another bite"—reposition the uphaul clamp down the main line—and pull again.

The uphaul team has fallen into a rhythm, unaware of the chaos on the litter, where Colin can do little to help and John can't manhandle the load around obstructions. The haulers pull away, steadily dragging Gwen up into the tip of a projecting tree root at the lip of the cliff as John frantically tries to muscle the litter up and over it. He finally manages to reach his radio and yell, "All stop! All stop!" before Gwen is run through. The up-haulers pause and wait for Ray Peritz, who is hanging near the top of the lower firefighters' rope, to clip in as the third man on the litter and help John.

> He [Ray] was on the lower rope and the other rope was above us. We were a good ten feet upstream [from Ray]. So I got a little uptight. I'm going, "Ray, it's not that bad, just walk across." But if he slips [on the scree], he's over the edge. He couldn't reach the other rope. I'm like, "Ray, just grab the rope!" He's like, "John, you're not thinking rationally."
>
> We couldn't get to it, we couldn't move, we couldn't do anything. I'm just trying to hold the litter out from the rocks, the litter was in really bad shape, cockeyed. She was getting dragged in the dirt. After a while Ray was able to come over, help us get out of the roots, get things out of the way, get big rocks out of the way. He eventually came onto the litter and I took the middle and he took the end. And then we started moving up from there.
>
> It was tough. We were still getting pounded with rocks.
> —*John Zell*

Hanging over the edge of the trail, I see three red helmets struggling into sight at the bottom of the scree slope. The three men dangling by their harnesses from the spider are working hard. The ragged wire on the litter's bottom cuts into their legs. Gwen looks terrible: dried blood around her nose, mouth, and eyes, her gray face badly swollen, her eyes fluttering open and closed. She is wrapped in a silver Mylar space blanket. Later we will learn her body core temperature when she arrived at Aspen Valley Hospital was in the eighty degree range—seriously close to the temperature that could have sent her heart into a deadly arrhythmia. The team has a cardiac defibrillator to shock a heart into restarting, but it is down in Rescue 1 with David Swersky, who as rescue leader is managing the situation by radio from the trailhead.

> You want to know what's going on all the time, and yet you know you have to keep your distance radio-wise because you don't want to be bugging those people whose hands are full every five minutes, "What's going on, what's going on?" They're working, they're all humping to get the system set up. The same with medical. We really like medical updates every fifteen minutes, and we can't always get them. Sometimes I wonder why we want them every fifteen minutes because we can't do anything about them anyway. It's not as bad being at the trailhead as it is sometimes being in the [rescue] cabin and being rescue leader, because there you've got the frenzy of that first half hour, everything is just going nuts, you're getting gear, you're getting organized, you want to figure out exactly what's happening, and then everybody vomits out the door and you're left there in this void of nothingness.
> —*David Swersky*

Gwen is moaning. The uphaul team pulls the litter within fifteen feet of the trail and has to stop; the rescue load is too wide to fit sideways through the narrow slot in the rock outcropping where the rope goes over the side. I am handed a saw and brush clippers and hang down below the lip, clipped by my harness into the safety line. I cut as many of the bushes and small aspen trees as I can reach. John, Ray, and Colin lean forward over the litter, trying to shelter Gwen from the gravel and dirt running down onto her. We clip a loop of webbing around the rail at her head and three people on the trail grab and lift, turning the litter head up and muscling it and the rescuers through the slot and onto flat ground.

While they do this, the litter rolls up forty degrees on its side and Gwen, held by straps, looks right at me, hanging a few feet in front of her. Through her half-consciousness, brought on perhaps by pain and fear, comes an awakening recognition as she tries to focus on me. "You're doing great," I say softly. Then she is past me and up.

Rick Deane, forty-eight, proprietor of the T-Lazy-7 dude ranch and two-decade rescue volunteer, has arrived with a small four-wheel-drive all-terrain vehicle. Several people lash the litter onto its front. Rick drives down the trail while four people trot alongside, holding on to Gwen. I run ahead, rolling logs and rocks out of the way. In a few minutes we are at the trailhead. We hoist the litter onto the ambulance gurney and push the whole mess into the back. Somebody closes the ambulance door sharply, and it clicks with the sound of finality, of completion, of success.

But two firefighters—Phil Caffey and Marshall Weitz—are still at the bottom of the hole, wet and hypothermic. It is time to rescue the rescuers.

David Swersky realizes that he has more trouble on his hands back in the hole. A light drizzle is falling. The uphaul system, partially broken down after Gwen was brought up, has to be rebuilt so the remaining rescuers can be extracted. David can do little but monitor the radio and wait as the operation drags into evening.

Chris is halfway up, having climbed one of the firefighters' ropes by using a pair of rope loops called prusiks, alternately locking one onto the rope with an adjustable friction knot, then sliding the other up. The lower ends of the prusik loops serve as stirrups. John, freed of the litter, rappels back down to help get the two remaining men out.

> They're numb, cold, really cold. I said, "Okay, do you know how to Jumar?" because I had two Jumars [mechanical devices used to climb a rope] with me. So one guy [Marshall] said, "I think I know how to do it." He's very overweight. So I said, "Okay, I'm going to clip you all up." While I'm getting him ready, I'm getting soaked, too, and I didn't go down with a jacket, which was a big mistake. I'm getting soaked; it's really cold.
> —*John Zell*

Marshall climbs fifteen feet up the rope, and then freezes. He won't go up, he can't come down, and John can't help him. Phil, watching with John from the bottom, decides he wants to cross the swollen creek and try to hike downstream out of the canyon.

> In a second he [Phil] is across the river, he's jumping [from rock to rock] across the river. The river's raging at this point. He drops his radio in the river. He's trying to get it. I see him trying to reach in the water, I'm like, "Forget it, forget it, you're not going to get it, you get caught in that you're dead." So he's on the other side, I'm screaming up to the top [by radio], "We're losing a fireman, he's trying to go on the other side, I don't know where he's going, he went around the bend, I can't see that he can get down." I'm trying to look around the bend from where I am, there's a rock wall, I'm looking around; the water's raging, I didn't want to get near it. He [Marshall] is stuck, he can't move. I'm like, "We're fucked down here, guys, we're really fucked." I thought I was gonna get out of here quick, have these guys up. I'm gonna freeze to death out here.
>
> So I'm screaming, "One guy's across the river, one guy's stuck, we need an uphaul." So [Debbie radios] "Okay, we've got to put it back together, it's gonna take a while." He [Marshall] just hung on the wall, frozen, he had a plastic bag over him, freezing, so cold he couldn't move. And he [Phil] is jumping around on the other side. I wasn't sure what his mental capacity was at that point from being so cold. He's looking at this rock wall across the river. I'd say it was maybe sixty feet. Steep rock wall. He's putting his hands on it and looking up. I'm like, "Oh my God, we're gonna have a dead fireman here." And I'm trying to scream across the river, he can't hear a thing, "Please don't try and climb that, please don't try and climb that. No way you'll make that, no way." Even if he was a really good rock climber, it's all wet at the bottom, and this guy is not thinking rationally if he's looking at climbing this. So he's walking around on the other side, looking at all these different routes, and I'm saying—I don't know what I was saying on the radio, but I was getting really nervous that this guy was going to do something really stupid because he was so cold.
>
> —*John Zell*

Chris rappels back down the upper rope and connects Marshall to an uphaul rope, which is used to lift him to the trail. Phil hops back across the creek and is uphauled, too. John is left to Jumar up the firefighters' ropes on his own.

You don't think well when you're really cold, I'm finding out. You just don't think as well as you normally would. So I'm struggling to get up this thing and not making fast progress at all. Then I get toward Chris. I'm dead. Chris was right above me, and he knocked down a rock. It was a really big rock [ten by twenty inches]. Luckily I had a helmet on, and it didn't hit me on the head, it hit me on the arm. Then I got to the second rope. I was really tired. The cold just sapped the energy out of me. Just drained the energy out of me. And I had trouble getting up the second line, which was easy. Chris helped me.

The cold just sapped the energy out of me. It was bad.
—*John Zell*

David Swersky sits in Pitkin County Deputy Tom Grady's Jeep with Grady and Steve Crockett, the county emergency services coordinator, listening to the radio. All the doors on Rescue 1 stand open in the rain, and the battery has gone dead. Everyone else who brought Gwen down to the ambulance has gone back up the trail. I close up Rescue 1, get Steve to give me a jump start, and leave it running with the heater on. The temperature drops toward the forties. I pick up a gallon of Gatorade and some Fig Newtons somebody has left by the truck, put on a heavy Gore-Tex coat, climb into the back of Grady's Jeep, and wait for people to come out.

Darkness fills the valley. "We're in the falling season," Steve says, staring out the windshield. David is frustrated. He is supposed to be running this incident, but he hasn't been able to get the volunteer firefighters under control or manage them effectively. "They were basically very helpful," he says later. "They gave her their clothes and saved her life, perhaps, but made themselves hypothermic. I can't fault them for that. I can't fault them for not wearing climbing clothes because they're not climbers. If I had been there first, I don't know if I would have had the presence of mind to say, 'Don't go, you guys can't go.' With our people, I can say that.

"The first rule is create no new victims," he goes on. "The only rule. Protect yourself, protect your teammates, protect the victim."

Gwen Garcelon has to be rewarmed with heated oxygen and warm intravenous fluids before she can be operated on at the hospital. She suffered from several broken ribs and fluid in her lungs. What would have killed her, though, was the cold. She would be readmitted to care later in the summer for a continuing fluid problem, and ultimately doctors would discover a small tear in her aorta, the major artery leading from the heart. The tear was a consequence of the impact.

Gwen would remember nothing of her fall or her rescue. "She's very lucky to have survived the initial fall," Dr. Marion Berg says later. "Ninety percent of those people die immediately." An emergency room physician from Louisiana in his early thirties who laughs easily at himself, Marion is the team's medical adviser and an active member. Ninety percent of people with torn aortas, Marion says, die within two days. All in all, she had a one-in-a-hundred chance of surviving.

Volunteers don't know any of that on the evening of June 6, as the rain comes down harder and colder. They know only that they have delivered her alive.

The Pitkin County Sheriff's Department buys Mountain Rescue dinner that night at Little Annie's, a downtown Aspen locals' hangout characterized by darkly varnished furniture, barn board walls, sports memorabilia, and an intermittently western motif. A score of people, many still in wet Gore-Tex and dirty, yellow, team-issue Nomex shirts, trickle in around nine o'clock. People sit on both sides of a long table made up of several small ones pushed together, wolf down steak and pasta and chicken, and politely thank John Hamwi, the rangy, elfin-faced proprietor.

"No. Thank you," he booms. "You're the unsung ones."

As ten o'clock moves toward half past and the rain drizzles darkly off the eaves outside, the group thins down—John Zell and Ray Peritz at one end of the table, telling each other their stories again, and a handful of us at the other. I get up to leave, but as I walk by John he tells me to sit down and help him eat his dessert, a huge mud pie. He is feeling expansive. I sit down not for the ice cream, but to bask in the aura pooled around the two men.

Slowly that aura draws the rest of the group over until we all sit close. The group has, over a few hours, experienced urgency, adrenaline, confusion, fear and risk, cold water and rockfall, noise and disarray. It has gone on to a giddy sense of relief and achievement, which has mellowed into contagious good feelings in this late evening decompression. The people here have tasted the rush.

Ray can't keep the grin off his face. He looks at John across the checkerboard tablecloth, under the yellow light. "Did we have fun today, or what?"

THE PAGER is
the size of a
deck of cards,
gunmetal gray.
It bears a faded
Mountain Rescue
sticker: white
cross on blue
mountains. I wear it on my right side, just behind the hip.

My first few months on the team, I jump each day at one
o'clock, surprised by the squawk of the daily test page: rapid
beeping, two tones, then the voice of a Pitkin County dispatcher:
"Mountain Rescue daily test page, test page only, WNRZ six-six-
three, time thirteen-oh-one." With time I grow accustomed to
that, but not to the other calls. No one ever quite does.

At twelve-thirty on a February morning the pager squeals to
life. I wake up the worst way—cursing—fling the comforter aside
(the cats have already levitated and disappeared), and flop onto
the floor. My girlfriend, Debbie Ayers, groans and rolls over. I
stumble to the bureau, pull the pager from the charger, and careen through the doorway into the hall, fumbling to turn down
the volume. "All experienced snowmobilers, call Chris Myers,"
the dispatcher intones.

"Yo!" Chris says after the first ring.

"What's going on?" I ask, naked but for the phone in my hand.

"Can you go out first thing in the morning?"

"Yeah, but I'm not an experienced snowmobiler."

"That's okay—I'll put you down."

"What's happening?"

"I've got to keep this line open. Bye."

I go back to bed and lie there. I need gas in my car. Don't forget the avalanche shovel left on the deck. I wish I had a thermos. Should I put hot tea in my water bottles? What should I make for lunch? What do we have in the fridge? Do I have enough snacks? Should I wear one pair of long underwear, or two?

The pager goes off again. This time it is lying by the bed. I hold it against a pillow.

"All Mountain Rescue members, you may stand down," says the dispatcher. "All Mountain Rescue members, stand down—the missing party has come out."

I wake up every hour for the rest of the night. By morning I am exhausted.

⋀ ⋀

Tom McCabe is poking around in the upstairs office of the Mountain Rescue cabin at 630 West Main Street, looking for something hidden in the disorganized filing cabinets. With his brush-cut hair, thickening body, and square face—a face that someday will be framed by marvelous jowls—Tom is beginning to show his forty-eight years. He runs a small appliance repair shop in Aspen, twisting wires and fixing vacuums for the rich and famous. Soft-voiced, thoughtful, Tom is a navy veteran possessed of an eleven-year-old daughter and a dissolving marriage. He shows the strains of his life through sad blue eyes and the small bags forming underneath them.

After nearly two decades on the team and three terms as its president, Tom usually manages rescues rather than charging into the field. Given a choice, he would—like most team members—prefer to be in the field. Today, Tom is happy. He is leaving for a weekend in the tiny San Juan Mountain town of Ouray, Colorado, to ice-climb with other rescue teams. He'll scale frozen waterfalls and drink beer afterwards with friends from all over the mountain west. He loves rescue work and the inherent camaraderie more than almost anything in his life.

"Aha," he says, holding up a shoulder patch insignia for the Grateful Dead rock band, a red, white, and blue skull bisected by a lightning bolt. Tom loves the Grateful Dead. "I brought my sewing kit along, and I'm going to sew it on my jacket," he says. "The Aspen team has a reputation to maintain." He throws me one and tells a story about a rescue convention that included some Finnish rescue volunteers.

One night, in a bar, the Finns ask Tom about the Grateful Dead patch on his Mountain Rescue shirt. What does it mean? "I said, 'You know how you go out on a rescue, and you get to some guy who's really beat up—you know he's going to die, you're going to work on him for hours and get him halfway down the mountain, and then he's going to die on you?' I pointed to the patch and I said, 'Well, I'm the guy who pushes him over the edge to save the trouble.' And the Finns just looked at me." He gives me a mischievous glance, his blue eyes twinkling.

> When I joined, my motivation was completely selfish. I had removed myself from real active, backcountry issues because of the [climbing] death of a friend of mine. Being married and trying to raise a family and buy a house and all that stuff, it was very easy for me to tie myself down. I didn't have a convenient excuse to get out in the backcountry. So what better excuse than to be a rescuer, right? Number one, I would be taken to places, in the course of doing rescues, that I would never think of going to on my own, so it was an exploratory kind of thing. You'd get to go to magical places in the county that you would never see, and I'm incredibly curious about every valley. I just never get tired of wandering around. The other thing was it was a perfect excuse. They ring the alarm bell, you can drop everything, you're a good person for doing this, you're a good person for dropping everything and running off into the woods. So for me, it was a good excuse. Jody [his wife] would have a hard time beating up on

me. It was really to keep one foot in the wilderness, and it was kind of adventuresome because you never knew what was going to happen.

—*Tom McCabe*

A half-dozen rescue teams gather for three days in Ouray. The volunteers from Salt Lake and Las Vegas arrive in shiny sheriff's vehicles with red and blue light bars on top. They carry weapons on rescues. They wear matching red or yellow Gore-Tex suits with "Police" or "Rescue" stenciled across the back. To Tom McCabe and John Zell, who has joined Tom, they're cop wanna-bes. They look like traditional cops. They act like cops. Tom and John don't like cops. They shy away from the other teams. The Aspen team is distinguished from many of the nation's two-score Mountain Rescue groups by its antipathy toward "cop-ness."

Rescue teams generally work under the aegis of local lawmen. In Aspen's case, the team answers to Pitkin County Sheriff Bob Braudis, a big-boned, gap-toothed Irishman. Six-feet-six and 250 pounds, Bob stands as one of the most liberal and politically as-tute politicians in a liberal and astute town. "I detest traditional policemen," he says, dismissing them as "bullet heads." He fa-vors "simpatico, liberal cops."

For many rescue groups, volunteering is a chance to play po-lice. But the Aspen team, organized in the early 1950s and one of the first Mountain Rescue groups in America, has always cher-ished its own identity. The team's job is dealing with emergen-cies off the pavement—"anyplace where the cops would get their shoes dirty" is how one rescuer described the criteria. Lost hik-ers, downed airplanes, fallen climbers, and drowned kayakers are the sorts of emergencies that merit a call to Mountain Rescue-Aspen, and team members like it that way. They don't appreciate the sheriff interfering in work that, rescue veterans believe, he doesn't know much about.

Sometimes local sheriff's deputies "think of us as cowboys with helicopters," says David Swersky. "We're not cowboys. We don't ask anybody to do anything they're not comfortable with, and if the pilot says he can't do it, we shut it down. We're the standard. I won't say we're the best rescue group in the country or even in Colorado, but we're among the best. We don't stand in anyone's shadow. I've been to the gatherings around the country, and we have a reputation as having one of the best rescue organizations in the country."

Such verbalized hubris is rare on the Aspen team. "There is little or no glory in Mountain Rescue, though there is great personal satisfaction," declares a handout given to individuals who want to join. "For the most part, participation in rescue or recovery involves long periods of waiting followed by long periods of very hard and disagreeable work. There is no member of Mountain Rescue above being assigned the most trivial job, from babysitting the vehicle on some back road to arranging for food and drink for those more actively involved in the rescue. Nor, because we are a small group, can we assure any member that he/she will be dismissed from the most unpleasant tasks, for example, a body recovery. Philosophically, Mountain Rescue is one entity, not a group of separate members. A successful rescue depends as integrally upon the member monitoring the radio in the cabin as it does upon the rescuer attending the victim on the mountain. For this reason, you will not be reading about yourself in the newspaper. Whenever possible we will stress the work of the group at the expense of the contribution of any single individual."

Van Kyzar (not his real name), a construction foreman in his mid-thirties, states the team's philosophy his own way one night to a half-dozen people who want to join the team and are taking the first step to do that, an introductory class taught by team members. An Emergency Medical Technician in charge of the team's medical training, Van spends an evening going through the medical equipment the team carries. Suddenly, he looks up from the trauma pack he is dissecting. "Don't anybody think you're gonna be a hero on Mountain Rescue," he says. "Anybody in this room who's got an ego trip, don't be on Mountain Rescue, because you don't build ego on bodies, and unfortunately, a lot of what we do is get bodies."

Joining some mountain rescue teams is difficult. Joining the Aspen team is, in 1993, relatively easy: show up for three monthly meetings, pass a class in advanced first aid, and an individual will almost certainly be elected by the board as a support member. Support members, if they demonstrate the skill and desire, may do everything full members do, except vote in meetings. After a year of participating—and completing trainings for rescues involving high angle (cliffs), scree (steep slopes), water, snow and ice, and avalanches, plus two classes on mountain rescue taught by Tom McCabe and other veteran members—support members are eligible for full membership. They are judged by full members, and almost always voted in—if they've made it that far, they're accepted.

Making the team, however, doesn't guarantee new—or even veteran—members the chance to charge into the field. The Aspen team is egalitarian in many senses, but it is a meritocracy when a rescue is under way. Part of a rescue leader's job is to know the strengths and weaknesses of members, and use them appropriately. Nobody is more aggressive about those judgments than Tom.

"Experience counts for a great deal in this game," he says, "and it's hard to come by that experience. Some years are real slow. The beeper goes off, you've got to show up. You've got to be there. And you've got to be there even if you've shown up four times, and you've left work, and you've come to the cabin, and nothing happens, and you have to go back to work, and your boss is pissed, and you've lost money. You can't show up twice a year and expect to be put out in front. That won't happen. If I turn around and you're there, and you're there, and you're there—you're going to go out in the field. And you're going to see shit maybe you don't want to see. But then at least you've had the opportunity, at least you've said, 'I really want this.' Then you can change your mind, then you can say, 'Nope, I don't need that, I don't want to respond to this kind of thing anymore.'

"But," Tom continues, "if my sense of urgency is real high, if I think it's messy, brutal, if I think somebody is going to die and scream and fight and leave us all with nightmares for a year, I'm going to send the people I think can handle it. If you're afraid of fire, and I send you out on a downed plane where there are six charred bodies, it's probably going to do things to your psyche

that I can't imagine. I don't want to do that to you. It is an interesting process, and we make mistakes because, unfortunately,
when things are very urgent, I don't always have the people I
want. The first six people that walk through the door may not be
an ideal team, but they may be a team who can get the job done.
You hope they don't come back so badly damaged they can't
ever function [on a rescue] again."

/\\ /\\

The pager is the only visible identifier for members of this team
that eschews uniforms, patches, similar haircuts. Once a mountaineers' clique, the team has broadened since the mid-1980s
into a collection of forty-five people who represent a cross-sec-
tion of modern Aspen. There are people who work outdoors: car-
penters, ranch hands, a cement contractor. There's a backcountry
guide, a few landscapers. But there's also a real estate salesman,
a nurse practitioner, a hotel maintenance man, a lodge manager,
two professional photographers, a phone salesman, a bartender,
a ski patroller, an auto mechanic, a biotechnology entrepreneur,
a jailer, a conference coordinator, two wives of wealthy attorneys, a couple of waiters, a restaurateur, a dentist, an appliance
repairman, two doctors, a lighting consultant. There are elk
hunters and vegetarians, dirt bikers and telemark skiers. Yet for
all their differences, they share a few key commonalities. They
are physically fit, often deceptively strong, and—like many Aspenites—thrive out of doors.

At the team meetings on the first Monday evening of each
month, a few new faces usually appear, a little lost amid the ban-
ter and inside jokes. Would-be members aren't expected to know
much about technical mountaineering or medicine, but they are
expected to be outdoor enthusiasts, comfortable and competent
in the woods. Rarely is there a backlog of such member hopefuls.
What deters most people who think they might want to join the
team is the commitment, which is far greater than they expect.
The technical skills they can learn, but the time and energy necessary to be good, to be there, to be called upon—these are beyond many people. The team, as a whole, volunteers for ten
thousand to fifteen thousand man-hours each year. The most

highly committed members may put in fifty hours or more on a busy month, what with meetings, trainings, work parties, fund-raisers, and rescue leader duty—plus rescues.

Each team member is assigned a numerical call sign, although almost all radio traffic is conducted informally, using names. The 501 ("five-oh-one") and 502 ("five-oh-two") positions—the boss jobs—rotate. These numbers are passed every two weeks to a fresh pair of trained rescue leaders—a half-score of team members who field all rescue calls and manage all rescues, near-rescues, and non-rescues. Their shifts may involve no rescue work, or a great deal. For every actual incident, many calls that amount to nothing—overdue hikers, missing hunters—are directed by the sheriff's office to the 501 on duty. They spend many late nights planning "bastard rescues" that never happen.

/\/\   /\/\

Aspen is a locus of what writer Edward Abbey called "industrial tourism." When Chicago industrialist Walter Paepcke looked upon Aspen in the aftermath of World War II, he saw a sleepy silver-mining relic that he believed could become a new Athens. It would be a place, he said, where men could be challenged intellectually, aesthetically, and physically. He and his wife, Elizabeth, founded the Aspen Skiing Corporation, The Aspen Institute, the Aspen Music Festival, the International Design Conference in Aspen, the Aspen Center for Physics, the Aspen Center for Environmental Studies, the Given Institute. Paepcke's vision—"The Aspen Idea"—largely has come to pass. Aspen today is a booming community that has dedicated itself to intellect, culture, and sport—and attracted a great deal of wealth.

The town has grown steadily into an international playground. Pitkin County, two-thirds the size of Rhode Island, hangs along the western crest of the Continental Divide, draped across the heart of Colorado's Elk Mountains. The town lies at seven thousand nine hundred feet. Some of the peaks rise above fourteen thousand. During the off-seasons—spring and fall—the community shrinks to five thousand people. At Christmas, close to twenty thousand tourists are in town, and the downtown core, thirty blocks, has the crowded feel of a city as skiers and shoppers mill along the sidewalks and cars crawl through the snowy streets, vainly seeking parking places. Come summer, culture and sports draw nearly as many people as ski season does.

Much of the town's architecture, even the new work, retains a Victorian flavor. Few of the buildings rise higher than three stories. In 1970 the first stoplight was installed; today there are five on the run into town and down Main Street. The town has sprawled beyond its original grid, laid out in the late 1870s on an alluvial bench between the Roaring Fork River and the base of Aspen Mountain. In recent decades development has crawled across the old mine tailings at the base of Smuggler Mountain on the town's north side, up the scrub-oak slopes of Red Mountain across the valley, and around Shadow Mountain into the mouths of Castle Creek and Maroon Creek, which converge with the Roaring Fork on the western edge of Aspen.

Sometimes Aspen feels like a little city. Other times it is a small town. When the tourist crush diminishes, when locals again can find a place to park downtown, a more relaxed atmosphere returns to Aspen. People walking down the street say hello to each other. It is out of this small town, this core community of friends, that Mountain Rescue-Aspen draws its members and its support.

For all its cosmopolitan qualities, Aspen remains surrounded by what, to most people, is wilderness. The backcountry is not as wild as it used to be, if only because more people travel into it. But it is still several hundred thousand acres of spectacular and bewitching beauty. Eighteen miles to the east, at the headwaters of the Roaring Fork River, lies the Continental Divide. North and east of Aspen are the drainages of Hunter Creek, Woody Creek, and the Frying Pan River, all running west out of the Williams and Sawatch mountains. Southeast is the northern edge of the Collegiate Peaks range and the valleys cut by Lincoln and Difficult creeks. South of town lie the Elk Mountains, core of the Maroon Bells-Snowmass Wilderness, encompassing the most popular peaks: Pyramid, North and South Maroon (together known as the Maroon Bells), Capitol, Daly, Snowmass, Sopris. Five passes—Schofield, West Maroon, East Maroon, Pearl, Taylor—run through the peaks to the town of Crested Butte and

Gunnison County, thirty miles south of Aspen. Some are traversed by dirt roads, others by foot trails.

Each year, hundreds of thousands of people come to these places to relax, to discover, to escape, to test themselves. The woods and mountains are an enormous part of the draw, and draw they do. The four ski areas (Aspen, Buttermilk, Aspen Highlands, Snowmass) count 1.5 million-skier days annually. The Tenth Mountain Trail system, a backcountry network of fifteen unmanned ski huts and lodges running north to Vail, and the Braun system, six huts running south toward Crested Butte, rent overnight lodgings to thousands of cross-country skiers. Thousands more hikers and climbers come to the Maroon Bells-Snowmass, Hunter-Frying Pan, and Collegiate Peaks wilderness areas. In autumn, hunters clamber through the woods in search of deer and elk. During summer, rafters ride the county's three rivers while mountain bikers careen down backcountry trails. Paragliders and hang gliders leap off the ridges to soar over the valleys. Aspen's airport, nestled in a valley amid the peaks, is the seventh busiest in Colorado. An average of three planes a year crash in the surrounding hills.

The 1970s and 1980s, with the "back to the land" movement and the growth in personal wealth and freedom, saw an explosion of urban adventurers seeking challenge, escape, and discovery throughout the world. The people who visit Aspen—and those who live here—tend to have the time, the motivation, and the money to get themselves into situations that are more than some can handle. As a consequence, Mountain Rescue-Aspen handles forty to sixty rescue calls annually, from finding lost hunters to recovering bodies on fourteen-thousand-foot peaks.

"Basically, what we do is go out and save people who make mistakes," says Debbie Kelly. "That's what we do all the time."

/\\ /\\

I awake on a late winter morning to the sound of rain. Not really rain but a snow smurr running off the roof and splattering on the metal sill by my window. It turns to wet snow during breakfast, more of the same in a week that has been generally gray.

I am working at my desk upstairs when the pager goes off. At first I think I have only leaned on it, which triggers it sometimes.

"Mountain Rescue members who are strong skiers. Mountain Rescue members who are strong skiers only, call 920-5106."

I get Tom McCabe—this week's 501—on the second try. Tom has a tired, almost weary, sound in his voice. He is quiet, nearly glum, when he answers the phone. His tone is flat: he has learned, after fifteen years in the game, to wring all of the emotion out of it. He'll deal with the emotion later.

"We've got a helicopter down. If we can find out where it is, and they're alive, I need six people ready to be dropped in. Gear on, packs in their cars."

"I can be ready in ten minutes."

"I'll put you on standby."

"Where are they?"

"We don't know."

"Do you have an area?"

"Pearl Pass."

"Oh, man."

Life on Aspen's rescue team involves a conscious choice to embrace disruption. A movie, a concert, dinner, business—all these may go by the wayside at any time. Sometimes, as I clip the pager on, I wonder if I'll spend my day as I plan to. Not every member responds to every page. Some are more gung ho than others, who pick and choose, weighing the severity of the incident. A page to search for an overdue hunter won't generate as much response as a call about a fallen climber on the Maroon Bells.

I keep my gear in the back of the Subaru or in a locker at the cabin. My summer pack weighs thirty pounds, my winter pack fifty. Inside is a medical kit, climbing harness, carabiners, rappel devices, webbing, prusiks, bivouac sack, insulated sleeping pad, Gore-Tex pants, gaiters, and parka. There's polypropylene long underwear, climbing helmet, goggles, extra socks, cold weather and climbing gloves, pile pullover, water purification tablets, sunscreen, balaclava, baseball cap, whistle, orange marking tape, notepad, freeze-dried food, emergency stove, and fuel. Depending on the mission, I will wear one of four pairs of boots and may also grab crampons and an ice axe, avalanche shovel and transceiver, skis, poles, radio, binoculars, or sleeping bag.

On this morning, at one moment I'm working on a magazine story and thinking about whether to rent a video tonight. A minute later I'm putting on a flameproof Nomex shirt (required for a helicopter flight), checking my Ortovox avalanche transceiver and strapping it around my chest. I change cotton socks to polypropylene and look out the window at the weather with a great deal more interest.

I step outside to attach climbing skins to my telemark skis. The wind is blowing hard now and spitting snow. The gondola up the face of the Aspen Mountain ski area has shut down because of gusts. Clouds churn over Shadow Mountain and West Willow Creek—the direction of 12,700-foot Pearl Pass. I can hear a plane somewhere, low—maybe Rick Deane in One Five Charlie, his single-engine Cessna 180, searching for the Alouette helicopter.

I keep thinking about the weather. I have time to think, and I'd rather not. The snow falls harder, blowing sideways across the sliding glass door, as I heat water to make tea for my water bottle. I tie up the pack's loose straps—don't want them dangling around a helicopter, where they might snag. I realize I'm scared. I don't want to go up in a bird in weather like this. If one has crashed, shouldn't that tell us something? I worry about what I'll do if I get dropped into a crash scene with people in trouble, how I'll react. I wonder if I'll freak out, or forget how to do something—how to do anything. Imagining the paralysis feels like a nightmare where I'm frozen, needing to run but unable to.

I spend an hour tinkering with my gear until it is more ready than it needs to be. I make myself eat a banana and toast and peanut butter, drink a couple glasses of water. I stare at today's *Denver Post* without comprehending.

There is no word, and nothing else to do. I finally make myself work again. Concentration is elusive. Half of my brain tries to deal with tasks like returning phone calls, while the other half wonders whether somebody is huddling alive above tree line in the hulk of the Alouette. Wonders what I might find and what I might do, suddenly dependent only on other team members, cut off by weather with critically injured people on our hands.

I sit in Gore-Tex and polypropylene, sweating slightly in a cool room, and tap at the keyboard. At twelve-thirty the pager sings again, a relief rather than a surprise. I shut off the Macintosh and put on my coat, but it is a stand-down page, not a call-out. I phone the cabin to ask what has happened. "One guy walked out Willow Creek, and we have three dead," Linda Koones tells me. "That's all we know."

"So we're not going anywhere today?"

"No."

I drive to the cabin anyway, curious. Linda, Debbie, Van, and Tom are there. They sit on high stools in the communications ("comm") room, a ten-by-ten-foot cubicle that serves as the nerve center for most rescues. Topographical maps, laminated and mounted on foam board, are stuck to Velcro strips on the walls. The base radio squawks occasionally. Yellow legal pads filled with notes lie on the white linoleum counter that runs along two walls.

The quartet is discussing whether Lycra tights are acceptable garb for rescues. "We okayed Lycra on the team," Debbie laughs. "Linda and Donna and Judy and I." Nobody seems particularly interested in talking about the helicopter wreck. I learn that the lone survivor walked out for eleven hours on snowshoes despite broken ribs, descending through heavy timber in Willow Creek until arriving at T-Lazy-7 Ranch. I am struck by the incongruity of the scene: four people shooting the breeze about nothing in particular, as if they are in a coffee shop—people who, only moments earlier, had been keyed up about the possibility of a difficult, bad-weather rescue. Now they decompress with humor and casual conversation.

"I'm around this weekend," I say. "I'll go do whatever needs to be done."

Van looks at me. A little bowlegged, inclined to talk out of the side of his mouth, like Popeye, he has hauled his lanky body up numerous harsh peaks, including Alaska's Denali. He makes his living in construction, one of the valley's booming trades. His straight brown hair and the blush on his cheekbones suggest late twenties, but he is older, father of several children. He has a vaguely manic look, thanks to widely spaced, very open eyes that seem perpetually surprised.

"Is this your first one?" He doesn't have to say what he means: body recovery.

"Yeah."

"You don't want to go on this one," he says. "Not as your first one."

"This one's a decap," Tom says as he shrugs into his overcoat for the drive down Main Street to the sheriff's office, located in the basement of the Pitkin County Courthouse. He'll get a briefing there from deputies who talked to the survivor. The helicopter's rotor struck a tree and pieces flew through the passenger cabin, he says. It's not pretty.

There is no urgency now. Tom asks Debbie to organize a small body-recovery team to fly in by helicopter to the crash site at the head of Willow Creek when the weather clears. "They've got to pick up the pieces," he says. "And if they're scattered and buried by snow, they'll have to probe for them."

I park downtown and walk around, walking farther than necessary to do my errands. I need a little decompression of my own; it's impossible to simply pick up where my morning left off. There's a running joke that Mountain Rescue volunteers are adrenaline junkies, and some truth to it. Whenever the pager goes off and I scramble to grab gear and get to the cabin, I feel alive. More than one Mountain Rescue member has been pulled over by a cop for roaring down Main Street during a call-out. I am, I realize, disappointed after the stand-down. Not only because people have died, but because the urgency, the drama, is gone. It is a rush that the more veteran team members say they learn to control but never escape.

"When I was new on the team, I just wanted to be a bat out of hell and flip the [rotating] lights [on Rescue 1] and do the whole thing," says Chris Myers. "That is a dynamic that is present in every individual. Some people grow out of it, and other people don't. People who don't grow out of it, either they get off the team or they don't grow in responsibility on the team. That's kind of how people grow into a rescue leadership position— whether or not they're able to be conservative in their calls. It's something that does need to be held in check."

"I still get the adrenaline rush," says Dave Lofland, a thirty- five-year-old carpenter and one of the team's mountaineers. "I just wait until I'm out there to get it. It used to be from the time my pager went off I'd be totally adrenalized. Now I'm calm until I'm on the scene, and then I go nuts."

Dave was elected to the team's board just as he became a full member. Nobody else wanted the operations position, so he took it on, agreeing to manage the team's vehicles, building, and equipment. Six feet tall, he hides his blue eyes behind mirrored Vuarnet sunglasses and sometimes pulls his dark, curly hair back into a short ponytail. Like many of the team's volunteers, he works with his hands, managing several condominiums. Like al- most all of them, he is effectively self-employed, able to drop everything and run.

"I think a lot of it has to do with the hurry-up-and-wait fac- tor," he continues. "You jump in Rescue 1 and you go screaming down Highway 82 or up Maroon Creek Road or up Independence Pass or whatever, and then you spend forty-five minutes at the trailhead. So I tend to just calm down because I realize as pumped up and everything as I'm going to get, typically we don't just race down there and go running out in the field to save someone's life."

The rush never goes away, but time dulls its edge. What keeps people on the team, what quickly becomes the overriding attrac- tion, is the team itself. Members simply enjoy each other's com- pany. "I've told friends I love this team," says Lori Hart, a petite, thirty-five-year-old pediatric nurse practitioner and former ski patroller with bright blue eyes and long dark hair. Someone nick- names her "Break-My" shortly after she starts coming to meet- ings, flirting with her last name. It catches on. She laughs and smiles and enjoys the attention.

Formerly a volunteer at high-altitude medical clinics in the Hi- malayas, Lori signed up with Mountain Rescue at the suggestion of Ray Peritz. "I love this group of people. I've really felt close, bonded. I feel like everybody cares. It's a group of people I just want to be around, and it's become a real significant part of my life. It's a feeling of belonging, it's a feeling of being loved and cared for. These are basic human needs that really do get fulfilled."

As with any team, the common bond is rooted in common experiences. Yet less than 10 percent—probably less than 5 percent—of volunteer time is spent on actual rescues. Most of what the team does is the mundane work of keeping a volunteer group organized and funded. People who join find they have a stable of new playmates, and soon are calling each other to go skiing or mountain biking or climbing together. Drawn by the thrill, they are held by the friendships.

A football or baseball team shares these characteristics. But those teams are public. What they do is for public consumption. It is viewed and appreciated by fans who understand the team's task, who may even play the sport themselves. Mountain Rescue-Aspen is not secretive, but few people understand what the team does or how it does it. Team members are uninterested in changing that. There is an unspoken belief that good people will come to the team of their own accord, and they will either have the personality to be team players, or they won't. There is no promotion, no recruitment.

Mountain Rescue members generally are self-effacing; the quiet ones in the back of the room are often the most effective and most respected. Machismo doesn't cut it. A handout given to support members promises that "personality differences," "a superior attitude," "placing yourself at unnecessary risk," or "lone wolf behavior" are all good ways to avoid being elected to the team.

"There are plenty of good climbers out there with great skills," says John Zell. "But they're also loners. We don't need those people."

John prides himself on being a team player, although he has little patience for people who aren't, in his eyes, up to his level. For those he likes, however, he'll go the distance and more. No one is closer to him than Scott Messina, a small, thirty-six-year-old mountain guide with boundless energy and seemingly unshakable good humor who has been the team's training officer since 1989. Scott and John share the intimacy of brothers but without the competition that so often fills the interstices of such relationships. There's a steady fondness between them, evident in the knowing looks and inside jokes. Sometimes they resort to pushing each other over or throwing snowballs. Each fills a niche in the other's soul.

Scott, in addition to running his one-man guide service, Aspen Alpine Guides, manages the Braun hut system for skiers. "I like to bag a lot of peaks," John says of how they came together, "and I said to Scott, 'If you ever need help with the huts, let me know.' One night he came into the Hard Rock and said, 'I think I can use your help on the huts this summer.'" It amounted to thirty hours a week, cutting firewood and doing maintenance. Now, Scott is training John to be his second guide. "Scott is one of my favorite people," John says. "I really like being around him."

In the 1990s, much of the work Americans do is vaguely unful-filling. In a world supervised by lawyers, limited by permits, and circumscribed by regulation, rescue work provides an uncommon commodity: a clear task, an obvious imperative, a direct result. When a page goes out, the job at hand is always different, yet al-ways the same: find a missing child, evacuate an injured climber, dig a body from an avalanche. The tasks vary: set up a helicopter landing zone, organize food for field teams, construct a litter brake system, treat the victim, relay radio traffic.

"I would just about guarantee you that everybody on Moun-tain Rescue is partially on Mountain Rescue because they see themselves on the other end of the line," says Chris Myers. "I think to some extent we're all risk takers, adrenaline junkies, whatever. I know out there I've taken chances I shouldn't have. Just after I joined Mountain Rescue, six years ago, I climbed three fourteeners [fourteen-thousand-foot peaks] in a day. A lot of climbing, a lot of exposure [to falling]. But I was like, 'Hey, I can handle this.' So I've taken risks. What Mountain Rescue's taught me is what's on the other side if I screw up. I'm mortal, I can die, I can get hurt. It's really put that in front of me."

"I think I froze my butt off enough out there, that might be a little bit of it," says Dave Lofland, who has climbed Denali and every major peak in Pitkin County. "I've been fortunate in that the mishaps I've gotten into I've managed to get myself out of, and I see how other people aren't as lucky."

"It's kind of a karma deal," concludes Scott Messina. "I want to do what I can to help somebody, to build up my backcountry karma, in case I ever need it. The enjoyment of being able to help somebody, and being able to, you know, save somebody's life—there's nothing more that can be said of that."

Rarely is there personal follow-up with victims. Sometimes a letter comes in, or a check with a brief thank-you note from a victim or relative. Gwen Garcelon sent homemade cookies after recovering from her fall into East Snowmass Creek. Yet nobody seeks victims out in search of gratitude, and nobody, it seems, misses it. They don't need to be thanked. They know inside themselves what they have done. That feeds a deep, instinctual need almost every human has—to help others.

It is the same instinct that causes strangers to plunge into burning houses and rescue people they don't know. There's no conscious desire to be a hero. It's a vestige of a tribal history, of a time when humans had to depend on one another for survival. With little but our brains to protect us in prehistoric times, we learned to work together. It is one of our most deeply innate characteristics as a species, and it forms the basis—unspoken, perhaps not even fully comprehended—for Mountain Rescue's mission.

In the early weeks of 1993 the pagers are quiet, but almost every month brings another training session. Some are highly structured: a night of slides and lectures about avalanches, then a day of fieldwork on skis, digging holes in the snow and study-ing avalanche hazards. Others are more laid-back: a six-pack of beer, a pizza, ropes and pulleys strung across the upstairs meet-ing room in the rescue cabin, working out a new rope system. Winter tends to be slow for the Aspen team, since most visitors are confined to the ski slopes and cared for by paid ski patrollers. As the days lengthen and people talk about the surge of action in the warm months, there is a sense of unreality about it all. On an intellectual level I can understand that we are getting ready for statistically probable events—events that, quite likely, will in-volve severe injuries and death. Yet, in my gut, I don't fully believe it. I feel like we're rehearsing for something that isn't really going to happen.

The team is preparing for intense, intimate, possibly tragic encounters with people. Somewhere in the world there is someone who will come to Colorado and get in trouble in Pitkin County. They may not even know yet that they will visit the state. We don't know who they are, but we are preparing with certainty to rescue them. There is an eerie sense of predestination, of knowing the future. It's almost as if, when we finally meet them, we could say, "We've been expecting you." To them, their mishap will be an accident. To Mountain Rescue members, it is foreordained.

So the trainings and meetings go on as the team tries to predict the unpredictable and be ready for it. What no one can see is that the first rescue of 1993 will be like no other. As February eases toward its close, Mountain Rescue-Aspen drifts unknowingly toward a rescue that will draw international media attention and badly shake the town and its team. The victims won't be the only casualties.

THE WEATHER REPORTS indicated it was going to be continually evil, possibly worse. We had eighty- to one-hundred-knot winds forecast for Sunday; there was three to five feet of new snow on the [Richmond] ridge. But the ridge was getting hit by wind, which scours a lot of it off. So what we were expecting was, in and out of the trees up there, you'd get certain areas that would slow us down and certain areas that would be pretty much blown clean.

Braudis was concerned it was unsafe. I called him on it Sunday night, when we sat down for the next operational plan, and we decided to go down the ridge. I essentially told him, in front of several witnesses, that we should have been doing that the night before, and that if we discover a body frozen in the trees because we didn't act, if there was a trial over why we didn't do some things, I'd testify against Braudis. As a state [Mountain Rescue] mission coordinator, that carries some clout. I'm one of the twelve people in the state that's recognized as being able to do this kind of shit, and having the experience to be able to do it.

There was no doubt that it stung him. I shouldn't have done it that way, but I get real emotional. I don't like to bullshit. I don't cope well with not getting my way under those circumstances, when somebody could die over it.

—*Tom McCabe*

It is a dream week in a skier's dream winter. In the first six weeks of 1993 Aspen has seen only ten days of sunshine. The winter storms trail across the weather map and out into the Pacific like freight cars, and nearly every day brings fresh powder. On the night of February 18, Aspen Mountain receives three feet of new snow. The skiing is fantastic, but avalanche danger in the Elk Mountains is so high that all the backcountry skiers planning to travel to the fifteen ski huts scattered throughout the high country in the Braun and Tenth Mountain systems cancel their plans.

All but seven.

After months of preparation, fifty-year-old Ken Torp parks his banana-yellow Cadillac at the end of Castle Creek Road. It is 10:00 A.M. on Friday, February 19. Joining the Denver resident are six friends from Colorado's Front Range who have driven four hours to be part of Ken's annual trip to the Goodwin-Greene Hut: Elliot Brown, forty-three; Dee Dubin, forty; Rob Dubin, thirty-eight; Andrea Brett, forty-two; Brigette Schluger, fifty; and Richard Rost, thirty-four.

Doug Bitterman, a guide at Ashcroft Ski Touring Center, notices the group preparing to ski up Express Creek, an avalanche-prone valley that climbs two thousand eight hundred vertical feet over six miles to an exposed saddle at the south end of Richmond Ridge. Another skier, Saville Ryan, explains the extreme avalanche danger to the group. But the group has a cavalier attitude; snow is what we came for, they say, and avalanches—well, you can't do much about them.

"That's probably going to be our rescue for the year," Doug tells a colleague as he watches the group begin slowly breaking trail up the valley.

⚠ ⚠

Scott Messina spends most of Saturday skiing on Aspen Mountain. He has canceled the backcountry ski trip he was to guide, and takes advantage of the best and deepest snow in a decade to ski black-diamond runs. The powder curls up over his head with each turn. Small, with curly, longish brown hair, a drooping mustache, and a vague resemblance to Dustin Hoffman, Scott has labored out of doors for nearly a decade as a hut-keeper and a guide. He works hard at keeping his guiding operation afloat, taking visitors backcountry skiing to various huts in the winter, leading them on hikes and up peaks in the summer. Although his business is often hand-to-mouth, Scott is not easily discouraged, and his steadiness and good humor earn him a lot of respect on the team. Says one volunteer, "I know who I look to for leadership: the little guy."

His sense about the backcountry; his intimate knowledge of the peaks and ridges and hidden gullies; his understanding of how, where, and when avalanches slide cause others to defer to his judgment. Volunteers work with Scott with an added sense of security and an understanding that he won't ask them to do something he wouldn't do himself. Beyond that, Scott is simply likable. Sometimes it is possible to see the shadow of a high-school troublemaker in his spontaneity, his inability to be too serious for very long, his capacity to spark those around him with humor.

Scott had spoken with a friend at Ashcroft Ski Touring Saturday morning and learned about the Torp group's departure into the backcountry the day before. "I thought to myself, 'Oh, Lord, what the hell's going on?' There wasn't anything I could do," he recalls. "There wasn't anything anybody could do."

At midday Saturday a series of avalanches rumbles down the west side of Richmond Ridge and across the two-lane road that twists twelve miles south up Castle Creek Road to Ashcroft. The largest slide surges across the road and blocks Castle Creek with hundreds of tons of snow and debris. In the next valley west, another huge slide thunders down Maroon Bowl into the Maroon Creek Valley, blocking Maroon Creek. Hal Hartman, the Aspen Skiing Company's veteran avalanche controller, inspects the sites and declares that the Roaring Fork Valley is experiencing a hundred-year avalanche cycle; slide paths that let go only once a century are releasing deadly white cascades. Valley residents are awed by the magnitude of the storm and the conditions it has created. Going into the backcountry now is phenomenally dangerous for travelers who can't pick routes that avoid avalanche trigger zones and slide paths.

The slides in Castle and Maroon creeks create a crisis in Aspen; the snow has blocked the source of the city's water supply. "We've got water for twenty-four to forty-eight hours, if we don't have a fire," deputy Tom Stephenson says. Avalanches on Highway 82 snarl traffic, and the slide in Castle Creek has, by blocking the road, trapped dozens of people at Ashcroft Ski Touring Center and the restaurant there, Pine Creek Cookhouse. Sheriff Braudis sets up a command post in the basement of the brick courthouse and begins trying to figure out how to restore water and open roads.

On Saturday afternoon, Jace Michael and I drive up to the Castle Creek slide to look around. With a windswept mane of strawberry-blond hair and a striking cleft chin, Jace is easy to spot in a crowded bar. Six feet tall, with the chest and arms of a swimmer, he has the casual athleticism of a quarterback. He is always eager, always one of the first to show up when the pager goes off. In his late twenties, he moved to Aspen from Los Angeles, where he had worked in a funeral home. Body recoveries, he says, are not a problem. In Aspen he landed a relatively comfortable job managing a small hotel, the Crestahaus, where he lives with his girlfriend, Barb. Occasionally the pair rides through Aspen on a tandem mountain bike, trying not to fall over from laughing.

Snow falls gently in the Castle Creek Valley. Through the clouds we can see other slabs and pockets of snow that look ready to fall down the steep western side of Richmond Ridge. The scene is unnervingly still. If a slide comes down, we are probably right in its path. Water from the creek backs up quietly behind the biggest slide deposition, a pile of snow fifteen feet deep covering a hundred yards of river and road. The place feels dangerous, and I am happy to get back to the rescue cabin.

Scott, the 502, and Tom McCabe, the 501, are both there, along with John Zell. There is no rescue under way. They are just hanging out. Waiting. We order a pizza. The phone rings. John answers. "Scott, it's for you," he says. "It sounds like Julie." He shakes his head and says to us, "It sounded like Julie, but she was really rude. She said, 'Who's this?' and I said, 'John Zell,' and she said, 'Let me speak to the 501 or 502! Let me speak to the rescue leader!'"

⋀ ⋀

Richard Rost and Andrea Brett stumble out of Express Creek at Ashcroft Saturday afternoon, cold, wet, and frightened, and begin digging their car out of the snow. Marshall Weir, who lives nearby, drives past and stops to help. They tell him five of their friends are lost up in the mountains. Marshall has more bad news for them: avalanches have blocked Castle Creek Road. They are stuck in the valley. He takes them to his house and calls Julie, Scott's wife, who calls the rescue cabin.

Scott telephones the Weir house and speaks with Andrea, who is near hysteria, and Richard. It is the worst possible situation. Torp's group of seven had reached the Express Creek saddle at 11,900 feet late Friday. From there they should have skied a mile and a half east, above the timberline, to Gold Hill and the Goodwin-Greene Hut, located on Gold Hill's north side. But the storm—the worst to hit the region in thirty years—has become a blizzard of ferocious proportions. Ken Torp and Elliot Brown are experienced winter mountaineers who have climbed Denali, but they get turned around in conditions so bad they can barely see. They lead the group south, rather than east, to an unnamed 12,430-foot knoll, mistaking it for Gold Hill. Unable to find the hut, facing darkness, the group digs in near a small group of trees in an open park south of the knoll. They try to build a snow cave, but it collapses, and they spend a cold, frightening night under the blizzard in an open pit. Only Rob Dubin manages to sleep. They have just one camping stove among them, since they had planned to spend their two-night trip in a hut equipped with a woodstove, bunks, and other creature comforts. They have light sleeping bags but no tents or waterproof bivouac sacks. Their dinner—chicken jambalaya and pizza—remains frozen and inedible.

By Saturday morning, with the storm still raging, they agree to call off the trip. Brigette Schluger and Andrea Brett are verging on hypothermia and move very slowly as the gale screams around them. Brigette's sleeping bag is soaked—she abandons it at the bivouac site. Ken and Elliot are the first to be ready. They climb north up the ridge to the high point on the knoll, trying to get their bearings. Richard Rost follows them, and the three men argue. "I can't be personally responsible for these people," Richard reportedly remembers Ken saying. Ken—who teaches classes in leadership—says he and Elliot are going ahead, down the north side of the knoll; if they don't return in twenty-five minutes, the rest of the group should assume the route is safe, and follow.

Richard is furious; he doesn't want to split the group. And what if Ken and Elliot are caught in an avalanche? But the two men ski over the knob and down the northeast side. It is the last Richard sees of them.

Richard returns to the bivouac site. He and the other four skiers agree to take a more circuitous route, retracing their tracks to the Express Creek saddle. Andrea is very, very cold. The wind blows so hard it knocks her and Brigette over. Visibility is down to ten feet, and snow fills their tracks in minutes. Richard and Andrea take the lead, seeking their trail from the night before, looking for the saddle that leads into Express Creek and back to Ashcroft. They believe Brigette and the Dubins are behind them and following, but they can't wait. Their choice is to move or die. They find Express Creek and ski for nine hours, breaking trail through fresh snow and crossing huge piles left by avalanches that slid across the route after the group ascended into their frozen hell the day before. They do not see the Dubins or Brigette again.

Scott Messina, his yellow and red North Face powder suit pulled down to his waist and the arms knotted around his stomach, chews on his mustache. He is glued to the phone, grilling first Andrea, then Richard. Richard doesn't want to tell Scott about the group's dissension on Peak Twelve Four Thirty, as the knoll comes to be called, but when Scott pushes him he explains how the group broke up. The dissension is a very bad sign.

Scott will spend hours on the phone with them; they won't get out of Castle Creek for two days because of the road closure.

They want to go back to Denver. At one point during the coming days, Tom McCabe will quietly let a deputy know he doesn't want them getting on the helicopter that has been hired to ferry people trapped at the upper end of the valley out to Aspen. He needs them—they can't be allowed to leave.

For Tom, Julie's phone call means he will be living at the rescue cabin for the next four days—sleeping upstairs on the couch, eating delivered food. Tom carries a weariness upon him, as if the mission is a great personal burden—and, because he is the rescue leader of the moment, it is. But this is also what Tom craves, and though he doesn't manifest it outwardly, the challenge of the search and its many details brings him alive.

Tom, Scott, and the rest of the team are hampered not only by the weather but by their inability to meet with Andrea and Richard. Without that, they have to assess the psychological state of the missing skiers over the phone.

> There's a good deal of guessing. You're assembling the information to the best of your ability. That means a ton of phone calls, and you're talking to people you don't know, and you don't know whether they're straight shooters and sane people, whether they're very emotional people—you don't have any idea. So you're trying to be a psychic, in a way. You're asking for very hard evidence from those people, and you're trying to pry it out of them. For key people you may go back to them time and time again. Hit them hard, let them rest, let them think about it, and maybe they'll remember something. Hit them hard again. If you don't think they're telling you everything, hit them hard again. Keep poking and poking. So we were doing that. We were calling next of kin. You assemble what you can in the way of a profile on each individual: what their equipment is, their experience, what kind of shape they're in, do they take medications, are they divorced, are they out of a job. You try to get a feel for that person so you can try to predict how they're going to behave under normal circumstances, and then you try to carry that forward a little bit to the abnormal. Is this person likely to remain sane? Are they likely to become excited? Are they likely to sit down and die? It's a real imperfect thing. It's just that's all there is to do. You have to start with that, you get as much information as you can, hoping that something in there will make a difference. And sometimes it does.
> —*Tom McCabe*

A search can't be mounted safely that Saturday night and probably won't do much good anyway, so a few members who have come by the cabin take the time to prepare carefully. "It would be ludicrous to try to find a needle in a haystack in the middle of a blizzard at ten o'clock at night," Dave Lofland says. Jace Michael, John Zell, auto mechanic Chris Herrera, and I spend a couple of hours double-checking gear. We go over the four snowmobiles in the cabin's garage, making sure they have gas, oil, spare parts, belts. We fill extra gas cans. We put gas and oil in Rescue 1 and in Rescue 2, an ancient Chevy Suburban that looks like a hearse but for the faded red-orange paint job.

Scott and Tom drive down to the sheriff's office to plan the search. Under the newly instituted Incident Command System, Mountain Rescue operations must be approved by an "incident commander"—a sheriff's deputy. It is here, on Saturday night, that the rescue first runs into trouble.

Scott and Tom have come up with a simple plan. Weather has ruled out most options; it is too nasty to mount an air search, and the slides in the Castle Creek Valley have blocked access to the Express Creek trailhead. The only remaining option is to open a route south down Richmond Ridge, which begins at the top of Aspen Mountain ski area and runs parallel to Castle Creek, forming the east side of the Castle Creek Valley. Rescuers could proceed south along the ridge from the top of the Aspen Mountain gondola. In six miles they would reach the Braun hut system's Barnard Hut. Another six miles would take them to the saddle at the top of Express Creek and Peak Twelve Four Thirty. This was the "last seen point" for the missing five, the place to start looking for clues.

Although avalanche danger is very high, there will be no risk for rescuers if they stay on broad, timbered Richmond Ridge, following the unplowed dirt road toward the Express Creek saddle. The plan is to push a pair of Sno-Cats—squat, tracked machines used for grooming ski areas and capable of traveling through deep powder—out toward the saddle Saturday night. They can pack down a trail other rescuers could follow Sunday on snowmobiles and cross-country skis.

These guys were nervous, they were twitchy, they were like bulls pawing the ground. They wanted to be out in the field, where they were comfortable. Why do these guys want to go out? What are they going to do? I know what you can see from the ground in a blizzard. Nothing. You can't even see your ski tips. If given the same amount of facts and information, I'll make as good or better decisions as anybody. And I'm not focused—I don't have blinders on.
  —*Sheriff Bob Braudis*

Scott and Tom return to the cabin at 8:30 P.M. with orders to try to locate a helicopter that can fly in bad weather; Bob has nixed their plan. He wants Mountain Rescue to work from the air. "I've got to find a Jolly Green Giant," Tom grumbles, flipping open a huge three-ring resource binder. He searches the binder for a military base that has one of the all-weather Sikorskys (nick-named after the animated emerald character featured in ads for frozen vegetables), while Scott sketches out probable routes for the skiers in red marker on a laminated topo map.

We had lost control of the situation to the sheriff's office. Traditionally, we have called the shots, and all of a sudden [under the Incident Command System] someone else is calling the shots. I think we've got enough competent mountaineers on the team, we could have sent a team of people up Richmond Ridge without putting anybody in danger. The bottom line is, if it gets too nasty you pitch your tent and crawl in. They're acting like it's certain death if we go in there. There's no avalanche hazard in that area, and if you get lost, you park your butt.
  —*Dave Lofland*

I drive home Saturday night through the darkened streets of Aspen's Victorian West End, its oldest residential section. The snow swirls around entombed cars, and I am glad for the Subaru's four-wheel drive. I try to remember what the streets are like during summer, when the cottonwoods are a rich green, the sun warms the asphalt, and the chick-chick-chick of sprinklers marks the quiet, neat neighborhood. It seems strange and alien.

It is hard for us to remember what it's like to live in nature, hard to realize, in our urbanized lives, how much control nature retains. The Weather Channel seems to civilize and cage it. People who live in Denver deal only with the occasional thunderstorm that delays a flight out of the airport or the bad plowing job that makes it hard to get to work. Rarely, in modern America, are we in a place where the weather can work its will on us, where we have no recourse, no refuge, no place to turn, no options. The missing skiers had options, but they didn't recognize them, didn't accede to the demands of the weather. Possessing some experience in the mountains, they ventured into the twilight zone made accessible by a little knowledge, that most dangerous thing.

Unconsciously, they behaved as they do in a city, thinking that if it gets too bad they can always turn around or build a snow cave. But it takes more than city skills to navigate a white-out, or build a solid cave, or sit out a half-week storm safely, and in the city you don't get wet and hypothermic and lose your ability to make good decisions. In the city if the weather's bad you stay home, don't go to school or work. If your car's stuck you take the bus or the train. The skiers need to do a hard thing: admit defeat at the hands of the elements, stay put, dig in, conserve energy, wait it out.

I stop at Clark's Market, picking up instant noodle soup, an instant dinner, a half dozen each of Hershey bars with almonds and Reese's Peanut Butter Cups. When I get home I make pasta, thinking about loading up on carbohydrates. I repack my pack, taking out climbing gear, adding the food I bought, maps, extra long underwear, and chemical heat packs for warming anybody we might find.

I lie in bed and listen to the wind blow. Although I want to condemn these people for bad decisions, I can only feel sorry for them. I pray for them, in a small way.

It is easy to wonder what they were thinking. What was going on as those who knew the way to the hut tried to find it? Did somebody make a wrong turn, insist on its rightness, and everybody else follow reluctantly? Why didn't they make dinner Friday night? Who built the snow cave, and why did it collapse? Were they panicked? Probably not until Ken, Elliot, and Richard argued and the group broke up. Could they see their tracks coming down, or were those blown away? Richard told Scott that the general consensus was to get the hell out of there Saturday, they didn't want to spend another night out, they were going for it. What happened to the last three, who had been only a few hundred yards behind Richard and Andrea? Did Brigette and the Dubins decide to stop again, dig in, hole up in the trees, light a fire? Or did they string out on the trek down the avalanche trap of Express Creek, lose sight of each other, falling down one by one backwards in the snow, lying exhausted in the soft powder, feeling better now, the flakes tickling their faces, looking up into impenetrable gray, unable to find a point to focus on?

Or was it an avalanche, the terror of the unseen rumble coming from a high, unknown place, coming like the wrath of God or Lucifer? Maybe they cried out, maybe they didn't know what it was. Maybe they tried to run, were frozen in their tracks, or simply fell over. That would be a hard way to go, in a rush of terror coming on top of cold and exhaustion, not even seeing your doom through the snow and fog. Better perhaps to lie back in the snow, to fall like an angel into the soft, welcoming arms of your match.

⋀ ⋀

Sunday morning I call the cabin at six-thirty. Bev Campbell, a Pitkin County jailer who helps the team out in the office and the comm room, tells me to come in. Another foot of snow has fallen overnight. The weather is still bad; there isn't much to do. Tom has not found a Jolly Green Giant, but a huge, two-rotor CH-47 Chinook helicopter is trying to fly over the Continental Divide from Fort Carson, an army base near Colorado Springs. If it can reach Aspen, I will be part of a team of six skiers to be deposited near the Express Creek saddle to begin searching. We must be prepared to be out in the storm on our own for several days if the weather stays bad.

I walk next door to get breakfast for team members from the Hickory House, a greasy spoon on the edge of Aspen that advertises "We cater to locals and other riffraff." I order thirty-five dollars worth of hash browns, coffee cake, muffins. The waitresses find a big camp thermos and fill it with coffee, dumping in pot after pot.

At the other end of town, in the basement of the Pitkin County Courthouse, Bob and his deputies want to bomb the Castle Creek Valley. They hope explosive charges dropped from helicopters will shake down any avalanches that may threaten the road; then they'll send plows in. Avalanche control experts from the local ski areas are skeptical. Avalanches aren't that simple, they say; bombing may not release all of them. Besides, the creek has eaten its way through the snow dam, creating a tunnel and alleviating the water crisis. Convinced, Bob decides to close the road until Tuesday, when the current avalanche cycle will have run its course and the risk of more slides will have dropped sharply. The tiny Bell 47 Soloy helicopter he was going to use for avalanche control work, flown in from Montrose, isn't needed anymore. Scott asks if he can use it, and Bob nods. The weather is still bad above twelve thousand feet, but Scott heads for the airport.

He has already been there early in the morning, flying in Rick Deane's Cessna, but the winds were brutal and the turbulence severe. Rick couldn't get the plane close enough to the terrain to see anything useful. Although the valleys are clear, a heavy ceiling obscures the peaks and ridges. Scott tries again in the helicopter, a turbine-powered insect flown by Harvey White. He lashes his rescue pack onto the outside of the machine and climbs into the Plexiglas passenger bubble. The first flight takes him up Express Creek. The winds whip out of the west, and Harvey has to fight to maintain control of the storm-pummeled bird. On the second flight, Scott wants to get over Richmond Ridge to the Goodwin-Greene Hut, to see if anybody is there. The wind and clouds, however, keep forcing them down.

> We were flying around, and all of a sudden the ceiling dropped down on us. The clouds came in on us, the visibility was maybe ten feet, fifteen feet, and Harvey, I'll still never forget him, you know, his voice saying to me, "Scott, can you see the horizon?" No, I can't. It blew in, and he just held it steady. He was just hovering. At that point, when it blew out, we were ten or fifteen feet from the ground, we had moved somehow, we were down. I said, "To hell with this, let's get out of here." Big-time pucker factor.
> —*Scott Messina*

As Scott begins his flights the ski team waits in the cabin, going through gear, repacking. Chris Myers, who is leading the team, looks at me: "So, how does it feel to sit here and know there are five people dying out there?" he says, as the wind whips snow down Main Street. I ask him how much of a chance he thinks they have. He holds out his left hand, forefinger pinched down on thumb, and looks at me.

Rescue volunteers wander in and out of the communications room, looking at the map on the wall, theorizing and rationalizing. Nobody wants to come out and declare, "They're dead," but the thought seeps out in small, low conversations. Then Tom steps out of the comm room. The skier team needs to get to the airport; the Chinook from Fort Carson is minutes away. Suddenly, the place is alive, the torpor gone. Jace runs around with a legal pad, checking out equipment. "Who's got stoves?" he asks. "Zell, do you have probe poles? Sign out the heat packs." Fuel, helmets, water, thermoses, maps, sleeping bags, food. Ray Peritz and John are dragging a little bit; we wait on them to get their gear into the truck. Tom walks out of the comm room, where Linda Koones; Rick Deane's wife, Landon; and David Swersky work the phones, taking notes on legal pads, speaking very softly, calmly, quietly. The more tense it gets, the quieter Tom's voice. "Hey, guys, get to the airport," he chides gently.

On the drive to the airport, Ray speaks up. Like so many in Aspen, he refuses to age. He bicycles and skis and lifts weights with a vengeance. His face shows the wear of almost five decades, but his body has the definition of a surfer's. The license plate on his red Saab commands, "SKI ICE." Ray rides ski slopes with grace and speed that leave good skiers half his age in his wake. Much of his time on a ski hill seems to be spent in the air, for skiing is, to him, about flying. Early in the morning, when Aspen Mountain is uncrowded, he loves to ski nonstop top to bottom, descending so fast he has to pop his ears. He used to market a ski resort in New England; now he ekes out a living brokering hotels to investors. The money isn't very good, but he laughs often, sometimes flashing a smile that reminds me of a rictus. Divorced, with a daughter verging on the teens, Ray is brash and fearless.

Now he raises his voice over the squawk of the radio in Rescue 1. "Who's making the call about diving down some hairy slope?" he asks. He does not sound fearless today. "Because I, personally, don't want to die. I'm a coward."

"Me too, so am I," everyone says. Nobody is joking.

We pull up to the small wooden building of Aspen Base Operations, the terminal for private aircraft at Aspen's airport. And we wait. We wait for two hours. No Chinook. The place is busy, jets flying in and out, rich people in furs walking around. Killing time, Alex Irvin—a stocky, dark-haired professional photographer from North Carolina and one of the team's better rock climbers—chats up a cute, twentysomething California blond with flawless brown skin and perfect white teeth. She is waiting with her mother for their private jet, and the three are in animated conversation when Chris Myers hangs up the phone.

"Braudis wants Messina to pull out, and he won't put us in the field," Chris says. "It's too dangerous." Everybody looks at one another for a moment, as if they've just heard a death sentence. Somebody says something about repacking Rescue 1 and rolling back to the cabin.

Sloan Shoemaker, a tall, easygoing ski instructor with curly brown hair and the good looks of a 1950s advertisement model, turns to Alex. "So, did you get a date?" he asks, and he smiles a sly smile. "I could have," Alex says, grinning back. "I could have been on their plane to California." The pooled tension ebbs away.

Bob has frozen the operation. The Chinook has been turned back by weather, and he won't allow ground operations along Richmond Ridge. John Zell, who's watching CNN on a couch at Aspen Base Operations, ponders the news that he may be assigned to stand by at the Castle Creek avalanche, ready to dig out snowplow drivers if there is another slide.

"Well, I'm going to have to stop at home and get my Walkman," John says, "because I'm going to have to be really, really zoned to watch snowplow drivers work."

"John, I think you have an attitude problem," Van Kyzar quips from his place on the couch.

"Me? An attitude problem? Just because five people are dying out there and we're supposed to baby-sit snowplow drivers? This is their one chance. We can get in there. If they stay out another night, they're dead."

Van is more low-key. "We're going to be at risk if we have to go in for a body recovery," he says, "in the helicopter if nothing else. Why don't we go in while they have a chance? Me, I much prefer the live ones. It's just a personal thing," he says, sarcasm rising in his voice, "but I prefer to find the live ones."

/\.\ /\.\

I wake up before dawn Monday morning to the sound of Tom McCabe's and Chris Myers's voices on National Public Radio's "Morning Edition." The media have discovered this drama and are converging on the rescue cabin. The temperature is six degrees. Roiling clouds hang on Mount Sopris and in West Willow Creek. A little snow falls as a gray light trickles into the interstices of the valley. I grab extra glove liners, sugar, and tea. I pore over the Patagonia catalog at breakfast, wishing I'd ordered this or that piece of winter clothing.

A dozen cars rest along the curb in front of the cabin; some team members have come in at first light to ferry snowmobiles up Aspen Mountain for the push back along Richmond Ridge. Scott and Tom have convinced Bob—following Tom's threat the night before to testify against the sheriff—to pursue the plan they had developed Saturday night. But the Sno-Cats don't move until 6:00 A.M. Monday because the drivers need sleep. Steve Crockett drives the Cat he owns; Mike Swanson, a driver for Rick Deane at T-Lazy-7 Ranch, pilots the second, a huge, articulated Prinoth capable of carrying a dozen people.

Reporters swarm the hut. Don Dubin, Rob Dubin's brother, has driven into town. He sits on the couch in the front room with his head in his hands, watching us morosely. His other brother, Marty, arrives shortly. Their presence discomfits team members.

"Having them there, it's tough to be able to say, 'You know, I think these guys are fucking toast,'" Scott observes. "You can't say things like that."

Tom monitors the Sno-Cats' progress down Richmond Ridge by radio; at 11:45 A.M. he sends the ski team to the Aspen Mountain gondola for the ride to the summit. I carry a radio and an avalanche beacon, which emits a signal other beacon wearers can use to find me if I am buried. I wear two pairs of socks, polypropylene top and bottoms, polypro turtleneck, fuzzy pile pants and pile pullover, yellow Nomex shirt, Gore-Tex parka and hood, lined Gore-Tex shell pants and gaiters, telemark ski boots, polypro glove liners, pile-lined gauntlet gloves, balaclava, and goggles. All that shows is my nose.

The gondola ride is supposed to take thirteen minutes, but lasts thirty due to wind. The car stops three hundred feet above the ground, bobbing and swaying. It inches forward, stops, bobs. Inches forward again. Scouring winds whistle through the gondola. These people are dead, I think to myself. It's a thought a lot of team members are having. We have been looking out our windows at home, checking the thermometers in the middle of the night, listening to the wind in the dark, thinking, "No way." Up here, the conviction digs into our psyches.

At the top we wait in the gondola building until word comes that the Sno-Cats have covered the six miles to the Barnard Hut, which will be our forward base. Chris Myers, leading the skier team, wants to be everywhere, do everything. The night before he had stuck his head in the planning meeting between Tom, Scott, Steve Crockett, and Rick Deane. Although he's not running the rescue he's acutely aware that he is the team's president. He pushes them, arguing that the Sno-Cat drivers should move Sunday night, not Monday morning. Now he directs who will ride on which snowmobile, taking fifteen minutes to organize six skiers and three drivers.

We load up, two passengers and a driver to each machine, plus a sled full of packs, and roar out into another world. Snow rises three and four feet deep on either side of our path, which twists and rolls through miles of Engelmann spruce and open meadows along the broad spine of the ridge. The snow falls steadily, but trees block much of the wind. We reach the hut around two, in time to see Steve's Cat churning out to the south across an open park, headed toward the steep hump on the ridge known as McArthur Mountain and the open terrain beyond.

It is a relief to be out in the field, to be doing something, anything. Rescuers clatter into the Barnard Hut, a simple building with eight bunks, a woodstove, and a small deck that looks west over a creek to an open bowl on the east side of McArthur. The snowmobile drivers have started a fire. Somebody shovels the roof. We eat lunch: water and PowerBars, gorp, cheese sandwiches. John, his brown eyes intent, huddles on a bench over his food, two days of thick beard drifting across the wide, granite jaw that helps make him a magnet for women. He cuts big bites off a huge hunk of salami. "I eat this for the fat," he says, flashing a wide grin that acknowledges his reputation as an inexplicably lean eating machine. "It keeps me warm."

Bob Zook, one of the snowmobile drivers, is in his own heaven. A big-wall rock climber, Bob at thirty has a wiry body, a large, egg-shaped head, a pronounced beak, and thinning, longish blond hair. He always carries a radiophone clipped to his belt—he sells them for a living. When Bob talks, listeners unconsciously seek a volume control. He laughs like a machine gun. Giggling, hunched over some piece of electronic equipment, he is a youthful version of the mad scientist.

Bob is naturally amped up, behaving at rest as if he had just consumed four cups of coffee. If he eats a piece of chocolate or drinks a Coke, he goes through the roof. His manner can grate on other team members. Bob knows this, and he makes fun of himself, sometimes playing up his foibles. Yet when a tough, technical rescue goes down, he's the one who gets the call. A ten-year veteran of the team, Bob is the climber who will swing on a rope under a helicopter or rappel down a rock face to reach an injured climber. "He's the one I'd want with me on the rock," says John, who has climbed with Bob in Yosemite. "He looks out for his partner, and he knows what he's doing."

Now, gnawing on his salami, John watches Bob with open amusement. "This is like Christmas for Bob," he says as Bob unpacks a sealed Motorola box, preparing to set up a remote radio station. "I think Bob's about to have an orgasm."

Bob assembles an antenna. Then he is out the door onto the deck, pounding into an eave, stringing cable through the window. He gets the base radio out of its box and quickly punches in the frequencies. He is talking nonstop, laughing his staccato laugh, a huge grin on his face, scampering around like a hunchback.

"I've made McArthur saddle," Steve Crockett radios in from his Cat. "Yes!" says John. "I didn't think he'd make it up that. That's great. That's great." Steve has bulled his way onto the open ridge, where the wind has swept much of the snow away. We hadn't expected the Cats to progress beyond the Barnard Hut, and figured we'd be on our own as skiers from there.

Rick Deane shows up with several other snowmobile drivers— friends who aren't part of the Aspen team but are helping in the search. Rick stands six feet and two hundred pounds, barrel-chested and heavily muscled, with blue, smiling eyes set in a deeply tanned face. He smiles with a corner of his mouth, heaving a cheek up and back to show sparkling white teeth. His dude ranch in the mouth of the Maroon Creek Valley seems to make money hand over fist, taking tourists snowmobiling in winter, horsepacking in summer. He spends his cash on equipment, all of which is available to Mountain Rescue. Horses, snowmobiles, and all-terrain vehicles are there for the asking. Rick, closing in on fifty, is the grand old man of the Aspen rescue team. He is friendly enough but keeps to himself; new members hold him in awe and find him unapproachable. He doesn't feel compelled to speak much; he is content to stand in the back and pay attention. More experienced members know he can be counted on even if he isn't going to do everything by the book.

Rick wears a fur-lined, earflapped baseball cap. John starts teasing him about his Gore-Tex pants and jacket, his polypro turtleneck. Rick always wears lumberjack plaid and blue jeans, even though cotton is verboten because it doesn't insulate when it's wet. "I have jeans on underneath," Rick explains, smiling.

Because Steve is able to push on, so is everyone else: two Sno-Cats, eight snowmobiles, six skiers as passengers. It is an unwieldy group. Riding the snow machines, we follow Steve's tracks to the top of McArthur. A mile away we can see his machine working. There is no color in this light. The distant ridges, a mile or so away, are white on white, their lines indistinct against the clouds and snow. The light is low; the effect is of a black-and-white photo: the wind-sculpted, stunted trees—krummholz—are dark, everything else shades of light. Every defect in my cornea, the lines and squiggles and dots, shows up in this world, and I chase them around as I look from snow to cloud to snow. The wind comes in hard from the west, and we stand in the lee of a line of krummholz. Drifts six and eight feet deep have formed here, with huge dry pockets blown between them. Posts every quarter mile mark the summer route. Our tracks fill quickly.

In the distance we can see a helicopter working the ridge that is Peak Twelve Four Thirty, the knoll Torp's group mistook for Gold Hill after making their first wrong turn. Tim Cochrane, Mountain Rescue's state mission coordinator, has come over from Vail to help and is taking a turn with Harvey White in the bird. Scott has convinced Tom that "a new set of eyes" might see something he missed.

He is right; Tim spots a pack lying on the snow near the northeast side of Peak Twelve Four Thirty and directs Steve to it. The rest of us follow, but the scene is chaotic. The Cat drivers and snowmobilers, chafing under Chris's tight reins, are doing their own thing, and Chris grows angry. He isn't familiar with the terrain, he is very worried about avalanches, and he wants everybody acting only on his orders.

Steve empties the pack inside his Cat. All the gear in it is wet and frozen. Down at the rescue cabin, the comm room team determines this is the pack rented by Brigette Schluger at an outdoors store in Denver. It is an ominous sign; people in advanced stages of hypothermia often feel marvelously warm and begin to shed gear and clothing just before they die. Tom, building his victim profiles, figures Ken Torp and Elliot Brown will make it out if they aren't caught in an avalanche, and the Dubins will stick together. Brigette is the odd person out, and the weakest. Without her pack, her chances drop toward zero.

Chris is not able to delegate. He wants to examine the area where the pack was found himself, and he takes me with him. At the moment he wants the job done, no one else is quite ready, and he doesn't want to delay. The fourteen other searchers sit in the Sno-Cats. We take our avalanche beacons and put them in "receive" mode so we can hear if someone is buried in the area—even dug into a snow cave that has drifted over. I follow Chris, looking nervously at the bowl above us on our right. I don't like it, and the light is so bad I can't tell how steep the angle is, whether there is a cornice hanging over it. With our avalanche beacons on "receive," not "transmit," we depend only on our spotters watching us, should the bowl slide and catch us.

The light is fading fast, but I am drawn up the knoll. Almost immediately, as I climb by foot up a windswept strip of alpine tundra running on the left edge of the bowl toward the rocky summit, I come across scraps of parallel snow, packed down on the grass. The wind has blown the loose snow away, leaving this. "Chris," I yell. "I've got tracks!" He comes up, then begins following them down to the east, near a steep rock face. I keep going south up the windblown section. I can see the tracks, at times looking like those of three or four people. There are no pole plants, and I discern a couple of sweeping turns. These seem to be descending tracks, as they move out into the snow-field and back over the wind-scoured grass, which must have had snow on it when the skiers came by.

We are running out of light. I want to get to the summit to see if there is any clue there. I am winded, but I keep pushing. I have my hood up and goggles down. The wind cuts bitterly, leaning on me from the right, but I am working hard and stay warm. I look back. Below, the spotters stand and watch. The two Sno-Cats squat on the open bench, looking like moon-landing craft in the white world. Their yellow lights flash. They are safety; they are the link home. Out here, it feels like another planet: the sourceless light, the cold, the steady wind and the inability to hear, the shortage of oxygen, the lack of color.

I keep climbing, up toward a pile of rocks that is the 12,430-foot summit. I look up again and see a body, fifty yards ahead. It is lying head downhill, face turned up to the sky, frozen into the grass. The wind whips the dirty blond hair, the feet point up. My heart already is racing from the altitude and the exertion. I am pulled forward but don't want to go. I try to stay calm and keep climbing. I don't want to radio back until I know for sure what I have. Jesus, I think, Jesus, I'm not ready for this. I am within ten yards now, peering through the blowing snow before I know I am looking at a couple of rocks and a tuft of grass. I have been able to see only what my mind expects to see. In sixty seconds I've gone through a week's worth of emotions. I feel deflated. Suddenly, I am very tired. Standing there, the wind whipping around me, the natural light fading, the beacons flashing on the Sno-Cats hundreds of feet below, I don't know whether to laugh or cry.

/M /M

At the Barnard Hut, people sit on chairs, benches, or the bunks against the walls. They don't move much. Clothes come off slowly and are hung to dry. The woodstove doesn't seem to be giving out much heat. I can't get my feet very warm outside my boots, so I put them back in, even though my boots are wet.

The mood is grim. We have been out in the conditions; we know what they are like. And we have dry clothes, food, warm Sno-Cats, support. It is the fourth night in the woods for the lost skiers. Outside, snow is falling again.

We hang two gas lanterns, one over the gas stove, one above the maps spread on the table. Bob Zook gets on the radio and starts calling the rescue cabin for supplies: food, water, batteries, spotting scope, Gatorade. Down in the valley, a chain of dozens of people works to keep the field team fed and equipped.

Chris Myers is agitated. He works over the map, explaining, discussing, theorizing. Thirty years old, tall and skinny and very pale, he has wide-set eyes and a nose that looks like it's been broken once. He grows paler when he is under stress, and he is feeling a lot of pressure today. Since Saturday evening he has been pushing Tom McCabe, the 501, for responsibility on this mission, and now he has it. In spades. Tom, Rick Deane, David Swersky—these are the old men of the team, and they are watching. Even Scott Messina, only a few years Chris's senior, is an expert in the backcountry. Chris is a six-year veteran of the team and an avid mountain climber. He is in his second term as the team's president, an administrative role that demands time although not backcountry skill.

The tired faces of the men leaning into the shadows against the wall look at Chris with skepticism, and he knows it. Three of the skiers are volunteers from Alpine, the Mountain Rescue team based in Denver. Sent to Aspen to help, they have been asked to do nothing because Chris doesn't trust them. On Monday morning he had sent them to run an errand in Aspen, and they took much longer than he expected. He knows the fault may be his, because he had not been clear about what he needed done. Nevertheless, he holds the confusion against them, and they are frustrated. Many in the cabin feel they have spent their day tagging after Chris, that their time and skills could have been better used. He has not earned their respect as a leader today.

Now he must formulate a plan for tomorrow. The group listens as he, Tom, and Scott talk on the radio, rehashing the day's discoveries, discussing options. He opposes the plans being passed up from the rescue cabin: drop avalanche bombs from a helicopter in the chutes above Express Creek to release any remaining slides, then send dog teams in on Tuesday to check for bodies.

> I hadn't been back there two minutes when Bob Zook's thrusting a radiophone in my hand and saying, "You've got to talk to McCabe." We hadn't even had a chance to debrief ourselves, to say, "What is your perception of what's going on out there," to just talk about it. We'd literally just come in from the cold, and all of a sudden I'm being told we've got bombs coming, we've got dogs coming, we've got the Fifth Airborne Division going to fly over, and by the way we'll have breakfast at 7:00 A.M.
> —Chris Myers

"I feel really strongly that this is the wrong thing to do," Chris tells the searchers in the yellow glow of the hissing lamps. "I want to hear from you guys, and then I want to put together a plan and present it to them." With the assent of others in the Barnard Hut, he works out an alternative plan for Tom and Scott. He wants no dogs, no bombing, no more people in the field to try to keep track of—"walking avalanche triggers," he calls them. He wants to use the people at hand to search the timber in the headwaters of Express Creek; to go back to Peak Twelve Four Thirty seeking the Friday night bivouac (somebody may have re-

turned and dug in there); to check out the head of Bowman
Creek, the drainage off the east side of Peak Twelve Four Thirty
that heads south to the Taylor River and Gunnison; and to make
sure no one reached the Goodwin-Greene Hut. The goal at this
point is to try to establish a direction of travel. Four drainages
flow off the open area where the skiers were last seen. They
could have gone down any one.

After half an hour of discussion, Chris radios the rescue cabin
and asks that the command team be gathered together to consider his plan. In the Barnard Hut volunteers sit silently, watching
him from the shadows as the stress turns down the corners of his
mouth. On Main Street, a similar grouping takes place: Tom
McCabe, Scott Messina, David Swersky, sheriff's deputies, Linda
Koones, and Landon Deane to take notes. Outside the rescue
cabin, the television satellite trucks are lined up along the curb.
The front pages of Colorado's newspapers have been filled with
oversize headlines about the search. Reporters prowl the cabin
and climb over each other to get an angle on the story. It is, one
team member says, "like the world is looking up our asshole."

The notoriety only makes Chris sweat more. The Barnard Hut
is braided with tension. Chris tears a page from the cabin's log-
book and writes his plan out in pen. He takes a deep breath,
keys the microphone, and calls the rescue cabin. He speaks for
several minutes, detailing his plan. Every few sentences he says
"Break," releases the microphone, and takes a deep breath. He
knows reporters could be eavesdropping on the conversation; he
speaks guardedly. When he is done, Tom tells him to wait.
"Stand by while we flip the tape," he says.

Chris's eyes get big. "They're taping this?" he asks. "Oh,
Christ."

The delay lasts for several minutes, but it is not due to a tape.
A hurried huddle is taking place at the rescue cabin. Rick Deane
has stepped outside of the Barnard Hut and reached Landon, his
twenty-eight-year-old second wife, on a radio frequency they use
for their T-Lazy-7 Ranch. Landon, who is helping in the comm
room, pulls Scott aside and passes Rick's message on. What
Scott and Tom hear is that Chris is floundering, that the field
team needs leadership.

"Rick called back to say, 'We need more leadership up here,'" Chris recalled later, "and then Landon got that message and said, somehow in the telephone operator game, 'Chris has lost it, things are falling apart up there.' So suddenly they make this plan to change command.

"They tried to do it very nicely. They said, 'Thanks for your plan, you're going to be relieved in the morning by Tim Cochrane, and he'll be there at seven o'clock.' I'm like, 'I don't think that's wise, we feel this search has a high sense of urgency, we're going to have a staging area out in the field with the Sno-Cat, just have him meet me there when he gets in.' I said, 'We don't want breakfast at seven, I don't want to wait to meet him, he can meet me at my, at the command post in the field.' They were like, 'No, you are instructed to stay, you are not to leave.' So I was told by the higher-ups not to leave. I was so frustrated."

> For him to do it right, he had to manage his span of control. And that's where he didn't. He panicked, he did not let go of control. He's a control freak, and at some point you have to have faith in the people you're working with.
>
> The teamwork thing's real important there. Nobody who was out in the field with Chris did anything to help him. They let him sit out there and struggle. There were other people out there who should've been picking up on it. When I got back the reports that I got, it was really desperate sounding. And I didn't know, really, what I had. But the people who were giving me the information were people I trusted, so I did what I could without ripping Chris apart publicly. I moved some things around, I tried to be as clear on the radio as I could without tearing him apart, because he wasn't listening, he wasn't picking up and didn't agree with what we were telling him to do, and I wanted to separate him from the command and control position up there. So I assigned Scott to him, said, "Have him break it down into smaller chunks, you stay with him and help him manage that smaller chunk, and if he gets out of control, Cochrane's there as the bad guy from another place to throw him out of the field." And my intention was, if Chris lost it, Cochrane was going to lock him up. He was going to be carried out of the field if he had to.
>
> —*Tom McCabe*

Just before going to bed in the Barnard Hut, John Zell calls his fiancée, Mariela Carcer, on his radiophone. Lying quietly in their bunks, everyone can hear their conversation. Her voice, unlike John's, still carries the twang of the East River, and is burdened with worry. "Where are you, honey?" she asks. "Are you okay? I'm worried about you. Be careful."

I lie in my bag and listen to the rumble of the idling diesels of the Cats outside and the wind blowing the snow against the window. I dream about finding bodies, a single and then three, dried-up husks, not really buried, only a few hundred yards from houses in an open field of stubble.

⋀ ⋀

Before we hit the trail Tuesday morning, Chris mutters, "Since I've been demoted, I think I'll rebel." But he doesn't. He waits at the hut.

Although the sky has lightened and the snow let up, in our minds these people now are surely dead. The valleys are avalanche minefields, the snow has been relentless, the wind brutal, and the last information we have was indicative of real trouble in the group. That was Saturday morning. This is Tuesday. We are starting to search not only for people, but for reasons to stop searching.

Rick Deane leads a group of snowmobilers down Express Creek. He goes all the way down the creek, despite warnings from Chris to stay out of the valley due to avalanche hazard. "That's Rick," Scott says later. "With Rick, you give him a job and say, 'This is what we need done,' instead of saying, 'Rick, this is the trail I need you to follow exactly here.'"

I go back to Peak Twelve Four Thirty with another skier, a member of the Denver Alpine team named Shane, and Dave Brown, who rides a snowmobile. There is an art to snowmobiling, and Dave rides his machine with grace and intuition, floating across terrain where everyone else bogs down. Quietly competent, patient, almost shy, Dave is comfortable and happy around machines, even though one, a carpenter's joiner, took off four fingers at the first joint a decade ago.

We work northeast from the peak toward Taylor Pass, which we think might have been Ken Torp and Elliot Brown's intended destination after they left Richard Rost on the knoll. The south side of the mile-long ridge rolls off into a huge and deceptive snow cornice fifty feet deep. We fear the two men could have wandered to the edge of the cornice, where it may have collapsed, then buried them.

The weather opens up slightly, but a new storm is predicted by noon. At Taylor Pass we are able to look back at the base of the cornice with binoculars. We see several avalanche debris piles and dark objects lying on the snow, but it is too dangerous to investigate. We take a break near the pass, sitting on a patch of dirt blown clean, eating frozen candy bars and scanning Express Creek below the other side of the pass with binoculars. We see nothing, but much of the valley is in dark timber.

The weather begins blowing back in. The ground blizzards grow fiercer and more constant. I have to lean into the wind and strap my ski poles to my wrists so they won't be whipped away. Back at the summit of Peak Twelve Four Thirty, I radio Scott. He has taken over from Chris and is running a forward base out of the Prinoth parked above the Express Creek saddle. Dave, I tell him, has cold feet—his boots never dried out the night before. He needs to warm up. Shane and I want to investigate the bivouac site, and with the weather coming in, we don't think we'll get another opportunity. "Okay," Scott says, "but I want to hear from you in thirty minutes." We will be out of radio contact behind the hill.

Dave takes the snowmobile back to the Barnard Hut. I turn off the radio. Shane and I ski down to the south, then turn west and head into the park. According to Richard Rost, the group camped at the highest clump of trees in this bowl. We think Ken and Elliot may have returned here and dug in, building a snow cave to wait out the storm. They could be oblivious to the search on the far side of Peak Twelve Four Thirty. I begin with one clump of trees, Shane with another. The wind is blowing harder now. We shout and hoot. We look for indications of digging, broken branches, the wet sleeping bag Brigette Schluger abandoned, anything to indicate seven people had camped there. We investigate fourteen tree clumps, and find nothing. I begin climbing back toward Shane, who is headed up the ridge to the peak.

It is blowing hard now, at least forty miles per hour, but I have my parka and my heavy gloves off—I am sweating, sucking wind in the thin air as I break trail up through the snow. I turn my radio on and hear Chris Myers calling me. He can't hear me back. Then I hear Scott calling. It has been forty minutes. I tell him about our fruitless search. "Chris and Herrera are up at the summit with snowmobiles to get you out. I want you back at the Cat to rest and warm up," he says.

"All right, we're headed up."

"Did you hear the news?"

"No."

"They found Ken and Elliot."

"Are they alive?"

"That's affirmative."

I yell up to Shane, standing thirty yards up the ridge. He just looks at me; he can't hear anything. I start plodding up as fast as I can, the wind whipping around me. I have to get within five yards for him to hear. He grins. Ken and Elliot, we learn later, ended up 180 degrees off course and skied twenty miles south to Taylor Reservoir, deep in Gunnison County. Tom had tried days earlier to get Gunnison County rescuers to send snowmobiles north past the reservoir to see if the skiers had come down Bowman Creek, but Gunnison officials declined, saying the avalanche danger was too bad.

On Sunday and Monday nights the two men found two different cabins and broke in to dry out and sleep. On Tuesday they reached a tiny store at the reservoir, having skied twenty miles from Peak Twelve Four Thirty. Ken is in good shape; Elliot suffers frostbite to most of his fingers.

The sheriff's office had apparently been called from Gunnison, and we get a message from the S.O. saying this is the number for the general store over in Gunnison County at Taylor Reservoir, call them up—two of our people are there. And I said, "What? Give me a break." So I called over there, and I'm talking to Torp. I said, "Are you the guys I'm looking for?" And he said, "Well, I hope so," so we bantered for a few minutes. I only kept him on the phone briefly. I said, "Tell me what your fingers are like, physically do you need anything, do you have waxy fingers?" So we talked about that. They were fine. They were sure they were fine. They sounded great and the Gunnison sheriff was going to get them down to the hospital, so I let go of that. I felt really good.

—*Tom McCabe*

Back at the search area a trio of skiers—Debbie Kelly, Sloan Shoemaker, and Drew Dolan, a slight, prematurely balding property manager—discover clues by a small clump of trees at the head of the open Bowman Creek drainage. On the east side of Peak Twelve Four Thirty they find water bottles full of orange juice and rum, and a red stain where wine has been dumped in the snow. The trio work their way a half-mile down the creek, following faint ski tracks through the scattered trees. At last the search has established a direction of travel for the missing three: south, away from Aspen.

Shane and I ride back on snowmobiles to the Prinoth with Chris Herrera and Chris Myers, who retrieve us from Peak Twelve Four Thirty. As I get off the machine, I feel the air vibrate. The wind is blowing forty miles per hour, but that isn't it. I glance north and see a huge, black apparition float over the next ridge: the Chinook. It looks like something from *Apocalypse Now.* The valley shudders with the deep thudding of its twin rotors. It barely seems to move, but it does, battering its way through the wind, a boxcar lumbering overhead. We can see faces in the windows. Slowly, slowly, the pilots bring the bird around to a rise fifty yards away, face into the wind, and start to settle the back end down. But something doesn't feel right, and suddenly they are up, then down, down, down fast, and settled into the snow. Tim Cochrane gets out of the Prinoth and goes up to talk to the pilot. Inside the aircraft, a dozen searchers from El Paso Search & Rescue, near Colorado Springs, wait. Help is pouring in now; news of the search has traveled as far as Great Britain and Japan.

After a few minutes Tim comes back. The Chinook will make an aerial search of Bowman Creek. "We have to make a human arrow and point the way to Bowman Creek. He doesn't know where it is," he says. So we all stand in a line out to the southeast, me still eating a roast-beef sandwich, Tim out at the front. The machine lifts off ponderously, pounding the air, and turns like a slow-thinking dinosaur. As it heads away we can see the rear cargo ramp slowly dropping to allow for better observation. The rotor concussion might bring down avalanches, but it may also wake anyone deep in the trees, deep in a snow cave. One of our fears is that so much snow has fallen, victims could be dug in and searchers may pass within feet of them.

Chris Myers and Chris Herrera take Tim and me back to the Barnard Hut. I want to go down to help with the search in Bowman Creek, but Scott insists I eat and warm up. There are other men in the hut, skiers and snowmobilers holding steaming cups, hoods thrown back from windburned faces and greasy hair. We strip off clothing and find hot drinks.

"Quiet!" Tim shouts suddenly from the radio. "They think they've found something."

Everybody freezes. Ten men stand there, cups in hand, radios strapped on chests or hips over heavy pants and coats, staring at the machine on the table. Tim lays his two hands flat on either side of the radio and leans over it, willing it to speak. It crackles. Nothing. Scott, in the Prinoth, is talking to the Chinook and relaying to the rescue cabin on Main Street. We can barely hear Landon making the cabin's transmissions.

"Scott, we copy that the helicopter has found three people. Are they the victims?"

Crackle. Silence.

"Scott, you were breaking up, we did not copy that. Are they the victims?"

Silence. Nobody moves.

"Jesus," Tim says. "What is this, a soap opera?"

"As the stomach turns," says one of the snowmobile drivers. Everyone laughs. Then they stare at the radio.

"Scott, you're breaking up again, we did not copy."

Chris Myers is standing very still behind me. "Please," he whispers.

Silence. Silence for two minutes. Finally Tim turns to Dave Brown, leaning in a chair against a wall, warming his wet feet by the fire. "Brown, you call in so I don't get in trouble for interrupting," he says. Dave smiles, but he doesn't move.

"Scott, we copy the Chinook is headed to ABO. Do you need medical on site?"

Silence. Crackle. Crackle.

Tim can stand it no more and picks up the microphone. "All right," he says, keying the mike. "Cabin, this is Barnard Hut, do you copy?"

"Go ahead, Tim."

"What news do you have for me?"

"The Chinook has found three victims, and is transporting to Aspen Base Operations."

"Are they our people?" Tim asks quickly.

"They are."

The cabin erupts with whoops. "Yes! Yes! Yes!" Everybody leaps off the floor. If they weren't alive, Landon would have told us. We have them all. *We have them all.* They've made it.

One of the Alpine team's skiers looks at me. "Happy day, man," he says.

The Dubins and Brigette Schluger had also turned south into Gunnison County, heading down Bowman Creek, following Ken's and Elliot's tracks. But they skied more slowly and spent Saturday and Sunday nights in open snow pits, sharing two sleeping bags. Brigette suffered badly and slowed the Dubins. But, defying Tom McCabe's victim profile, they did not abandon her.

When the trio first separated from the rest of the group Saturday morning near Peak Twelve Four Thirty, Brigette was able to travel only ten feet at a time without resting. You have to move faster, the Dubins insisted. The gear in her backpack was wet and frozen—it would do her no good. So she dropped it where searchers eventually picked it up.

Rob Dubin took charge, forcing Brigette to keep moving, organizing the trio, pushing them on. Brigette had no gear beyond the clothes on her back. The Dubins shared theirs with her. By the time they reached the first cabin Monday evening, Brigette and Dee Dubin had badly frostbitten fingers and toes. In three days they had covered less than ten miles. They learned from a note that Ken and Elliot have been there. They flew the American flag upside down from a flagpole, stamped "HELP" in the snow, and waited. The Chinook pilot, running low on fuel and about to turn around, spotted the upside-down flag—a universal distress signal—then saw a person waving. Rescuers had to carry Dee Dubin onto the bird, but her husband and Brigette could walk.

I feel like I have just been sprung from a trap. It is as if I had been wrapped in steel bands, my whole body, and they have exploded off me. Relief pours from people's faces. We don't know these people, but it was our job to save them, and somehow they have come out alive. All the focus we had on that outcome suddenly is released, and it flows out in absolute giddiness.

Down in Aspen, the local radio stations broadcast the news. The bells of St. Mary's Catholic Church peal. People drive up and down Main Street, honking their horns.

> I remember people looking for chairs. There were weak knees, and a variety of us were choked up and tearful. It was hard to talk for a few minutes—different people at different times. Not everybody collapsed at once. There were still telephones and all kinds of people asking questions, there was still stuff to be done. It wasn't confirmed, so it was almost like you're guarding against letting yourself collapse. But once it was confirmed—once they said, "We have three people on board and we're flying in"—then they gave me the codes for their condition [two Code One and one Code Three]. And of course we stopped using the codes years ago. I thought I knew, as a mission coordinator I'm supposed to know. I thought I remembered it, and I did remember it correctly, but I didn't want to say it over national TV and be wrong. So I didn't say.
> —*Tom McCabe*

Tim Cochrane and the snowmobilers depart back toward the Aspen Mountain ski area, leaving Chris and me at the Barnard Hut. Chris gets up on the roof to shovel off the half not shoveled Monday. "I've got to be outside," he says quietly.

⋀ ⋀

Evening is settling on the town when we get off the gondola at the base of the mountain. It is like surfacing from scuba diving, the sense of coming back into another world. Suddenly I remember I have a girlfriend, a calendar, a list of things to do, obligations and chores. Our time in the woods has been a very industrial wilderness experience, built around internal combustion, maps and aircraft, radios and Gore-Tex. It has been a fight with nature and time, not an appreciation of them. Now, suddenly, we are returned to the unreal world of Aspen.

Jace is all grins as he shakes our hands. Chris and I throw our packs in the back of his truck and head to the cabin. As we come up Main Street we see three satellite trucks, their television lights bathing the cabin in a mercury glow. Jace avoids them by driving into the alley. We barge into the cabin through the back door. It is all a blur. Reporters are packed into the main room, mixing with Mountain Rescue members from the El Paso, Vail, Alpine, and Aspen teams. Tom is weepy, giving one TV interview after another. Everybody is shaking hands. It is the best reunion I've ever been to.

There are cans of Bud and Coors in the fridge, and I grab one. Linda Koones comes up and offers me champagne. I still have one hand free. Sure, I say. Linda and Landon have worked evenly, steadily for three days, and they are still handling the phones, but now they are smiling.

People are ebullient. The place is exploding with noise and festivities. At six o'clock there is a press conference at the courthouse. I go over to watch and sit in the courtroom pews with Chris. Bob Braudis speaks for a moment, and then Tom. Elliot Brown, who has flown over from Gunnison with Ken Torp, speaks the most, waving his bandaged fingers for the cameras. There must be sixty reporters. They clap when Elliot comes in. The Mountain Rescue members do not clap. They sit or stand, many with their arms folded, and watch.

Bob catches Chris Myers in the hallway outside the courtroom. "What the hell is going on over at the cabin?" he demands. Chris has no answer. The situation has become a media free-for-all. Bob doesn't know what's going on, and the incident he and his deputies are supposed to be commanding—the rescue now getting worldwide attention—has been running on its own momentum. Control and management have fallen into Mountain Rescue's lap, especially Tom McCabe's. Tom has been more than happy to run the rescue himself, without much interference from the sheriff's office—particularly since he feels the sheriff made bad decisions early on, and he felt like he had lost control Sunday to Bob. The seesawing command structure in the face of

Bob's desire to get a firm hand on Mountain Rescue will return to plague the team in coming months.

We catch a ride back to the rescue cabin with a friend of Chris's, who shakes our hands. He pulls up in front of the building. Television lights wash over the facade. Through the car's passenger window I see a TV reporter look at us, and realize I'm still wearing my radio chest pack and yellow Nomex shirt. I hear her say, "Here come two rescuers; they're going to come up and hug him."

"Fuck that," Chris says before opening the car door. Rob Dubin is being interviewed on camera directly in front of the door to the cabin. I walk up to him, into the lights. I introduce myself. He thanks me. I don't know what we say. I introduce him to Chris. Then Chris and I walk inside.

The party is truly roaring now. Nobody is really drinking, but everyone is giddy. People still are trickling off the mountain, with the big Prinoth coming last, rumbling down the face of the ski area. John Zell comes in and says, "What the hell, why don't I hug everybody!" We are waiting for the Prinoth, seventy people crammed in the building and spilling outside, howling. Drivers passing by honk and cheer in the darkness. Finally, word comes that the snow machine is clattering through town with a police escort.

We go out and stand among the TV trucks, climb up the snowbanks, and slip around on the sidewalk. The police lights flicker in from a side street, and then the articulated Prinoth follows, clattering slowly up Main Street, past the white Aspen Police Saab that has stopped to hold traffic. There are beer cans set on top of the TV cars, people are whooping and waving their arms. Mike Swanson double-parks the Prinoth in front of the cabin. Scott jumps out, shaking hands and hugging. Rick Deane gets out, then Drew Dolan and a half dozen other people. We haul out all the gear, dragging it into the cabin. TV reporters stand in the street, trying to get an angle. Everyone ignores them. One newswoman, microphone in hand and camera rolling, shouts, "Does anybody want to tell us how you feel?"

"ALL FIVE ALIVE!" trumpets the *Denver Post* in a banner headline. Denver network TV stations produce half-hour specials about the rescue, to which they attach the lurid but enduring moniker "Miracle in the Mountains." Newspapers throughout the state devote page after page to every aspect of the saga, from Ken Torp's personally authored account of events to how Colorado mountain shops can't keep avalanche transceiver beacons in stock. Yet by Friday—only a week after Ken and his group had set out from Ashcroft—people are angry.

The whiplash is vicious. The elation over the successful rescue quickly ferments into anger, resentment, bitter recrimination, and sardonic jokes. In the ski patrol shack at the top of Aspen Mountain, Ken Torp finds his way into the local lexicon. A hand-lettered sign there coins the verb "to torp: to lead your friends, without consideration, into difficult circumstances and then abandon them." It is immediately adopted throughout town.

"Hey," somebody will say at the top of a lift, "don't torp me—I'm still putting my skis on!"

"After seeing some of the people who were rescued on TV, I was really irritated," Peggy Hanks, a local, tells the *Aspen Times Daily*. "They weren't humble in the least, considering the time and money people spent looking for them. They should have to pay everyone back."

Mountain Rescue-Aspen has an annual budget of about seventy thousand dollars. A little less than half comes from Pitkin County, as a line item in the sheriff's budget. The rest is generated through fund-raising events staged by the team and through donations. Money comes in the mail every month, some of it anonymously, some in response to the occasional fund-raising letter sent to people who have given in the past. Some comes from victims or their friends and relatives. All of it goes into a kitty to pay the electric bills, buy new ropes, keep the vehicles running, send team members to advanced trainings. There's depreciation on trucks and snowmobiles, contents insurance, new radio batteries. Every year a couple thousand dollars is spent on pizza and beer for work parties, on board meeting dinners. Topographic maps tear or disappear, the mountaintop radio repeaters break down, the phone system in the cabin dies. Six-hundred-dollar radios are dropped. Carabiners vanish.

Every year the team spends most of its budget without paying a dime to the members for their time. There is no money, when all is said and done, to pay for the actual rescues.

The Torp rescue cost Pitkin County approximately twenty thousand dollars for food, fuel, overtime for sheriff's deputies, and a hundred other things. The army's Chinook helicopter cost the nation's taxpayers $2,400 for each flight hour, running up a five-figure bill. Sloan Shoemaker, skiing down the face of Aspen Mountain as rescue teams were pulled from the field after the last of the missing skiers had been found, tore a ligament in his knee. That injury would cost Pitkin County—which is self-insured—nearly forty thousand dollars in medical and disability bills. If anyone in the lost party had owned a Colorado hunting or fishing license, many rescue costs would have been covered, since license fees contribute to a state rescue fund. But no one did. "We are getting calls from taxpayers saying, 'We are not paying for this,'" a sheriff's office employee tells the *Denver Post*. There is no mechanism to force victims to pay for the cost of a rescue, which makes critics of the skiers even angrier.

Again and again, in conversations on the streets, in letters to the editor, Aspenites complain bitterly about the "arrogance" of the skiers, especially Ken Torp, who had once been chief of staff for former Colorado Governor Richard Lamm. Tuesday afternoon, after being examined in the Gunnison hospital, Ken and Elliot Brown fly in a private jet back to Aspen. A television reporter interviews Torp on the plane for the five o'clock news. Ken is headed to Aspen's Ritz-Carlton Hotel and is ready, he says, to party. "We're going to light up Aspen," he promises, grinning from behind dark, square sunglasses he seems never to shed. Many locals, seeing Ken for the first time, find him repugnant. He doesn't have to get down on his knees, they say, but a little humility and a heartfelt thank-you would go a long way. Ken's manner rubs many Aspenites the wrong way, and it is all downhill from there.

The next evening, on NBC's "Nightline," Ken dodges questions about the wisdom of undertaking the trip in the first place. On Thursday, the *Aspen Daily News* reports how Saville Ryan had warned the group about the avalanche danger before they set out. "Well," someone in the group reportedly replied, "Express Creek is always a crapshoot anyway." Nor did the severity of the storm seem to concern the skiers, in particular Elliot and Ken. They came for snow, they told Saville, implying the storm was just what they wanted.

Locals feel like they have been slapped. The alpine tradition of helping people in need, and of graciousness on the part of both rescuers and victims, seems lost on the Denver skiers. Sheriff Braudis had told a reporter, before the skiers were found, that rescuers venture out in hideous conditions to look for people they don't know "because we love them." Tom McCabe, fighting waning odds of the skiers' survival, had said "these are our kind of people."

Tom still holds a grudging respect for Dee and Rob Dubin, who kept Brigette Schluger alive and didn't abandon her. But few outside the rescue community have anything but contempt for the "Miracle Five." "Why should people have to put their lives on the line for these idiots?" wonders Aspen resident Jan Carney. When Ken suggests holding some kind of fund-raiser in Aspen to defray costs, Mountain Rescue members quickly turn him down—Aspenites feel like they've paid for the rescue once, and have no intention of paying for it again.

Friends and family of the Dubins give Mountain Rescue more than a thousand dollars. Sixteen months after the incident, Elliot Brown sends the team two hundred dollars. Seventeen months after, Ken sends two hundred and fifty. But what irritates Scott Messina most is the people outside the incident, heavy hitters in the state government and friends and family of the missing skiers. "The whole thing was, 'Do whatever it takes, everything is covered.' Where are those fat fuckers now, when everybody turns out fine and they just made some bonehead mistake?" he fumes months later. "These people all make these commitments, and where are they? It [the money] doesn't have to go to me or the team or whatever. We're all paying for it [the rescue], you and me as taxpayers, and that's the infuriating thing."

The disintegration of the Torp group becomes almost comic. While the skiers insist they split up by mistake during the blizzard, their sniping and backbiting in the days following their rescue strongly suggest otherwise. Producers besiege them with proposals for made-for-TV movies, and the group splits into factions, retaining different agents. One day members try to downplay their reported disagreements; the next brings a new accusation about how things had gone wrong and who was to blame. Brigette Schluger, the Denver art dealer who found herself skiing with Dee and Rob Dubin, complains they treated her "like a Roman slave girl." In Aspen this is met with hoots of derision. *Outside Magazine* commissions a feature story about the greed and media frenzy. The title: "I'm Lost in a Blizzard, Let's Do Lunch."

For Mountain Rescue-Aspen's volunteers, the end of the rescue means trying to pick up their lives again, going back to doing the things that pay the bills. But it's not easy. Wednesday morning I find Scott repacking his huge backpack at the cabin.

He has been called by a TV producer, he says, who threw out a figure of ten thousand dollars for Scott's story, plus twenty-five thousand dollars to be a "technical consultant" on a movie. That didn't sound too bad, Scott reflects.

He has just unpacked his pack for a TV crew that wanted to do a story on proper winter camping gear. As that wraps up, another cameraman barges in. He doesn't bother to introduce himself, and he doesn't ask names. He just starts talking. He is a freelancer hired by a Denver station, he says. He really needs to do an interview, he tells Scott; can we do it now? But Scott is exhausted. He has to get home and take care of some business. Okay, the TV guy says. How about later today? I've really got to have this today. Scott, who has given more interviews than he can remember, sighs. Okay, he says, later today. Are you in the phone book? Yes, Scott says, I'm in the book.

"What's your name?" the cameraman asks Scott. Scott looks at him. He looks at me. He looks at the cameraman again and sticks out his hand.

"Tom McCabe," Scott says.

⋀ ⋀

That evening people gather to help clean and organize gear at the cabin. Several have received calls about movie and TV prospects. There is cautious interest; the figures are enough to garner attention: numbers like fifty, a hundred, a hundred and fifty thousand dollars are bandied about. "The question is, do we all want to prostitute ourselves?" someone asks rhetorically as a group stands in the comm room. Dave Brown, sitting quietly in the corner as usual, shrugs and gives his trademark half-embarrassed grin. "I don't know," he says, pondering the wisdom of the television world and the fact that the skiers essentially saved themselves. "I don't think we did anything that great."

Over the next few days, phone lines buzz as team members discuss the movie deals. Dustin Hoffman will play Scott, someone quips; Danny DeVito will be a perfect Bob Zook, although a little old. Tom claims Schwarzenegger as his double. But beneath the jokes, tension grows. Some people who had been major players might stand to make a lot of money. Others may not. This potentiality collides head-on with the team's avowal to give no individual credit to members. Even if all the money goes to the team, some people would get more billing than others, or be more involved with the production. Who will get what? Who will be in control? Issues that didn't exist a few days ago suddenly have become big problems.

In the days leading up to the March 2 team meeting, Scott changes his mind about helping to make a movie. "No money," he says, "is worth the integrity of the team."

Chris Myers, who has received more calls from producers than he can count, agrees. "That's not what we're about," he says.

The monthly meeting, held only six days after the skiers were rescued, packs the room above the garage. The board's cluttered office is at the top of the stairs; a left turn past the shower leads into the beige-carpeted meeting room. Team members crowd in on the two couches and dozens of white plastic chairs. They stand on the landing of the stairs. Linda Koones, Dave Lofland, Chris Myers, Debbie Kelly, and Scott Messina sit grimly at the board's white linoleum folding table, their backs to the French doors at the rear of the room. Scott, as usual, has a plastic water bottle on the table before him. A strip of yellow tape on the cap marks it as his, and he drinks from it throughout the evening. Unstuffed sleeping bags and a pair of boots clutter one corner, several sets of skis another. Along the left side, red and tan lockers reach up to the vaulted white ceiling. Bob Zook's locker door is decorated with a postcard of Yosemite's Half Dome. Bob has traced in blue pen a route he climbed up the sheer granite. A few doors down is Tom McCabe's locker. He has taped a "Far Side" cartoon to it. In the comic, the reader peers over the shoulder of two pilots looking out the windshield of their plane. Directly in front of them a mountain goat peers back through a hole in the fog. "Hey," one of the pilots asks, "what's a mountain goat doing way up here in the clouds?"

As the meeting gets under way, Chris asks any nonmembers to explain who they are and why they're here. It is a standard ritual to introduce people who may want to join the team and have come to learn more. But this time, Debbie adds something: anybody who is a member of the press will be asked to leave. No reporters have attended previous meetings, but this one could be different—the air is pregnant with expectation about "the movie." Moreover, the skiers haven't been the only people criticized in local papers. A columnist in the *Aspen Daily News* has written, "Mountain Rescue thrives on this kind of thing. They get off on it. It feeds their egos. It's why they do what they do. . . . For the Mountain Rescue members who blasted several of the skiers' reasons for going out, take a good look at your own. Without their arrogance, you couldn't fuel your own."

In another article, the paper has questioned whether the rescue was run as well as it could have been—a criticism that hits close to home. And in a third, disparaging remarks from team members about cooperation from the Aspen Skiing Company on the incident have been printed, causing consternation. Caught up in the media swirl, feeling misrepresented and uncomfortable in the public eye, team members seethe with anger at journalists.

Part of the problem has been the team's own making. By the end of the rescue, reporters were crawling all over the cabin, getting in the way, tying up the phones. Neither the sheriff's office nor Mountain Rescue had appointed a spokesperson, so reporters had roamed at will, interviewing anyone who would talk to them. "They'll take one tiny thing that you say, something they're looking for, and play it up, use it out of context," Debbie laments.

Ray Peritz, who has found himself at the heart of the story criticizing the Aspen Skiing Company, is bitter that the reporter chose to ignore all the good things he and others said about the firm. But Tom doesn't seem too concerned—in fact, he admits, he was not happy with the Ski Co., which hadn't run its ski lifts as late as he wanted on Tuesday. That was why Sloan Shoemaker had to ski down Aspen Mountain at the end of the rescue, which led him to blow out his knee. Tom concedes he had wanted his criticism to get into print. Debbie—who works for the Ski Co. as a backcountry powder tour guide—had been furious with Tom when she found out, yelling at him in the comm room. Now she pleads with the team to "go through channels" if there's a problem.

Bob Braudis comes in at the beginning of the meeting to speak to the team. The sheriff is haggard and tired. His dark hair, swept back in waves from his head, flows down to his collar. Everything seems oversize on Bob, including his pug nose and the David Letterman-like gap between his front teeth. He is tan, but his brown eyes are rimmed with red. He stands up and fills the front of the room, stuffing his hands deep in the pockets of his khakis, and rocking back on his heels against the weight of his ample belly. It has been, he says, "the craziest week of my life." He's here to thank Mountain Rescue. But, he adds, he has told his deputies they won't be selling their movie rights to anyone. "If they take money for their movie rights, they take that money as they leave my organization," he says in a broad-voweled, methodical voice with just a hint of a lisp. "We can't forget who we work for," he says before departing, "and that's the people of Pitkin County."

It is almost nine o'clock by the time routine business is out of the way. Chris runs his hands through his dark blond hair, takes a deep breath, and begins to talk about the proposals for a television movie. The board met with TV producers this afternoon, he says. But the board needs to hear what the membership wants to do.

"Let's all vote to support the board, no matter what their decision," Van Kyzar insists. People agree, but reluctantly; the room is claustrophobic and tense. Members who have had less time to consider the movie concept seem more likely to embrace the opportunity. Those who have thought extensively about the idea seem more inclined against it, fearing for the team's integrity. "I think this goes against everything we stand for," says Rick Deane. Rick never speaks at the meetings. Once employed as a Marlboro Man model, he is the classic strong, silent westerner. The fact that he speaks up now causes many in the room to pay close attention. "I think this will just divide the group," he continues, pushing back his dirty baseball cap, exposing white skin above dark tan. He stands balanced, feet apart, thick fingers wedged into the front pockets of his dirty jeans, wrists rolled forward. "This isn't what we're about, and I just can't say strongly enough how much I'm opposed to it."

But Tom, leaning against one of the lockers, makes a slow pitch for taking the money. It could be, he says, an endowment for the team. There will be some criticism from other rescue teams that don't get money, sure, but it could be a real bonus for the team's finances, he says. Athletic, dark-haired Dave Goldberg, who runs the Silver City Grille, and chunky, tonsured Dave Polovin, a backcountry guide and bicycle shop owner, both like the idea.

"What's all this talk about money?" asks Bert Fingerhut, the fifty-year-old president of a biotechnology firm who sits on the boards of several nonprofit groups. "This team doesn't have money problems, not seriously. If you need money, the community provides it." That's not true, somebody counters. Chris checks a notebook in front of him and finds that the team received $31,700 from donations and fund-raisers in 1992—about half its annual budget.

If the team does become part of the movie, it will have something to defend, argues Lee Hewey, a wrangler at T-Lazy-7 Ranch. Whatever makes it on-screen will be a far cry from the truth, he's sure of that. Remember *Aspen Extreme*, he says, and *Zenith: Murder in High Places*, two abominable movies recently filmed here. "If we stay out of it, we can just sit back and laugh."

The discussion seesaws, many of the participants clearly at war with themselves. Nobody joined Mountain Rescue-Aspen or its board for monetary reasons—in fact, people sign up with a clear understanding that volunteering will cost them money and time. No one is prepared to deal with the problems brought on by fistfuls of unexpected cash. This unwelcome debate has been thrust upon the team, and because so much money is involved, the offers can't be brushed aside. No one in the room is especially rich—many are close to poor, by Aspen standards—and the potential for cash has made a lot of people sit up and take notice. The team has never had to deal with greed before, but there are wisps of it in the air now, evident in people's eyes as they ponder what they might get, what someone else might get. Even those who advocate taking money only for the team's coffers understand there is something dirty about the whole business. The true nature of the debate in the steamy room isn't about splitting up the pie, but about whether to take a bite at all. It's about what's right and wrong, about selling out.

The American greed of the 1980s has been especially evident in Aspen, where locals have been displaced by wealthy second-home owners, where fancy boutiques have overwhelmed more pedestrian shops. One of the characteristics of Mountain Rescue-Aspen that makes the team so broadly popular in the town is its fundamentally communitarian nature. Any team that saves people's lives earns goodwill; this one has garnered an additional measure by stalwartly remaining a volunteer organization of local residents, a bulwark of small-town values in an increasingly glitzy resort community. Being part of that makes many of the team members proud. Stooping to grasp a few dollars for something they do out of love feels like whoring.

After thirty minutes, Chris calls for a vote. He had hoped for a clear consensus against the movie but hasn't seen one. Rather than relieving his stress, the evening has only worsened it, and he is not handling the strain well. "Some of the board members have been away from their jobs for a week," he says bitterly. His paycheck for the past seven days has amounted to all of a hundred and twenty dollars. "I want to get on with my fucking life." He tries to cobble together the question, but is so overwrought he cannot. Finally, Debbie helps phrase a proposal that the board pursue movie offers.

"All right," Chris says, his mouth turned down in a hard, dark grimace, "we can vote, but I have to say, I've just got to say, for whatever it's worth, that if we go ahead with this, I just don't think I could fucking live with myself." His voice breaks and his eyes brim over with tears. He slumps back in his chair and puts his hands to his face. No one says anything.

Debbie calls for the vote. "All in favor of pursuing the movie, raise your hands." Chris sits up and begins to count. Some people raise their hands only tentatively. "Put up your fucking hands!" Chris yells. Hands go up a little higher. The results are inconclusive: fourteen in favor of pursuing a movie, nineteen opposed. The board will take the vote under advisement at a meeting the next day.

Scott perks up from his slouch at the end of the board's table. "On a lighter note," he says, "the Braun huts have brought some beer and wine for everybody. Go have some."

/\\ /\\

The next day I run into Debbie. I ask her what the board decided.
   "We decided," she says, "to fuck the movie."

/\\ /\\

In mid-March team members receive a letter from Mountain Rescue's board. Unlike the typically chatty newsletters sent out each month, this one has the smell of a lawyer about it. "Any member who contracts to profit monetarily from any involvement with movie or television production will jeopardize their position on the team," the letter intones. "The mission file and any other documentation are the exclusive property of Mountain Rescue-Aspen and are not to be used by any member for profit."

   "It was directed at everybody," Scott Messina concedes, "but it had one person's name on it, mostly."

   The name everyone saw, but no one had to speak, was Tom McCabe.

   Chris is still reeling from the way Tom treated him during the search for the five skiers, and Tom doesn't feel too good about the way he was treated either. "That particular mission was the worst one, from an internal dynamic, that I've ever been on," Tom says. He believes the board's memo about the movie is a slap back at him. "Some things went down that I wish hadn't gone down, and some feelings were hurt, not the least of which were mine."

   Tom's relationship with the board chips and curls around the edges during the following weeks, and not only because he was hammered over the movie—which, ultimately, is never made. For more than a year, Debbie and Chris have tried to get Mountain Rescue to work more smoothly with the sheriff's office. Bob Braudis, who is legally responsible for search-and-rescue operations, had decided in 1992 that he wanted more control over the team's operations and began to seek it. Tom, who served as president three times—most recently in 1991—and was accustomed to a lot more latitude, doesn't like the idea of surrendering any autonomy.

> It used to be they just went out and pulled bodies out of wherever they were, pulled people from wherever they were. They weren't too concerned about the risks to themselves, they weren't concerned about the care they gave these people as far as whether or not they [rescuers] were Emergency Medical Technicians or Advanced First Aiders, or whether they did everything right or not. Just the fact they got them out of whatever situation they were in was good enough. I think a lot of it stems from the "sue me, sue you" thing in this country—that's why the team's had to change, and I think it really bothers McCabe and some of these old guys, because it used to be so much easier. They did everything themselves, they didn't have to answer to the sheriff's office, they didn't have to fill out reports.
> —*Debbie Kelly*

Bob Braudis, first elected in 1986, is a different kind of lawman from his predecessors. Under Colorado law he can be held personally liable if Mountain Rescue screws up. He wants to make sure the team doesn't cost him money; he plans to do it by putting his people in control. Tom has chafed as the team's board, led by Chris Myers, acquiesced to more control of rescues by deputies. At Bob's insistence, deputies are now appointed "incident commanders" during rescues, even though many of them have no rescue experience. What matters is that they can be trained as managers. "I see the paid professionals, as opposed to the volunteer professionals, coming out of the sheriff's department," says Steve Crockett, Bob's emergency services coordinator and right-hand man. "They'll be the people who are in the key positions, because we can control them, we can get a return on that investment. They're going to be the helicopter managers, the helispot managers, the incident commanders, stuff like that. Not to replace the technical expertise Mountain Rescue has in certain areas, where they're the leaders in the industry and stuff like that, but if we need to manage something, we need to get our people in there."

To the deputies, being incident commander generally means sitting in the comm room and watching Mountain Rescue volun-

teers do their jobs, but it also gives deputies veto power over rescue plans and decisions, a sharp departure from the hands-off
approach of a few years previous. "I've probably been on three
hundred rescues," says David Swersky. "I've probably managed a
hundred rescues. It's offensive to me to have a paid person from
the sheriff's department looking over my shoulder, telling me
what to say and how to do it."

During the saga of the "Miracle," Tom, as rescue leader, took
the opportunity to try to reestablish some autonomy for the
team. He argued vehemently in favor of going out when Bob and
Steve wanted to hold back. There is a perception—particularly
on Bob's part—that Tom is a renegade. In the dirty backwash of
the "Miracle," Debbie, Chris, and Scott are frustrated with Tom.
While they aren't happy about the sheriff's office becoming more
involved in rescues, they are resigned to it as a reality and have
been trying to make the relationship work. Tom has disrupted
their dance, cutting in and waltzing away with the team, leaving
Bob to steam.

> I kept control of that incident at great, fucking personal cost—twenty
> hours a day, no sleep, but I did keep control of it because it was not
> really managed well. He [Steve Crockett] has moles, and the moles
> in Mountain Rescue say McCabe's the biggest problem in Mountain
> Rescue-Aspen. I think I could work with anyone, and I could work
> with Tom McCabe, but it takes a certain amount of give-and-take.
> What I don't like is lip service and then a stab in the back. I like to
> get stabbed right in the front. Let someone come up and stick the
> fucking dagger right in your chest and say, "You prick." But getting
> stabbed in the back hurts a lot more. Shit, I was so disappointed
> when I heard about all the bad-mouthing that McCabe was engaged
> in after stroking the shit out of me. [He'd say] "Yes, I agree with
> you," and then I'd leave the hut and go home, and then he'd say,
> "Fuck the sheriff, he doesn't know what he's doing."
> —*Sheriff Bob Braudis*

Angry with the board, targeted by the sheriff, Tom is not having a good spring. To top it off, his fifteen-year marriage to Jody
is unraveling, but Tom has said he'll stick it out for now because
of their eleven-year-old daughter, Merrin. Unhappy about the
way the movie idea has been handled, frustrated by what he sees

as the board's failure to stand up to meddling by the sheriff's office, Tom grumbles to the board about taking some members and starting his own rescue team.

> He has always felt like it was his team, and I'm not sure why he gave up being president and got more people involved. He's always wanted to control the team and have it be his team, do things his way, and he's always been real opposed when things didn't go his way. Tom and I have knocked heads a little, but I think we both still respect each other a great deal. I know I still respect him—he has an incredible amount of knowledge. I don't want to see him go away. I want him to be part of the team.
> —*Debbie Kelly*

In the end, nothing comes of Tom's ruminations. He pulls back and tries not to create further trouble with the sheriff.

> After the "Miracle in the Mountains" I essentially stepped out. In the most ancillary way, perhaps, Debbie would talk to me or Chris would talk to me or Lofland would talk to me, and I'd give them an opinion, but there was really very little energy. There was almost no criticism. If I take that excuse away from them, if that's no longer a part of the equation, it's not something Crockett can use as a crutch. He can't be beating Bob up over the fact that McCabe is the source of all the sheriff's difficulties vis-à-vis Mountain Rescue. If McCabe's not there, that argument falls apart, okay? You can't say McCabe is orchestrating, that McCabe is doing this, that McCabe is doing that, because McCabe is not there.
> —*Tom McCabe*

⋀ ⋀

Steve Crockett, the sheriff's Rasputin, is tall and loud, his hands chapped and red. An electric-orange nest of hair circles and twists above his crimson face, wrestling itself to a draw. In 1988 Steve—sardonic, sharp-witted, a no-bullshit, blue-collar intellectual who moved to Aspen as a 1960s dropout—came into the public eye and ran for Aspen City Council on a radically anti-growth platform. "Too many rats in the cage," Steve said; that's what's wrong with Aspen. The town hadn't had such an exciting election since the drug-addled journalist Hunter Thompson came within a few votes of winning the Pitkin County sheriff's race in 1970.

Steve Crockett and a slate of no-growthers won, their victory coming at the crest of the greed and development wave washing through the upper Roaring Fork Valley in the late 1980s. But nine months into his term Steve was thrown out of office in a recall election. He was smart, and about many things he was right. But he was no politician, and his foes capitalized on his rough manner and the slights he had inflicted on the town's elders to force him from office.

Steve went to ground, disappearing—some say to the Utah desert—for a month. Soon he reappeared with a job in the Pitkin County sheriff's office: emergency services coordinator. He and Bob Braudis had been close friends and hard-drinking buddies for decades. Bob had worked diligently to get him elected; now he helped put Steve back on his feet. It started as a five-thousand-dollar contract to analyze the county's mutual aid agreements with other counties and federal agencies. Soon it was a thirty-five-thousand-dollar annual salary.

In 1990 Bob and Steve convinced the various agencies in the county to agree to work under the formal Incident Command System. ICS, as it is known among emergency services cognoscenti, was developed by the federal government to coordinate large, multiagency efforts to fight big wildfires. In recent years it has insinuated itself into many government organizations that deal with emergencies, for it has a basic appeal to logic. ICS is a standardized command-and-control management chart, easily adaptable to incidents of almost any size. The positions on the chart—incident commander, operations section chief, logistics section chief—have a paramilitary feel to them. They are positions that never change, regardless of the size of the emergency. On a small event—a twisted ankle a few hundred yards from a road—all the jobs might be covered by a few people. On a big one, dozens of personnel may be slotted into management positions.

Big emergencies—forest fires, floods, earthquakes—are like wars. Success depends much less on a quick, heroic action than on a methodical, organized attack. In big incidents, what makes the difference isn't heroism. It's logistics.

During the "Miracle," casual observers saw television footage of helicopters flying out on searches, or snowmobiles transporting rescuers into the woods. That's what a search looks like from the outside. What they didn't see was all the other efforts that put and kept people in the field: marshaling food and fuel and water, organizing and managing vehicles to be in the right place at the right time, running and logging communications, tracking finances, talking to the media, handing off control at shift changes. These tasks are usually manageable when a single rescue team or fire department tackles a problem. But when other groups become involved, operations crumble. Each organization has its own lingua franca, its own way of doing things. ICS provides a common template so that everyone can mesh together, from the Snowmass Village Fire Department to the Bureau of Land Management.

That's the theory, anyway. The practical effect was that Mountain Rescue agreed to learn to use the Incident Command System, then forgot about it. Bob let the lapse slide until after the "Miracle." Then, shaken by what could have been a disaster, enraged by what he and Steve perceived as Mountain Rescue's insubordination, he decided to change things. Mountain Rescue was going to work under ICS, with deputies in charge. And Steve—with his ham-fisted political skills—was going to make it happen. "His methodology," Bob says, "is ram it down MRA's throat."

> Bob [Braudis] was as autocratic as I've ever seen him. He said, literally, "I've had enough, we're going to do this, and if you don't do this I'm going to take your charter, I'm going to tear it up, and you will cease to exist, you will get your shit out of this fucking cabin, and you're done. You have no liability insurance, you have no workmen's comp coverage, you have no toys, and your phone doesn't fucking ring. You're not a search-and-rescue group anymore—at best, you're a hiking club." And it was "Yes, we'll get in line, we'll do what we're told, we understand, we've been bad boys."
>
> I was the messenger. I was Spike saying, "I'm here, and you get me because you were bad. I'm the jail keeper here." Well, they didn't

like it. Imagine that. No more autonomy. Picked up the phone, squawked to Bob.

  —Steve Crockett

Steve had been aching to get more control over Mountain Rescue. He had portrayed the team to Bob as a bunch of adrenaline-crazed dilettantes in Lycra, just waiting for the chance to do something stupid and bankrupt the county. Now he browbeats Bob for complete authority over search and rescue. "Make it right," Bob finally tells Steve, who promptly proclaims, "I'm the SAR czar," to the rest of the sheriff's office.

> Bob needs some feedback from me to counterpose Crockett, and he's not getting it. I'm very pissed off at Braudis on the one hand; on the other hand, I can understand. He's got to have faith in me. Our track record as a team and my track record as a person, as a key decision maker, it's been almost impeccable. It's been, like, plus-plus-plus. We don't lose. We've been winning these things for years and years and years, and our track record's excellent. Crockett's track record is spotty. Why's it so hard to believe us? Where's the breach of faith?
>   *—Tom McCabe*

> In my business, you're measured by what hasn't happened, rather than what has. The disaster that never happens, how do you measure that? I'm in the business of keeping us from killing people. What they're advocating is the classic "wait until it breaks" before you realize it's time to fix it.
>   When you have an organization that's steeped in tradition, that's the town darling, that has the preponderance of evidence on its side that they're still conducting business in a safe, appropriate, cost-effective manner, and somebody is suggesting that this is not the case and they need to change and these traditions need to be revised and amended, that is very threatening, and that causes the potential for confrontation.
>   *—Steve Crockett*

As the spring progresses, Steve becomes increasingly involved with the Mountain Rescue team. He holds classes to teach the basics of ICS to team members. He starts showing up at rescues, filling out forms, giving advice on how to do things. And he begins to get on people's nerves. When the team's board tries to organize a training on how to work around helicopters, Steve flies into a rage. Furious that the board didn't go through him to arrange the training, he challenges the course instructor's credentials and gets in a shouting match with board members. He hasn't approved the training, he says; he will order the county's risk manager not to insure it. The board, angered but with no other option, cancels the class.

"Crockett," says Debbie, "is an incredible human being; he knows a lot, he can do a lot. It's just that he's got this huge ego that he's got to deal with. All of a sudden he just kind of steps off the level playing field and does something that pisses everyone off. Crockett's going to slit his own throat."

Not everyone is so sanguine. "Braudis thinks he has an MRA president he can manipulate," Van Kyzar says one spring evening as he stands under the flowering apple tree in front of the rescue cabin. Van is convinced the sheriff wants to do away with the volunteer team and expand his department to include a paid search-and-rescue team—and Steve is going to make that happen. "You," he tells me, "may get to write a book about the elimination of one of the best rescue teams in the country."

THE UTE TRAIL switchbacks up the forested side of Aspen Mountain, starting from a dead-end street on the south side of town. The narrow footpath is one of the most popular exercise routes in Aspen—accessible, steep, scenic. Every day dozens of people hike or run up it, following the sharp switchbacks that cut across the pinched avalanche path at the bottom, then through spruce and fir in the upper sections. In thirty minutes a fast hiker can stand on Ute Rock, a promontory that seems cantilevered over Aspen, nine hundred feet below.

The trail is rocky, and hikers must watch their step as they move through the alder and aspen trees at the bottom. Higher up, the trail repeatedly crosses a narrow gully, a pipeline for rocks kicked off from above. Nearly every year, Mountain Rescue gets called to the Ute Trail.

The spring has been relatively quiet. There have been few incidents. With the exception of Gwen Garcelon's plunge into East

Snowmass Creek and a drowning in Lincoln Creek, they have been minor. Saturday, July 3, that changes. The page at 11:30 A.M. sends me tumbling out of the house, but John Zell, as usual, is ahead of me. We become part of the "hasty team," the first group sent out the door. John is cheerful as he slides behind the wheel of Rescue 1. "I was just thinking," he grins as he kicks the truck into gear, "how I wanted to spend some time with the guys."

"Aren't I one of the guys?" Debbie Kelly asks with mock petulance from the seat next to him.

"Of course you are, dear," John says tenderly.

Debbie was born in Shreveport, Louisiana, but her voice reveals no trace of southern accent. She grew tired of her classmates at Colorado University making fun of the way she talked, so one day she simply changed her speech. Debbie had expected to give, not to get, when she joined Mountain Rescue in 1988. When she found how gratifying the work was, she came to care deeply about the team and its fate—a commitment that, in 1993, leads her to put in more hours than anyone else on the roster. The excitement and adrenaline of rescue work were, she says, almost unexpected—although not unwelcome.

> People have basically accepted me, and I think it's because I'm capable. As long as you're as capable as the next person, then you're basically allowed to do whatever they're allowed to do, and no one says, "Don't send her because she's a girl." You've got to prove yourself, and sometimes to prove yourself you've got to prove you're not only as good, but you're better at certain things. I'm not as fast or as strong as a lot of the guys, but I can keep up, I can keep close enough so that people aren't waiting for me. I don't want to be waited for.
>
> I want to be one of the guys in the sense that I'm just another one of those people that get picked as your strong group to go out first. I just want to have my name right up there on the same level as, you know, the hasty team people, the people that you say, "Okay, these people know what they're doing, they can get there fast, they've got their equipment together." That group of people that's up on the top of your list—I just want to be there.
>
> —Debbie Kelly

The other two passengers in the truck are Ray Peritz and Bart Bowers, a twentysomething carpenter who likes pointy cowboy boots and slicks his black hair back in a pompadour. A relatively new support member, Bart is still tentative.

"Damn!" Ray says suddenly. "I was supposed to meet my daughter on top of Aspen Mountain for lunch."

"You can forget that!" John crows as he careens through dense holiday traffic.

Someone has been hurt on the Ute Trail by a falling rock, badly. Scott Messina has driven straight to the trailhead from his home, and we can hear him on the radio, breathless as he talks and climbs the trail at the same time. "I think it's a pneumothorax," John says after listening to Scott's report. "No breathing sounds on one side." Although the truck has red rotating lights mounted on the roof, Bob Braudis won't let the team turn them on, ever. John resorts to other tactics to get people out of his way. He drives like the practiced New Yorker he is, waving people aside, weaving through traffic, simultaneously talking on the radio and chasing his portable phone as it slides around the dash. John heads straight through town along Main Street, then turns off toward the base of the Ute Trail. The drive takes three minutes.

As Rescue 1 pulls up behind the Medic 4 ambulance, Scott reaches Evelyn Hoffman, a fifty-three-year-old tourist who has been struck in the back by a basketball-size rock. The ambulance paramedics, first on the scene, have brought their own litter up the trail and are working on her, but the trail is much too steep to carry her safely down to the road. There is urgency in Scott's voice as he radios Debbie; Evelyn is not in good shape. "Let's get some people to beat feet," he says.

Two weeks earlier, the team practiced lowering a litter down from the Ute Trail. As luck has it, Evelyn has been felled exactly where the training was staged; we know precisely how to rig the rope system. Getting her down means placing her in a litter and lowering her and the litter team straight down the fall line of the gully and the avalanche chute.

I grab a three-hundred-foot rope. Bart follows with a brake bag. By the time we reach Scott, we are sweating hard. Evelyn and the medics are on a thirty-five-degree slope below the narrow slash of trail. The hill lies at the angle of repose, the delicate balance between gravity and inertia. Scott ties an end of the rope to the head of the litter while I scramble uphill with the rope bag. Bart follows, crawling on all fours up the steep slope to the base of a tree. In a few minutes we have attached a rope brake around the base of the large Engelmann spruce.

The brake is a four-inch-diameter steel tube, fourteen inches long, with a large hook of half-inch-thick rod welded perpendicularly onto either end. A triangular steel ring runs through the uphill end of the tube. We tie loops of nylon webbing around the base of the tree and clip the triangular ring to them with a steel carabiner. The tube lies parallel to the rope leading to the litter. We take four wraps of rope around the tube; the hooks keep them from slipping off the ends. The friction of the rope curling around the tube allows the brake operator to control how fast the load is lowered as he lets rope out across the brake; the more wraps or the tighter he holds them, the more friction. The load is transferred through the brake to the anchor—in this case, the tree. With this arrangement one person, with one hand, can hold a victim and six litter-bearers—twelve hundred pounds—on the hillside.

For safety we tie two heavy-duty prusik loops around the rope just below the brake, and clip these separately into the anchor. The prusiks—loops of thinner rope—are knotted loosely around the main line, and don't impede the lowering operation. But if the brakeman were to let go of the rope above the brake, the prusik knots would tighten around the speeding rope and catch the falling load within a foot or two.

Ten minutes after we reach Scott he signals us to begin lowering. Six rescuers have gathered around the litter; each wears a climbing harness, which he or she clips at the waist onto the litter rail with a carabiner. By leaning back and standing up, the rescuers pick up the load without using their hands. This way they can carry a litter long distances without tiring.

"Down slow," Scott radios, and Bart and I begin paying rope out through the brake. The litter team pulls against the brake; we let them down as fast as they can walk. Because they can lean against the tension in the rope, they can walk relatively comfortably down steep and rocky slopes.

Two hundred and fifty feet below, Ray has set up an identical brake. Below him, Jace Michael and Ron Bracken, a handyman at the Silver Queen condominiums, have arrived and built a third brake station. They wait, watching the litter team bull down through the alders and scrub oak of the hillside. A few minutes after starting down, the litter team reaches the second brake, places the litter on the ground and holds it in place.

"Off belay!" Scott radios. We release the tension on the brake and uncurl the rope from the tube. Ray wraps the litter's rope tail around his brake, ties his prusiks in place, and in seconds the litter team is headed downhill again.

Scott believes he can reach the bottom with three brake stations. "Pack it up," he radios. Washed of urgency, Bart and I begin casually collecting gear and repacking the brake bag, which contains the brake tube, several dozen lengths of webbing, eighteen carabiners, heavy-duty cargo slings, gloves, a handsaw, prusiks, a tarp, and other tools for building brake systems. Just as Bart closes the bag, Scott calls on the radio, his voice much tenser than before. "I need you down here, fast," he says. "I need another brake station."

Bart scrambles down to the trail with the brake bag as I put on my pack, and we break into a trot. "Where are you?" Scott calls.

"We're moving," I say into the Motorola bouncing in my chest pack. "It'll be a couple of minutes." Bart races through a rock garden, nearly twisting an ankle. A few switchbacks below we pass Ray; a few more and we come to Jace and Ron. The rope is stretched taut from their brake across the trail and down the slope. "Keep going, keep going!" Jace yells.

We race around several more bends to find the litter team crossing the trail. Scott stands on the switchback below. "Come to me," he says calmly. We duck under the rope as he points to a tree. We are still a couple hundred feet from the ambulance.

Down here the aspens and willows are fifteen feet high—or would be if they stood straight up. All bend sharply downhill, holding the memory of avalanches in their curve. We thrash our way down through the thicket to a big spruce and have the brake built and ready to go in less than two minutes. The litter team reaches us a moment later, with only a few feet of rope to spare. A quick hookup, and they're off. As Evelyn passes I get my first look at her, motionless under the oxygen mask, eyes closed.

By the time Bart and I dismantle the brake again and reach the trailhead, the ambulance has left. I ask Scott how the patient is doing. "I don't know. Not so good, I think," he says. Evelyn suffered nine broken ribs, a broken collarbone, a collapsed lung, and other internal injuries. She would spend a week in the hospital. But the mood here is anything but somber. Sweating in the bright July sun, sitting on truck bumpers drinking Gatorade, the team is elated. The rescue was fast, it was smooth, it was efficient. Even Steve Crockett, waiting at the trailhead, can't take that away. Team members are wary around him, careful of what they say, watching out of the corners of their eyes as he declares, "You guys did great, despite our best attempts."

Chris Myers rolls his eyes. Steve has been dogging him at the trailhead, telling him which ICS forms to fill in, how he has to record who arrived at the scene in a government vehicle, who arrived in his own car—or "personally owned vehicle." It's a "POV" in the acronym-laced world of incident command, and Steve is a fumarole of jargon and abbreviations.

"Hey everybody? Everybody?" Chris calls sarcastically as people repack gear and strip off sweaty shirts. "I fucked up, okay? I yelled at a police officer. Steve tells me I should have had the incident commander yell at the police officer for me."

The team trickles back to the cabin. Turkey and tuna and roast-beef sandwiches have been delivered by the sheriff's office, along with grape soda and Coke and potato chips. Steve—rarely seen inside the walls at 630 West Main—walks in, steps up to the fridge, and grabs a Miller, the lone beer inside. Everyone else drinks soda. Leaning against the wall near the front door, he jokes and laughs, telling stories, making nice. Rescuers who had been on the hill sit in a rough circle, eating on couches and in chairs, listening, not talking.

In the garage at the back of the building, as several people reorganize the equipment in Rescue 1, somebody comments quietly on Steve's presence. "He can't mend fences," Dave Lofland says, "with all the bridges he's burned."

ᐰ ᐰ

At six-fifteen the following morning my pager jumps and squeals. The cats scatter off the comforter. It is the Fourth of July, but the sky is gray, the day cold. The temperature will not rise above fifty-six degrees in town today. The dispatcher announces a search on Richmond Ridge. Heavy frosting lies on the high ridge above West Willow Creek. A dark and violent thunderstorm filled the valley last evening; up high it left half a foot of summer snow.

Thirty-two-year-old Charlie Eckart, a recent arrival to Aspen, lately of California, had decided at midday Saturday to take a mountain bike ride. His route: three miles and 3,200 vertical feet up the face of Aspen Mountain, twelve miles back Richmond Ridge, six miles down Express Creek, and thirteen miles of pavement home. He carried water and a vest, but no clear understanding of what the terrain would be like as he rode into the rising storm.

When he didn't return by late Saturday evening, friends called the sheriff's office. Deputy Skitch Rounsefell called Tom McCabe, the designated 501 for the first half of July. Tom and Chris Myers, the 502, stayed up until 2:00 A.M., planning the morning's search by phone with Skitch and Steve Crockett. If Charlie hadn't found shelter, he could be dead. A storm like the one that blew through Saturday takes a summer day in the Rockies and whips it into winter in half an hour.

"Full winter gear," Tom prescribes over the phone. The columbines outside my door are in full, glorious, improbable bloom as I throw skis, boots, and snowshoes in the Subaru. At the cabin, Scott is parking the Unimog by the apple tree outside the front window. Designed as a troop carrier, built a generation ago by Mercedes-Benz, the Unimog looks—and drives—like a dull red shoe box on four-foot wheels. It has twelve gears, eight forward and four reverse, and a top speed of fifty miles per hour, downhill with a tailwind. Anyone riding in the rear compartment will emerge reeking of exhaust. All the directions are in German.

The driver needs a copilot to operate the radio, since it takes both hands and feet to manhandle the machine.

The Unimog is rarely taken out, for the battery often seems to be dead, and it's so slow the rescue is usually over by the time it arrives. But Tom, who arranged to buy it several years ago, is fond of it, and it can go places no other rescue vehicle can. The new snow, plus pockets left over from the hard winter, means tough going up on Richmond Ridge. In fact, the road Charlie wanted to ride has yet to be traversed this summer by a vehicle. The Unimog is prepped and stoked.

I help Scott load gear: snowshoes, blankets, heavy-duty sleeping bags. Scott is in a jovial mood. "Where are those bivvy sacks?" he asks me, grinning with mischief. "You know, those heavy-duty black bivouac sacks?" I hand him a black plastic body bag.

Scott, a plastic mug of coffee in his hand, runs maniacally around the cabin as Tom hunkers somberly over the phone and radio in the comm room. Scott puts on a goofy hat designed to look and act like a small umbrella. "Do you think it's going to rain today? Do you think it's going to rain today?" he asks, scampering through the building like Groucho Marx.

Rick Deane took off from Sardy Field at about seven o'clock in One Five Charlie to fly along Charlie's planned route. Tom Grady, the deputy who took over at dawn from Skitch Rounsefell as incident commander, is content to sit back in the comm room and let Tom McCabe run the show. The two monitor Rick on the radio while Scott and Debbie organize ground teams. Suddenly Steve Crockett's voice comes across the radio. He and a friend, Chris Cohen, a bartender at La Cocina, are up on Richmond Ridge, making progress along Charlie's route in Steve's battered black Willys jeep.

Tom is stunned. Debbie, who has just stepped into the comm room, is incredulous. Sometime between 2:00 A.M. and 6:00 A.M., Steve—who has been insisting for months that everyone in Mountain Rescue do everything by the book, the man who helped plan this morning's search—decided to go out and search himself.

"Who am I working for?" Steve radios blithely. Tom's jaw is tight as he picks up the microphone. "You're working for me," he says. He turns to Tom Grady. "I'd like to register a complaint," he says quietly. "Crockett asks us to play by the rules, and now he's out there freelancing. Nobody knows he's out there. He's got his radios off. We don't have any control over him." Tom Grady says nothing.

Steve, in fact, believes he had gained approval for his foray from Skitch Rounsefell the night before, saying he wanted to do some reconnaissance. But Skitch and Grady did not connect at the dawn shift change, leaving Grady in the dark.

> These guys briefed like two Liberian oil tankers in the night. From McCabe's perspective—his uninformed perspective, which was no fault of his—he was right on. He's right. But is that McCabe's fault? No. Is it my fault? No. It has to do with how we run the sheriff's department and with Grady and Skitch. I slipped through the cracks, and I took the fucking hit for it.
> —*Steve Crockett*

Rick radios in. He has spotted someone waving outside the Reveille cabin, a small hut Rick owns on a Richmond Ridge mining claim. Rick circles slowly and pitches a drop radio to him. The radio, packed in a red foam container, allows someone on the ground to talk to Rick. Rick has a deadly aim, and has nearly hit people with the radio during previous air searches. This time he backs off a little bit, and puts it about twenty feet from Charlie.

"How are you?" Rick asks.

"I'm okay," says an unfamiliar voice. It is full of relief. "I've got a fire in the cabin."

Rick tells him Steve should be coming down the ridge from the north in a few minutes. Tom has already sent Scott and John Zell up Express Creek in Scott's pickup truck to approach from the opposite direction. The idea is for Steve to keep going to Express Creek, which is closer, rather than backtracking. The two vehicles should meet near the saddle at the top of Express Creek.

In a few minutes, Scott radios in—his truck is having problems. "There are strange smells, and I swear they're not coming from John or me," he says. Tom launches the Unimog to back up Scott and John. Debbie drives; I take the other front seat. Dave Brown and Carl Ellerbrook, a beefy, friendly carpenter of prodigious strength, climb in the back. They get almost no view in the steel compartment, and grow nauseous from the fumes and swaying of the Unimog.

Debbie powers the twelve miles up to Express Creek Road at twenty-five or thirty miles an hour. We stop to stretch at the turnoff. Early morning light reflects off fresh snow on the Elk Mountains to the south. On the nearer slopes, the rich green of spruce contrasts with the lighter shades of aspen groves. A few abandoned buildings from the ghost town of Ashcroft scatter across the middle distance. In the meadow just before us, irises—perhaps planted decades ago by a miner's wife—bloom purple and white.

Debbie starts up the dirt road. Fresh snow hangs wetly on the aspens, brushing inside the open windows of the Unimog. On the radio we can hear Scott and John; they have bogged down in an old snowdrift and are shoveling fiercely, trying to get through. They can't raise Steve on the radio. We are within a mile of them when Steve reaches them from above. Debbie turns the Unimog around while Dave and Carl—looking a little green around the gills—get out to admire the view. In a few minutes Scott and John retreat down the road and stop.

"I really let Crockett have it," John says, biting off his words and waving his hands in agitation. "I said, 'You fucking piece of shit, what the fuck are you doing up here?' I just laid into that fucker. That piece of shit. I said, 'We're out here shoveling, busting our asses, you've got your radio off. We don't know if you're in trouble, you shithead.' I asked him what he was doing up there, and he said, 'You guys wouldn't have made it.' What a piece of shit."

"I can't believe it," Debbie says. "It's just more ammunition to take to Braudis."

Scott, however, is grinning. He knows Steve is in trouble.

Steve pulls up behind in the open jeep carrying Chris Cohen and Charlie, who seems fine. The three vehicles start down, and Debbie succeeds in keeping Steve penned behind her all the way to the cabin, forcing him to breathe the Unimog's blue fumes. She's proud of that.

Charlie doesn't seem to understand how dangerous his situation was. Tom sits him down in the comm room to talk about what happened. He had departed late in the day with no map, no food, no matches, no bad-weather gear on a ride that takes a strong, healthy rider five or six hours. He found the Reveille cabin—which Rick Deane never locks—only by chance. There was wood and matches, so he managed to warm up and dry off. At one point, as evening was coming in, he decided "to make a break for it." He rode his bike a half mile out into the storm and became so cold he dropped the bicycle and ran, frigid, back to the cabin. He volunteers brightly to Tom that Mountain Rescue should make sure cabins all over the woods are open and well-stocked.

"No," Tom says, poking him gently in the chest. "You don't understand. That's a private cabin; it belongs to the guy who was flying over you. There's no system of cabins out there. We want you to carry matches and food and warm clothing."

Steve stands by the apple tree, talking to Chris Cohen and Dave Brown. Inside, Tom bends over a counter, carefully penciling a letter of complaint to Bob Braudis. Even from behind he looks angry. He shows the note to Chris Myers, who tells him to send it. It is an opportunity, Tom says later, "to smack them on the side of the head and get their attention."

ʌʌ ʌʌ

"Crockett's out of here," Debbie says, giggling. The board—Debbie, Chris, Scott, Dave Lofland, and Linda Koones—has gathered in late July for its monthly meeting in the front room of the cabin. A menu from Paesano's Italian Restaurant is being circulated; the first order of business, as always, is getting dinner delivered.

"It happened Thursday," Debbie explains. "But I had this dream four days before. We were all at the cabin, it was a work party or something, only we were working like dwarves in *Snow White* or something, and singing, 'Dingdong, the witch is dead!'"

She laughs again. "Crockett did it to himself," Chris says. He and Debbie had met with Sheriff Braudis and complained about

Steve, who disappeared from view after rescuing Charlie Eckart and has been relieved of his role as "SAR czar." Team members believe Steve shot himself in the foot by going out on his own to get Charlie.

Steve, however, tells a very different story. "The support rug was pulled out from under me, again," he says later. The problem, he believes, is structural: Bob Braudis gives him responsibility to deal with Mountain Rescue, but no authority. Tom McCabe complained to Bob, and Bob pulled Steve back, rather than supporting him. It is the fourth time Braudis has done this, Steve says, and he is fed up with the treatment he is getting from his boss and twenty-five-year friend. "Bob is the most wonderful human that walks the planet. I mean, the guy is nice, unfortunately, to a fault. He just can't hurt people. He can't tell people what they don't want to hear. In his worst fucking nightmare he can't tell people shit they don't want to hear. I believe he is virtually physically, psychologically, emotionally incapable of this. And it's like all things, the thing that makes you great is the thing that will eventually kill you. It's his Achilles' heel."

No one explains Steve's story to the members of Mountain Rescue. As much as possible, Mountain Rescue members have been avoiding Steve, who has come to represent the institutional Antichrist, and so no one on the team asks him his story, either.

"Our biggest role is to educate people," Steve continues. "I've tried, in those fits and starts with Braudis and myself. I begged Chris Myers. I said, 'I need the opportunity to get in front of you guys and talk about this shit and sell this program and sell me. I need to talk to you about the relationship between you and the sheriff's department, and I need to talk to you about Steve Crockett and get this shit out on the table. We need to start establishing a relationship.' I was not afforded that opportunity. They wanted me to fail and they set it up to fail and the sheriff fucking helped it fail. And it failed."

> Steve will tell you it falls down on the political level, that I don't support him to the extent that he needs my support. I'll say it falls down because he's totally unwilling to compromise. His rigidity hurts him. I don't know if we'll ever resolve that, but it's coming to a point now where I'm going to say, "Steve, get this done. This is what I want,

four or five simple things. Get it done. If you can't do it, you've
failed." That's where it's going.
—*Sheriff Bob Braudis*

Scott promises to meet soon with Tom Grady, who will—in
Steve's absence—be the team's liaison with the sheriff's office. "I
want to rebuild their confidence in Mountain Rescue," Scott says,
indicating he'd like to do more training with the Incident Command System, but on the team's terms.

The teapot tempest over the Eckart rescue is important to the
principals, but it's a fight among bureaucrats. For that reason it
is significant; Mountain Rescue members are struggling for turf
and autonomy. They have not had to contend with this before.
Even as they worry about what will happen to the team under
Steve Crockett and Bob Braudis, team members are forced to
fight on the sheriff's terms. Resenting bureaucracy, they are re-
sorting to it.

Hour after hour, the board wades though the pile of minutiae
that makes up a team, the little things that need to be done
quickly but get done slowly, the balance between catching up
and looking ahead. Linda goes over the month's donations.
Debbie comments on how few rescues there have been this summer. Someone observes that Van Kyzar hasn't been doing much
work as head of the team's medical committee; the board wants
to put another person in charge, probably Dr. Marion Berg. Dave
makes a pitch for more radios, and the board tries to sort out
whether it is over or under budget on communications expendi-
tures. Scott wants to set up an avalanche training seminar for the
team in January, bringing in outside instructors. Chris and Scott
discuss designs for name tags to sew on the Nomex team shirts
and for a team baseball cap. Scott proposes an old ski patrol slo-
gan for the hats: "You Fall, We Haul."

At regular intervals, Scott starts whistling the tune for "Dingdong, the witch is dead," and everyone laughs. He is characteristically fidgety, like a teenager. He hops up to write the phrase on
a blackboard screwed to the wall. Later he goes back and scrawls
"CROCKSAR" underneath it. Then he adds "SPIKESAR." He
takes a handsaw from his pack and cuts a little at the table, then

at a projecting piece of the building. He looks around in mock guilt, a class clown seeking attention. He pokes fun at Chris, picking on him, tossing out one-liners. Much of the humor goes by Chris, who easily gets caught up in his own seriousness. Chris looks a little lost or stunned when Scott quips about a point he is discussing. Scott likes to dart around Chris, to take verbal jabs at him, but tonight especially, he needles Chris with fondness.

"I'm always in a good mood," Scott says. "Sometimes I'm in a gooder mood than others. Life is too short not to be in a good mood."

RAY PERITZ and Van Kyzar have a new toy, a Hare traction splint.
The device looks like the stainless-steel outline of an ironing
board. It is used to pull traction on a broken femur and stabilize
a victim's leg. Ray and Van have removed the splint from its box
and are down on the brown carpet in the front room of the rescue
cabin, toying with its various adjustments, when Bob Zook walks
in. The door has been left open in the early evening of a late July
day, and Bob was wandering by. He lies down without being
asked, and the other two begin strapping the splint around his leg.

Bob never stops talking. Tom McCabe, who has been watching
Ray and Van, makes small talk. The topic turns to the relatively
low number of rescues and the dearth of difficult peak rescues
this summer. Maybe, someone says, it's because the heavy snowpack—the heaviest in a decade—has been slow to melt out, dis-
couraging many people from trying difficult peaks like the
Maroon Bells and Pyramid.

"Maybe the education we're doing is actually working," Tom muses. The team has, for the first time ever, published a slick little brochure titled "This Booklet Could Save Your Life." The pamphlet describes hazards of summer travel in the mountains and how to prepare for trips into the backcountry. Five thousand copies were printed, and local outdoors shops keep calling for more.

"There's a lot more self-rescue going on," Bob suggests as Ray lashes Velcro across his thigh.

"Maybe," Tom says, chuckling, "after people saw what we did to that asshole Torp, they don't want to call us."

Whatever the reason, the slow pattern holds through the end of August, a month that sees relatively few calls: a couple of broken ankles, several lost hikers and overdue climbers, a boy with a church group who thought he'd broken his hip but, in fact, had not. Still no big peak rescue. But every day could bring one. At the monthly meeting and in casual encounters, the word is the same: keep your pager on, keep your pack ready.

On a Thursday evening late in the month a half-dozen people gather at the cabin to work on a rescue system called a Kootenai carriage highline. The previous autumn several team members spent a week with a Canadian rescue trainer, learning new rope rescue systems, including this one. Those techniques must now be integrated into the team's protocols.

Different rescue teams have, over many years, developed different habits for rope-based, or "technical," rescue, the genesis of mountain rescue work. Much has changed in the decades since the German climber Fred Braun first started hauling victims off Aspen's neighborhood peaks while wearing hobnailed boots and carrying a hemp rope. Vague industry practices have been developed for rescue systems, but there is no school, no institute where they are standardized. Much knowledge about ropes and rope systems has come from experience and practice, and sometimes from fatal error. Very little comes from controlled testing. Some of the "rules" are simply wrong, and rescuers who delve into technical work spend endless hours studying one another's systems and tricks and arguing their merits.

Many of the changes have been produced, like so much in rescue work, at the behest of the legal industry. Product liability lawsuits and a general awareness among climbing-gear manufacturers of the need for greater safety have produced enormous improvements in the quality of ropes, harnesses, and hardware. So has the growing commercial demand for climbing gear to outfit new legions of climbers. Dozens of types of ropes, cord, and webbing, each engineered for specific tasks, have come on the market. So have myriad carabiner designs, pulleys, brakes, and ascending devices. Nevertheless, rope systems remain a study in basic physics, and nothing can change that. As the sun drifts toward Mount Sopris, the upstairs room of the rescue cabin becomes a place to practice, to learn, and to remember. Because no two rescues are ever the same, because every one requires quick adaptation to the situation and the environment, a handful of men have dropped by this evening to remember and understand the rules, the limitations, and the physics of the tools at hand.

Chris Myers sits in the upstairs office. Ray Peritz drifts in, then Dave Lofland. As they chat their pagers crackle with a message about a possible mission: an overdue climber on Capitol Peak. The reaction is a collective yawn. Nobody does anything—it's up to the 501 to decide if a team will go out, but the good weather suggests nothing will happen unless the climber doesn't show up by dawn. The phone rings—a reporter from the *Aspen Times Daily*, listening on his scanner, heard the page and wants to know what's happening. Dave answers. "We have two Siamese twins," he says, trying to keep a straight face, "one climbing North Maroon, one climbing South Maroon, and they have become separated."

A few minutes later the pagers hum again—the late climber has appeared, safe, at the trailhead. By now Bob Zook, Ron Bracken, Jace Michael, and Drew Dolan have arrived for the training. Bob sits at the linoleum table in the middle of the room and carefully arranges a pile of Gummi Bear candies into rows. Chris walks by and grabs a handful. Bob eats a Bit O' Honey bar, grinning, hoping someone will gripe about him consuming sugar. He behaves, as always, like a small child on caffeine.

Chris passes out a photocopied diagram of how to construct the Kootenai carriage highline. After studying it for several minutes, Dave looks up, puzzled. "Let's just build it," he says, shrugging. A highline typically stretches more or less horizontally between two points. It might be used, for example, to span a river and reach a swimmer stranded on a rock. The Kootenai carriage is a system of pulleys that runs along the taut line, pulled one way or the other by attached tag lines. A litter or a rescuer may be suspended from the pulleys. The whole system is fashioned so that once the rescuer is over the stranded swimmer, the main lines may be slackened, lowering the rescuer to pluck up the victim, then tightened through mechanical advantage to raise him back up.

Although the concept is simple, its design involves a measure of art, tempered by the physical limits of an operation. Because rescuers usually carry their gear on their backs, the highline must accomplish a great deal with very little. It must incorporate a ten-to-one safety factor: the weakest link must have a breaking strength ten times the weight of the load. It must be redundant. In the Kootenai system, two lines are independently anchored and tensioned absolutely equally to form the main highline. It must be designed to incorporate dynamic rather than catastrophic failure; that is, if the system is approaching failure, something must give rather than break, to serve as a warning. And it must be quick to set up and easy to adapt.

Soon the room is a nest of orange rope. A roof post forms one anchor, a bar across the French doors the other. Tom walks in, a cardboard twelve-pack of Labatt's Blue under his arm. Bob has pushed the table out of the way, but his Gummi Bear display remains intact. "Have some sugar, Tom!" he chirps.

"Fuck you, Bob," Tom shoots back, a grin in his eye. "I'm an adult." He starts tossing out cans of beer. The balance of the twelve-pack he hangs by a carabiner from the pulley carriage: the rescue load.

The sky outside runs to black and the first stars come out. For two-and-a-half hours the crew drinks beer, eats Gummi Bears, and tinkers with the system. Here's the place to set the prusik-minding pulley. This is the proper order in which to slack one side and tension the other. Here's how to over-tension the system when setting it up. This is how the force changes when you alter the angle of the load. "If people saw this," says Ray, surveying the scene with a beer in his hand, "they'd say you guys are weird."

The details go on into the night under a fluorescent lamp in the back room of the small building on Main Street. By ten o'clock Tom is sitting on the couch in the back of the room, smiling at some private joke. He breaks wind and looks pleased with himself, raising his eyebrows and nodding gleefully. "He who farts in church," Tom giggles, "sits in his own pew."

Hunched over the table at the other end of the room, Chris buries his face in his hands. "Jesus," he says. "We need a rescue."

THE SHERIFF used to live in the basement [of the Pitkin County Courthouse]. Every time there was a rescue his wife would get a loaf of white bread and bologna and make sandwiches. She always made as many as were in a loaf, and she would get juice and stuff like that and take it over to the rescue cabin. The sheriff was always very supportive because he didn't have the personnel. His deputies wore cowboy hats and cowboy boots; this was the Old West. They were no dummies; they realized if they were going to have to hire ten or fifteen people for two days to go do a rescue, and buy their medical equipment and rent a helicopter, that it was going to cost four thousand, five thousand, six thousand dollars. "Well," they thought, "we've got these crazy Europeans and climbers around here that are willing to do it. Let's do everything we can to help them." And so it was a totally hands-off, supportive relationship.

—*Dick Arnold*

For decades Fred Braun *was* Mountain Rescue-Aspen. A tough, hardheaded German who immigrated to the U.S. in 1928 after learning to climb in Europe, he moved to Aspen in 1951. He had retired from an engineering business in Chicago and, with his wife, Renate, bought the Holiday House, one of four Aspen lodges then in business. He helped found a chapter of the Colorado Mountain Club and in the mid-1950s pulled together Aspen's rescue team. In 1965 he built the rescue cabin on a plot of land the city leased to his team for two dollars a year. That same year he incorporated Mountain Rescue-Aspen, a team he would lead until he retired from rescue work in 1980.

The rescue team and the Braun huts, a half-dozen cabins he built south of Aspen, were Fred's passion, and in 1978 he was declared "best crusty old altruist" by *Aspen Magazine*. He complained about skiers burning too much wood at the huts and leaving too much of a mess behind, but he loved getting people into the backcountry. When he grinned it was a sort of elfin smile—he didn't always show his teeth—in a round face under a close mustache and a Karl Malden nose. He had just a few wisps of hair on the top of his head by the time the city celebrated Fred Braun Day on June 20, 1975, but a good patch of white ran around the back from ear to ear. Furrows trickled like mountain rivulets down his high forehead to black eyebrows above deep-set, dark eyes.

Fred's influence ran so deep that a half decade after his 1988 death the Aspen team was still printing T-shirts with his caricature on the back. "Support Mountain Rescue" urged the front of the shirt. The back declared "Get Lost!" and featured a squat, cartoonish climber, his oversize wafflestompers stepping over peaks, an ice axe in one hand, a feathered, peaked Bavarian cap on his head, a Mountain Rescue patch on his shoulder.

The Aspen team was, simply, Fred's team. Fred believed in autocracy; if he liked you, you got in. Dick Arnold, a strong climber and ski instructor who received extensive medical training in Vietnam, came to Fred in the late 1960s and told him he'd like to help Mountain Rescue.

"Oh, okay, that's nice," Fred said.

Nobody carried pagers then. They hadn't been invented. If there was trouble in the backcountry, the sheriff would turn on a beacon atop Shadow Mountain, visible for miles up and down the Roaring Fork Valley (and a popular target for local .22 shooters). If Fred needed a team, he'd telephone people, but he never called Dick. If Dick knew a rescue was going down, he would stop by the rescue cabin, two doors east on Main Street from Fred's house, and offer to help.

"Yeah, okay," Fred would say.

It was Fred's way of weeding out the dilettantes. Only the people who really wanted to be team members got to be team members, and then only by showing a lot of commitment in the face of seeming indifference. "You came to the team fully trained," Dick recalls, "or you weren't welcomed. They didn't try to bring new people in and recruit and foster and all that. If you were a climber then you could be on the team, and if you knew how to ski then you could be on the team."

"Fred would call and you didn't say no. You went. Fred called, you went," recalls Jim Ward, a twenty-year veteran who left the team in the late 1980s. A mountain guide in the 1960s, Jim was part of a crew that relied more on stamina and strong backs than on technical gear or advanced planning to get the job done. "When you'd come off the mountain you'd have a little schnapps, say 'good rescue' and 'see you next time.'"

Finally Fred invited Dick Arnold to go out on a rescue on the Maroon Bells. A fused brace of thick, pyramidal fourteen-thousand-foot peaks south of Aspen, the Bells for decades have been the region's primary challenge to mountaineers. Ascending them is difficult, requiring crampons and ice axes to work up steep, snowy couloirs, ropes to belay across exposed ridges, helmets to protect against the rain of rotten rock that pours down the gullies and faces. For decades the Bells have killed climbers. For decades they have been the sine qua non of Mountain Rescue-Aspen's technical challenges.

After that rescue was over, Fred handed Dick a piece of paper. It was an application to be on the Mountain Rescue-Aspen team, proffered after Dick had been helping out for three years. "That was the end of the initial interview process," Dick recalls. "That was to get in the front door."

⋀ ⋀

Although the American West is mythologized as a land where rugged individualists made it on their own, the truth is that success in this often harsh country came to those who cooperated. That was how the Mormons settled and irrigated Utah, how wagon trains traveled through hostile bands of American Indians, how railroads were built and mines were dug. In the wake of the Second World War, Europeans brought to the Rockies a love of the mountains and a desire to climb them. They grafted the European mountaineering ethic onto the American rural tradition of neighbor helping neighbor. A social compact evolved in which residents of small mountain towns came to accept the risk-taking of those who would challenge the peaks, and went to their aid when they needed it. Climbers, for their part, generally took responsibility for their actions. Fred Braun and the other climbers in Mountain Rescue-Aspen went out to those in need because it was the right thing, the human thing, to do. In the 1990s, that is still why people clip on a Mountain Rescue pager. What has changed is the expectations of victims.

Dick Arnold worked for the Aspen ambulance service in the early 1970s and suggested to Fred Braun that Mountain Rescue-Aspen should think about taking medical supplies on its rescues. We've got to at least splint the bones and stop the bleeding, Dick argued, but he made little progress with the conservative German.

"You didn't do that," Dick recalls. "You just sent the strong climbers up on the mountain and they brought the victim down. If he was still alive when he got down, then fine, the ambulance got him. There's a certain selection there: If the guy falls and he gets reported two or three hours later and the team gets up there four or five hours later—remember, this is all climbing, no helicopters—and he's still alive, he's probably going to live another couple hours."

"The neat thing about Fred," recalls Jim Ward, "was he had this uncanny sense to know whether anybody was in real trouble, or if it was going to be fine to wait until morning. He'd been around and he'd seen so much of this stuff that he could tell people, 'Okay, this is the way it's gonna be,' and you didn't get a lot of argument. You just didn't argue with him a lot."

This approach had worked well for years, and Fred saw little reason to change it. But as the 1970s drifted toward the 1980s, change came not from within but from without. Mountaineering was not immune to the trend in American society toward the quick lawsuit. The idea of a "standard of care"—a phrase never heard during Fred's day—insinuated itself into rescue planning. The task was no longer simply to send strong people up the hill but to send people with the right training, both medical and technical, and to send them quickly.

"One of Fred's problems was he had to climb the mountain to help," says Dick. "Sitting in the office and organizing, calling and preplanning—it was never done that way, because the pressure was less and there were fewer rescues. He knew who was on the mountain, and once everyone [the team] was all in his house, they all just went up the mountain. They'd come down a day later with the victim or the body."

The social compact between mountain towns and climbers slowly began to mutate as more people, many without good grounding in the ways of mountains and mountaineering, ventured into the woods and onto the peaks. No longer was rescue a favor to a victim, lawyers contended; it was an obligation upon the rescuers, and pity the volunteer who made a mistake at a victim's expense. By the 1990s lawyers had come to overshadow much of Mountain Rescue-Aspen's planning to the point of ludicrousness. If, for example, a rescuer is a trained Emergency Medical Technician but his certification has expired, legally he must stand and watch a victim suffer, even die. If he tries to help and the victim dies anyway, he and Mountain Rescue, the sheriff, and Pitkin County all stand an excellent chance of being sued for negligence.

These changes have arisen over the past two decades, but even in the mid-1970s Fred Braun could see them on the horizon. "I know that Fred did a pretty good job of handling those guys," Jim Ward says of the various sheriffs. "There was a certain amount of that, and it probably grew progressively as the years went along and more attorneys got involved, more insurance. It was probably something Fred couldn't handle. As you get older you have less tolerance for that stuff." Fred was in his seventies. He decided it was time to hand over the reins.

"It took five of us to run the goddamn thing, to replace him," Dick Arnold recalls. "We had no idea how much time he was spending."

Much of the weight fell on Dick and Greg Mace, both in their late thirties. Greg, the son of Stuart Mace, was Fred's heir apparent. Stuart was a veteran of the army's Tenth Mountain Division, which trained near Aspen during World War II. He returned from the war, during which he had been stationed in Alaska, and settled in the Castle Creek Valley. Ted Ryan, another Tenth Mountain veteran who owned land around the Ashcroft ghost town, gave him a lease for as long as Stuart and his wife, Isabel, were alive.

Stuart loved all things Alaskan and soon was running dogsleds in the valley, taking tourists for rides and serving them simple alpine fare for lunch. He and Isabel started a restaurant in town, Toklat at Aspen, that featured Alaskan cuisine, right down to the whale blubber.

Greg and the other Mace children grew up in the mountains around the family compound at Ashcroft, also called Toklat. It was while in school in Switzerland that Greg truly fell in love with the idea of living in and being a part of the mountains. In the summer of 1969 he came home to help in the Aspen restaurant. There he met his first wife, Krisi, a student Stuart had hired as part of the staff. After another stint in Europe and one in Utah, Greg and Krisi came home for good. In 1973 the couple opened the Pine Creek Cookhouse, a rustic restaurant amid the cross-country ski trails that made up the Ashcroft Ski Touring Center.

A mile up the valley from the Mace home, the last inhabited building, the Cookhouse was a natural base for rescues in the surrounding mountains. Fred Braun and the rest of the small, tight-knit rescue team stopped in often, and Greg and Krisi always fed them for free. One day during their first winter a call came in to the Cookhouse. There had been an avalanche on the trail to nearby Hayden Peak. A skier had been caught. Would

Greg go up? He raced to the site but was too late. Digging out the body of a sixteen-year-old boy, Greg decided he wanted—he needed—to be part of the rescue team.

Greg and Fred Braun became best friends. They found they were kindred spirits. They spent long hours in the Cookhouse and at Fred's home in Aspen, drinking schnapps, talking about rescues. They shared a mutual respect for the mountains and for each other's abilities in the backcountry. Fred knew Greg was capable, and over time they came to love each other.

The Cookhouse and the home Greg shared with Krisi and their two small children filled with the sound of radio traffic as Greg grew move involved with the team. Greg would drop anything for a rescue. He would head out on the busiest night of the year, leaving Krisi to clean up the restaurant—sometimes with the help of the Cookhouse's regular customers. Once he went out on a rescue near the Maroon Bells, leaving Krisi particularly distraught; she had been planning a surprise birthday party for him that night. Later, as the celebration got under way, she radioed him. "You're missing your own party," Krisi said.

Mountain Rescue was Greg's passion. Fred knew Greg would work as hard as he had to build and support what he had begun. Everyone else on the team knew it, too. Fred would pass the mantle to Greg. That was as it should be. The future would be like the past. In the wake of Fred's retirement a board was formed and the workload spread around, but Greg was destined to carry on as Fred had, shouldering the bulk of Mountain Rescue's work, molding his life around the team.

In the years after Fred's retirement the Aspen team slowly started to expand its mandate beyond rescuing mountaineers. The new board began to incorporate water rescue for the fast rivers veining the valleys. The team began to search for lost hikers and hunters. The Aspen team started employing a select few helicopter pilots from time to time to help with rescues. Veteran pilots from Vietnam had set up small companies around western Colorado, flying into the state's nooks and crannies for oil and gas companies. They got work around Aspen dropping rescuers on ridges, carrying victims and bodies from peaks. It was challenging, demanding flying, and only a few pilots were good enough for the Aspen volunteers to willingly get in their fragile airships—or worse, dangle on a cable below—and soar through the thin and turbulent air to thirteen or fourteen thousand feet.

For all the changes, though, through the early 1980s Sheriff Dick Kienast generally left Mountain Rescue alone and rescuers continued to push hard, to do as they had done.

"We were on that knife edge of being responsible, professional, clean, well-shaven, all those good things," remembers Dick Arnold. "But we had one foot over into the shaky, crumbly rock, rotten ice: 'Let's go for it, let's push a little further.' A lot of people are alive today because of that attitude."

⋀ ⋀

In 1980 Julie Hesse took a leave of absence from a Boston architectural firm and hitched a ride to Santa Fe. The ride she got went as far as Aspen. Although she continued on to New Mexico, she—like so many who settled in the Roaring Fork Valley—came back for a longer visit, and soon she had a job.

Greg Mace was in the middle of running a rescue when he met Julie. He was the permanent rescue leader; he ran all the missions. Greg talked on the radio while interviewing Julie for a waitressing position at the Pine Creek Cookhouse. She got the job, and not long after that she started seeing Greg—tall, athletic, with thick brown hair, a wide smile, and bright blue eyes—as more than a boss. His marriage to Krisi had failed, and Julie—attractive, lanky, with short dark hair and piercing brown eyes—was there. In late 1985 they married. Their lives seemed set. Greg had full custody of his two children, and the four of them lived in a small yellow house at the head of the Castle Creek Valley, a mile beyond the Mace family home.

"I don't think that Greg got out as much as he would have wanted to," Julie says, "because of the Pine Creek Cookhouse in the summer. Having it open six days a week, there wasn't a whole lot of time."

When the opportunity arose for Greg to climb the Maroon Bells in July 1986, Julie—who by then had become a Mountain Rescue member and was serving as secretary on the board—encouraged him to do it. Several Mountain Rescue members wanted to reconnoiter the peaks for good helicopter landing areas. "I said, 'Why don't you go?'" Julie recalls. "I said I'd take care of the Cookhouse that day."

The group met at a parking lot not far from the base of the Bells before dawn on the twenty-sixth. The sky was full of thunder and rain, but they decided to go at least to the base of North Maroon and see what happened. After an hour the sky cleared to a beautiful morning. They started up: Greg Mace, Tom McCabe, and David Floria, along with two men not on the rescue team: Flint Smith, a guide who knew the Bells well, and Jerry Begley, one of Flint's employees. Because Greg was the permanent rescue leader, he always carried a radio. Yet he'd left his at home this day: it wasn't working properly. Tom, expecting Greg to have a radio, didn't bring his. It wasn't a big deal; they would climb without one.

They made good time up the standard route, reaching the 14,014-foot summit of North Maroon around noon under a brilliant sky. Flint pointed out good places to land a helicopter, routes to use to access various points on the mountain. At the top he pulled out a golf club, sent a ball sailing out into the wilderness, and everyone laughed. Then the group headed south, traversing the notch separating the two peaks and up the ridge to 14,156-foot South Maroon Peak, reaching it by early afternoon. After Flint dispatched another golf ball they continued south off the peak, heading down the ridge and back to the valley floor.

The quickest descent route was a snow-filled gully called the Grand Couloir, not far from the peak of South Maroon. The steepest pitch, at the top, reared up to about fifty degrees, an intimidating angle for anyone standing on top of a twelve-hundred-foot-long snow and rock pipeline. A cornice hung over one side of the gully, which curved to the right out of sight and eventually opened onto a more gently sloping snow bowl. The group discussed continuing down the ridge and then hiking down a trail to the wooded valley far below, but opted instead for the quicker couloir descent. Flint offered to set up an anchor in the snow and belay anybody who felt uncomfortable hiking down the steep slope, but everyone decided they could make it down safely unroped.

While Tom and Greg stopped to lash crampons onto their boots, David and Jerry headed down. They "plunge-stepped," slamming their heels into the soft corn snow to make foot holes. Flint went off to the right to inspect the cornice. Down below, David and Jerry practiced self-arrests: they purposely fell, then rolled over onto their stomachs and used their ice axes to stop themselves from sliding. With one hand on the shaft of the axe, the other wrapped around the head, they would face uphill, pull themselves up over the axe, and dig the long pick into the snow as a brake. A climber who isn't wearing crampons can get up on his toes as well. But if he is wearing crampons and lets his toes drop toward the snow, the front points of the crampons will catch and flip the sliding climber violently up and back into an uncontrolled tumble.

By the time Greg and Tom started down, David and Jerry were almost five hundred feet below.

> We were talking and I had my head down, watching my foot, when I looked up and Greg, he had already stumbled and was in the process of doing a self-arrest. I didn't see him stumble, I just saw him in the process of falling. At that point he rolled over and executed a standard self-arrest, but he did so with a great deal of vigor. He planted the axe very deeply. It sank in very well. It stopped right now. It didn't slide or rip out or anything. It stopped so suddenly, and he had a little momentum, that his hands slid down the shaft of the axe. His hands started at the top of the axe, and his [wrist] leash and his hands all slid down together. When the leash hit the stop, the shape of his hands on the axe was such that the profile of the hand was probably at its narrowest, and the leash—although it wasn't snug tight, it wasn't floppy loose, either—it went right over his hand, just slick as a whistle, and that was it. It just took a moment, and he didn't have an ice axe to use as a tool at perhaps the very steepest part of that pitch. It took him very little time to gain quite a bit of speed. He probably slid on his stomach for twenty yards. He was trying to slow himself down, and then he started to tumble. I don't know whether his crampon caught. I suspect that's what happened, his toe dropped and he started to flip. Once the tumbling began there was no recovery.
>
> —*Tom McCabe*

Tom yelled. Flint, up on the cornice, screamed to Greg to use his ice axe to self-arrest, unaware the axe remained plunged into the top of the couloir. David and Jerry, looking up, stepped into Greg's path, but then got out of the way as they realized there was no way they could stop Greg, who hurtled by at thirty miles an hour. Greg tumbled into a deep groove, worn like a water slide in the snow by climbers sliding down the slope and by the summer sun, and careened around the corner to the right and out of sight.

David and Jerry stumbled down to where they could see around the corner. "He's alive!" they shouted, then ran and skidded out of sight. Flint ran around the cornice and leapt into the couloir, then glissaded down, skiing on the bottoms of his boots and disappearing around the corner.

"I was freaked," Tom says. "I picked up Greg's axe, I turned around, and I front-pointed all the way down. I was rather flipped out. I was really pissed. I was really scared."

If Greg had cleared the corner, he would have slid out onto the snowfield. But he hadn't. He had slammed into a pile of rocks. By the time Tom reached the scene, David had already started down for help. He would run for ninety minutes before reaching the parking lot, then drive seven miles down the valley to make a phone call. David, Flint, and Jerry had picked Greg up and placed him on a tiny rock ledge above the snow. He had hit the rock on his left side and was spitting blood. It was clear he had broken his shoulder, a number of ribs, maybe his hip. What the group couldn't tell was whether he had punctured a lung or lacerated other organs.

Greg was in a lot of pain. Flint had a good medical kit with him, but he wished he had more equipment. The most medically experienced in the group, he lamented not having the tools to drain fluids from Greg's chest. The three men repeatedly had to roll Greg up on his left side and suction fluids out of his throat to prevent him from choking.

> I was filled with dread and foreboding. I'm Greg's understudy,
> essentially, and we used to talk about how I had appointed myself

his understudy and he was the teacher. You don't expect your
teacher to get hurt. He's semi-invincible.
—*Tom McCabe*

The nearest helicopter was based an hour's flight away, in
Montrose. But Tom had learned the night before that there was a
helicopter, hired for some project, sitting in Basalt, only a few
minutes away. He had written the pilot's phone number on a slip
of paper and left it sitting on the dashboard of his car. He hadn't
had a chance to tell David about it before he departed down the
mountain, but he thought someone else on the team would
know about the aircraft.

"You just had to listen to him breathe once, and you knew he
had a problem," Tom says. "But after we got him a jacket and
put it on to keep him warm, and we got the little rocks out from
under him to where he was fairly comfortable, he lay quietly for
quite a while. He was restless for a while, and then, as his medical condition started to deteriorate and he was less aware of
things, he became progressively more quiet. I was thinking that
he was finally calm. He had been very agitated, asking 'why me?'
kinds of questions, 'God, why did this have to happen? This is
really bad.' He was, I'm sure, thinking of the fearless leader, too.
And he knew he was the fearless leader. I have a feeling he was
thinking in those terms, too. He never mentioned the thought of
dying. I mean, we didn't talk about it at all. It didn't come up."

As the sun settled the waiting trio watched the shadow of the
Bells creep up the west face of Pyramid Peak on the opposite
side of the valley. There was room for only one person at a time
to be with Greg, so they rotated. Just above where he lay they
cleared an open spot on the flat, laying out smooth stones. They
would move him here when the helicopter arrived and load him
into the litter.

The way he was situated on that ledge, there was nowhere to be except at his head, and I was just right there, kind of holding him and
making sure he was warm. He'd been quiet for a while, and I don't
think I even noticed him passing away. I suspect what happened
was when he passed away and his body relaxed, his hands—he had
crossed them over his chest—his left hand kind of fell out from un-

derneath the jacket. That had happened a couple times earlier, and I would tuck it back under. About the third time I think I realized something was wrong. That might have taken a few minutes. I checked his pulse and shouted to the others, "Come on down, we've got to move him!"

—*Tom McCabe*

Flint rushed over and checked Greg's pulse but got nothing. The three of them heaved Greg up to the flat spot they had prepared in the rocks and began cardiopulmonary resuscitation. Flint tried a couple of paracardial thumps on Greg's chest. After twenty or thirty minutes, Flint gave up. They could keep working, he told Jerry and Tom, but it wouldn't make any difference. They stopped. Three-and-a-half hours had passed since Greg had tripped. A few minutes later, in the distance, they heard the whap-whap-whap of Bert Metcalf's helicopter coming up the valley.

David Floria was the only passenger, riding in the tiny bubble with Bert to show him the way. No one else on the rescue had known about the helicopter in Basalt, and so Bert had come over from Montrose. A litter was suspended on a cable underneath the bird. Bert flew in over the three men and Greg's body, hovered, set the litter down, and pulled up a few feet. Tom waved the helicopter off—he didn't want to work in the rotor wash.

David gave me a shrug, like "What's going on?" I gave David the signal, that slit-your-throat kind of signal. Just shook my head. I thought David was going to fall out of the helicopter; the door was off on that side. They did not expect that.

We got the radio out [of the litter] and I called the staging area down at the parking lot. Jack Gabow was on the radio and he wanted to know what the status was. Everybody was very concerned, of course—"How's Greg doing, how's Greg doing?" I knew Julie might be at Ashcroft with a radio nearby, and I knew that probably quite a few people were listening on their scanners, and from somewhere, from Greg's training undoubtedly, back in the recesses of my little brain, I remembered the ten-code for "call the coroner," which I've never used before or since: ten-ninety-eight. I remembered that. I said, "Ten-ninety-eight, ten-ninety-eight." Jack said, "Wait a minute." And then Jack came back and he said, "Tom, let me get this straight, could you repeat that? Do you know what that means?" And I said, "Yes, do a ten-ninety-eight." That's when they knew. Apparently that was a very bad place to be at that moment.

Let's face it, Greg was the overwhelmingly acknowledged leader of the group, and we depended on him so much that it was unimaginable. It was just, "This can't happen. It can happen to anyone else, it just can't happen to Greg." So it was a very strange place to be, and I felt empty. I felt like I'd been hit over the head and stunned. It was just like you had all your emotions taken away, ripped right out of you.

—*Tom McCabe*

⋀ ⋀

"God, I was going through so much," says Julie Mace. "You know, to lose your husband, lose the place that was your home, your job—and I really felt I was losing the children, too. I felt like I lost absolutely everything. At that point the only ties I had were Fred [Braun] and Mountain Rescue."

The Mace family owns a cabin near the timberline at the base of Castle Peak, six miles up a rough track from Toklat. Greg was buried there, under the deep shade of spruce trees. Stuart would be put to rest next to him seven years later. Two years to the day after Greg's death, a contingent of Mountain Rescue members climbed a 12,033-foot mountain south of the cabin and lit a bonfire on the rocks just below the summit to celebrate the act of Congress naming it Mace Peak. A golden eagle came to sit just above the rescuers, on the true summit. When the wind rose he would spread his wings and play, clinging to the summit. Then he would launch, riding the thermals up along the ridge, putting on a show for the bonfire team. It may be Greg, Tom thought as he watched the bird. It may be Greg.

Greg's death stunned the team and the town. For want of a good radio, because of a poorly adjusted wrist strap, Greg was dead at the age of forty-three—dead because of the work he did to help others. Julie, who was twenty-eight, went into hiding. She arranged with Greg's parents to move into the Mace Hut and run it as a winter ski hut. It became the only hut among the fifteen scattered across the region occupied by a hut keeper. She catered to skiers with hot meals and hospitality. For six winters she ran the Mace Hut, mostly living alone, skiing or riding a snowmobile down past the avalanche paths to the road, hauling supplies back up. For the most part Mountain Rescue members left her to deal with her grief alone, too.

Instead of abandoning Mountain Rescue, however, Julie soldiered on. She became passionate about the team, particularly about training. Training had never been a big part of Mountain Rescue's history, but Julie demanded it be given more emphasis. She wanted to force team members to go through mandatory training on how to conduct rescues on snow and ice, in rivers, on cliffs and scree slopes. She stepped on toes, and when she was elected to the board again in 1988, she kept pushing. Many veteran team members didn't agree with Julie. They hadn't joined Mountain Rescue to spend their weekends practicing knots. But she did find an ally in Tom, who became president in 1986 and later served as training officer.

"I was a clique buster," says Tom. "I really wanted to open the team up to a lot of people in the community. More and more people are participating in the backcountry, larger numbers, more rescues over what we had forty, thirty, twenty years ago. You start to establish more standards. Because of the litigation, a higher degree of professionalism is expected. You're a paraprofessional, and the training is the only way you have to check people out."

Like Julie, Tom—who had been on the team for a decade—stepped on toes. Politics on the team were sometimes unpleasant in the late 1980s, and many of the old-time members left—frustrated, fed up, or just tired of the growing demands and expectations.

"I think there were some people who just didn't like Tom," says Dick Arnold. "Didn't put up with his shit. He ran that very autocratically. We had our elections, but he needed that sense of power. He was very dominant."

A few veterans—Tom, Rick Deane, David Swersky, Neil Camas—rode out the turmoil. Dick Arnold, David, Tom, and Jack Gabow alternated the presidency of the board until 1992, when Chris Myers took over. By then, like so many others, Jack had retired and Dick moved away. Chris, who had joined the team just after Greg's death, represented the Third Wave, the third generation after Fred Braun and Greg Mace. He bought into the idea of training, of standards, of cooperating with the sheriff in the litigious world of the late twentieth century.

It had taken the better part of a decade, but the lessons of Greg's death and the demands of a rising standard of care had penetrated deeply into the team, in large part because new members had replaced so many veterans. Still, it wasn't the team Julie Mace had known in the 1980s. In 1990 she quit.

"Realizing Mountain Rescue isn't going to be everything that Greg wanted it to be, nor maybe it should be," Julie says, "I'm finally allowing myself to let go of some of my feelings and some of the things he was doing and letting other people take over.

"I probably didn't have to do what I did, and I know a lot of people didn't like what I was doing, but to me it was really important, and it was a way I could try to keep his memory alive. When I felt I wasn't able to do that I finally gave up."

/\\ /\\

Scott Messina strides up a gentian-dotted slope in Cooper Creek. The valley, one drainage east of the Mace Hut, lies in morning frost and shadow. On a small, bald knob, gazing up at Mace, Star, and Cooper peaks, he stops. The ridges are dusted with snow, the aspens running to gold. A hundred-pound piece of rough white quartz sits on the ground at his feet.

"Say good morning to Fred," Scott says cheerfully, slurping from the plastic coffee mug in his right hand and smiling at the view. Around the quartz lies the white residue of Fred Braun's ashes. Those ashes have lain on the moss and lichen of the overlook above the Lindley Hut for five years. As the breath of winter creeps down the high valley, Scott thinks about running for president of the team.

Scott met Julie at his first Mountain Rescue team meeting, only a few months after Greg died. Julie lived at the Mace Hut, fifteen miles south of Aspen. Scott had taken up housekeeping in the Gates Hut, twenty-five miles north of town. Twenty-nine years old, a native of Denver, Scott had just escaped his second bad marriage. An aunt who lived in Aspen suggested he apply for a job as a roving hut keeper for the Tenth Mountain Trail

Association, which manages a string of a dozen ski huts stretching from Aspen north to Vail. Scott wanted to get out of Denver. He was hired for the job by Jim Ward and began to spend his days skiing the three hundred miles of trails that compose the Tenth Mountain Trail system, repairing huts, checking on guests, calling the basement of the Gates Hut home. Jim dragged him to a Mountain Rescue meeting a few weeks before Christmas.

"I was just impressed that there was someone else out there who was living kind of like I was," Julie recalls. "I think it was something that kind of bonded us, because there aren't too many people who are really living like that."

Three years later Scott and Julie eloped while on vacation in Nantucket. For two more years Julie lived at the Mace Hut during the winters, but she finally gave it up. During her fifth winter at the hut, a local skier, Lynn Durr, was killed by an avalanche that thundered across the Castle Creek Valley. Lynn had been skiing on the trail that leads to Julie's cabin, a route exposed to a half-dozen avalanche paths.

"The stress of the avalanches was really getting to me," Julie says. "I realized I was probably the one person that went underneath that avalanche path more times than anybody else." She wasn't making any money at the Mace Hut. A year after Lynn's death she was offered a job managing a vacation home owned by several wealthy men, and the caretaker's apartment that went with it. She took the job and, with Scott—who had bought a small mountain guide service—moved to Aspen.

By the fall of 1993 Scott has become one of the stalwarts on the team, and pressure is growing on him to run for president. The presidency has taken on added significance because of the bitterness following the "Miracle in the Mountains" and the struggles with the sheriff's office over control of Mountain Rescue operations. Chris Myers is burnt out, engaged to be married the following summer, and won't seek the post again. There is an unwritten understanding that if someone runs for a slot, almost never will anyone else run. To volunteer for a position on the board is to get it, so if Scott can be convinced to run for president, the matter probably will be settled. Tom, however, is making noises about running for a fourth term as president.

"I have a feeling if I threw my hat in the ring, if I wanted to be president, I could be president, and if I was president I could run the show," Tom says. "For me personally it's a matter of shit or get off the pot. I can either run for president again and make it again in my image, or I can practice what I've been preaching: 'Let's not have another dictator, let's not have another Fred Braun, where everybody kowtows to Fred and his ideas hold sway almost universally.'"

His musings worry some members of the team. Several people, including Ray Peritz, have been trying to get Debbie Kelly to take on the presidency, but she is very reluctant.

> I almost feel like I don't want to be president of Mountain Rescue. I don't know why. I don't want people in the community to say, "Oh, yeah, there's Debbie Kelly, president of Mountain Rescue." I don't know why that is. I'm a leader of the team, making decisions for the team, the direction it's going, but at the same time not letting anyone know that I'm a leader of the team. Because most people in the community just think I'm probably one of the people that's pretty involved. I've always liked that, that individual recognition is not part of the deal, it's always a team thing.
> —*Debbie Kelly*

"Tom's vision, at times, has not been good for community relations," says Dave Lofland. "He's pissed a lot of people off, and I think the work we've done within the past two years has really put us in a better position within the community. I think we're going to get a lot farther. I think we'll accomplish our goals more easily if we're working more in harmony with the sheriff's department."

The late summer and early autumn of 1993 form a turning point for the direction of the team. The choice, although not often articulated and never broadly discussed, seems clear: back with Tom or forward with someone else. Going back appeals at some level to almost everyone, for the team is frustrated. Steve Crockett, the Incident Command System, and the increasingly tight rein Sheriff Braudis has put on the team are topics of constant griping. To fight, to act, to demand lines and decisions and definition is much more attractive than negotiating, maneuvering, politicking.

And yet . . . and yet. Those who are thinking hard about these questions—Tom, Debbie, Scott, Chris, Ray, Dave—all agree that they need to rise above short-term and personal considerations and try to divine what course of action will make Mountain Rescue-Aspen better at saving lives. With resignation Debbie, Scott, and Chris decide that as viscerally satisfying as a knock-down-drag-out turf war with Bob Braudis would be—a war Tom seems very much to want—it won't solve things and could make them worse. The Third Wave of leadership is convinced that cooperation and compromise, not confrontation, are the way to proceed. Sheriff Braudis is politically savvy, and although Mountain Rescue maintains enormous good favor in Aspen, so does the sheriff. With the exception of Tom, no one on the team has much stomach for a public fight to defend the team's autonomy.

As the summer weeks meld into fall, Tom drifts away from the lure of the presidency. He and Jody have separated, and he is worried about Merrin, on the cusp of adolescence. He has to re-think his priorities.

"I've too much of my own stuff going on right now, and I just don't need the aggravation," Tom says. "Mountain Rescue will survive with or without me, no matter what. It's important to me. I've invested a lot of time in it, but it is becoming increasingly clear to me that there are other things in my life that are suffering, and I need to pay attention to me more than I do to Mountain Rescue. The team is more important than McCabe. I've preached that for years, and I believe it, and sometimes it is hard for me to practice it."

While Tom makes these decisions, Scott angles the other way. "I think I'll probably run," he says, although he sounds as if he's explaining why he won't. "I don't want to run because I don't want it to be an ego thing. I don't want them to come out and say, 'Scott Messina saved my life.' Mountain Rescue-Aspen saved your life. I don't really want to be singled out. I'm not in it from a hero's standpoint. That's why I hesitate to run for president."

He is running, he admits, in part to keep Tom out of the presidency. "It's been a big-time power thing for Tom," Scott concludes, "and it's time to back off. We've stopped some of it, and we need to maintain the reins on Tom. If he does get back on the board, things are going to change back again. After all the effort we've put in, I don't want to see that happen. No way."

"I knew it was coming," Julie says of Scott's decision to run. "I mean, I could see it coming a mile away." Greg wasn't president in 1986, the year he died, although he had been previously. The parallels are a little uncanny all the same, Julie concedes. "You can wonder, 'Why did I put myself in this position again?' But you know, it's funny how we go after the same kinds of people. I don't know why we put ourselves in the same position."

"I'm glad Scott wants to be president," Debbie laughs after Scott admits, more than he declares, that he'll take the office, "'cause it takes the pressure off me." Chris, she says, was putty in the sheriff's hands, and Tom is too rigid. Scott isn't the model of diplomacy, he stumbles over his words and often has trouble articulating his thoughts, but she hopes he can find a middle ground. Almost everyone except Tom seems relieved that the issue is settled and tries to believe that Scott will do well.

"I trust him in the field," Tom says of Scott, "but as an administrator I don't think he'll be terribly effective, because I think he lets a lot of shit slide. Who knows? It's a game, and what you have to do—from my perspective, getting to be an old fart in the organization—you've got to just let go and say, 'Okay, do what you think's best and see how it works out,' and if it doesn't work out, you know, don't beat him up over it. Just say, 'Let's try something else.'"

When the election comes at the December team meeting, all of the maneuvering and prodding and worrying of autumn is long past. The vote is a fait accompli, with Scott as president, Dave Lofland moving into Scott's old position as training officer, Ray coming on in charge of operations. Linda and Debbie take renewed terms as treasurer and secretary. Nobody votes against anyone. In fact, David Swersky, who orchestrates the raucous five-minute nominating and voting ceremony, doesn't even bother to call for votes, just "a standing ovulation" for the uncontested 1994 board.

After the cheers die down, Tom pipes up, an impish grin on his face. "Isn't that supposed to be followed," he asks, "by a standing insemination?"

JUST FROM the whole way the situation was going, the way the day was going, it just seemed like there was some reason for me to be out there. I just felt like there was a possibility I was going to find him. We were in our [search] area, so we had to really look, we had to pay attention to clues, any kind of findings, and so all of a sudden things started getting more and more focused, more and more energized. We went up this really intense, steep, rough terrain with heavy packs on, and I wasn't at all physically exhausted. It didn't bother me a bit.

—*Lori Hart*

The call comes on a glorious Indian summer day in mid-September: a search for a missing hunter in the Hunter-Frying Pan Wilderness. John Zell, working far up Castle Creek at the

Lindley Hut hauling firewood, is scornful. "AFH," he says. "Another Fucking Hunter. I'm not going to bust my ass for a lost hunter." Hunters are almost always fine, John says, usually sleeping in their tents when rescuers find them. Although many team members hunt themselves, some—especially John—see hunters as generally boorish and incompetent.

Down at the rescue cabin, however, David Swersky and Tom McCabe are thinking very differently. The hunter isn't only missing—he'd last been seen Sunday. This is Wednesday.

Mark Lobsinger, thirty-nine, and Terry Phillips, forty, both Oklahoma residents, hunt together every year near Aspen. Mark, a father of five children, has a terrible sense of direction and often gets lost. But he is in good physical condition. He trained to be in shape for the venture, which coincided with Colorado's archery and muzzle-loading rifle seasons for elk and deer. The two men set up camp among the rocks near Scott Lake, a pool perched at twelve thousand feet, just above timberline in the Williams Mountains. Two ridges east lies the Continental Divide.

On Sunday they set out to hunt in different directions. When Terry returned to the tent that evening, Mark wasn't there. Terry wasn't worried; they had agreed that if one of them was trailing an animal he wouldn't be back. Terry wanted to hunt on the next ridge east. He left Mark a note saying he was going to set up his own tent a few miles away, and headed out.

That night it snowed, but when Terry looked through binoculars at Mark's camp Monday morning, the tent had no snow on it. He assumed Mark must be there, and went on hunting, eventually killing a deer Tuesday. Only after hiking back to Mark's camp Wednesday morning did he find Mark had not returned. By early afternoon, Mountain Rescue knows it has a problem.

"When you're notified on a Wednesday that somebody was last seen on a Sunday morning, and in between two big storms came through and the temperature plummeted and this guy's from Oklahoma, all of a sudden you think, 'This guy's dead,'" says Tom. "My gut feeling is this is not good, this is serious, we need to move immediately."

Tom heads to the airport, where he joins Rick Deane and takes off in One Five Charlie to search from the air. David calls

Richard Dick, a wiry, weathered man of indeterminate age who wears sharp-toed cowboy boots, favors snap-button shirts, and flies a Bell 47 Soloy helicopter as well as anyone in Colorado. It will take the better part of an hour for Richard to fly from his home in Montrose to Aspen.

By the time Scott, John, and I reach the cabin after a morning of stacking firewood at the Braun huts, David Swersky has already sent eight searchers up Highway 82 toward Independence Pass. Mark Lobsinger disappeared in a valley known as Lost Man; on the wall of the comm room, the eastern flank of the Williams Mountains above the valley is carved up with Magic Marker like a butcher's diagram of a pig. Each of the four search teams will try to cover one pork chop before dark, then make camp and start again in the morning.

"I still had hope," recalls Jace Michael. "'Hey, maybe he's bivouacked somewhere; he might be injured and we can find him.' I think we all kind of felt that way, and I think we all evaded that final decision that he's dead, we won't find him alive."

When Richard Dick is only a few minutes from the airport, David sticks his head out of the comm room and looks at me and Kevin Hagerty, a blond, sunburned carpenter and ski patroller. One of the team's rescue leaders, Kevin is universally known as Hags.

"You're going," David says. We climb into Kevin's battered pickup truck, pushing tools out of the way, and drive the three miles to the airport. The day is calm and warm, the valley filling like a bathtub with limpid, late afternoon light. But we are sweating in our gear. We must wear as much as possible, in the event we somehow are separated from our packs during the helicopter flight. Although we strap the backpacks into the cargo racks on the side of the helicopter, sometimes packs and rescuers fly separately to keep from overloading the tiny machine at high altitudes. There is no guarantee they will end up in the same place.

We fly slowly east up the valley, fifteen hundred feet above the winding road. The three of us fill the Plexiglas bubble of the cabin, which affords a view from our toes to the rotor mast behind our heads. Kevin connects the headsets and dials in the

Mountain Rescue radio frequency so we can hear the ground teams. Our plan is to be dropped in high, up on one of the thirteen-thousand-foot ridges above Scott Lake. As the other teams search up, we will comb the high ground, then bivouac for the night. In the distance we see a flicker in the sky—One Five Charlie banking in a turn as Rick and Tom crisscross the Williams Range.

> We were looking for footprints, and we followed tracks. Unfortunately, because of the number of people who happened to be working that area—guides had taken a variety of people in there—there were horse tracks and people tracks all over the place, and we were trying to fly them down and see where they led us. They led us into some pretty far-flung drainages, and then you're looking for any individuals, you're looking for color, you're looking for movement. It's real basic, but it's surprisingly difficult from an airplane to see things, even when they're trying to get your attention. And if they're not trying to get your attention, if they're unconscious or down in a snow cave or something like that, when there are very few visual clues, it's a whole lot more difficult than you might think.
> —*Tom McCabe*

Sloan Shoemaker is driving back to Aspen from Boulder when he passes the Lost Man trailhead and sees Rescue 1 parked there. He stops to help and soon is running the staging area. Now, when we are only a few miles from the mouth of Lost Man Creek, his voice comes over our headsets in the helicopter. "Cabin, this is staging," Sloan radios. "Team Two reports contact with the victim at 11,300 feet in Jack Creek."

"What's his condition?" Tom breaks in from One Five Charlie.

"Go to channel eight," interjects Dave Lofland. He is half of Team Two, along with Lori Hart, who is on her first mission. I open a topo map and point to Jack Creek, a Lost Man tributary south of Scott Lake. Richard banks the helicopter into the mouth of Lost Man Valley and the shadow cast by the Williams Mountains. Kevin fumbles with the radio to find the alternate channel. Dave's cryptic comment is not a good sign. Team members learn to guard their conversations on the assigned Mountain Rescue radio channel, assuming that reporters or others are listening in. More obscure channels are used for bad news.

By the time Kevin changes channels the brief discussion between Dave and Tom is over.

"What do you think?" I ask.

"I don't know," Kevin shrugs. "He could be alive."

Down in the Lost Man Valley, we see searchers heading up the trail, bright in their red climbing helmets and yellow Nomex shirts. Richard flies past Jack Creek, circles around, banks left and into it. Our altitude is 11,500 feet, only slightly higher than Dave and Lori's reported position. As we turn west the setting sun fills the cockpit, refracting off the Plexiglas bubble and all but blinding us. Richard flies toward a cliff band that protrudes from the ridge north of the creek; the terrain comes up sharply before us. With only a few hundred feet to spare he gets the bird under the ridge's shadow, and for a few seconds, we can scan the scattered openings in the timber along the creek. Then he banks hard left and heads back out.

He repeats the maneuver, and this time, looking down between my feet, I see a body clad in yellow, sprawled on the ground near a tree. It is facedown, left arm and leg cocked out. Dave Lofland is standing near it, looking up. It is a singular experience to look down at a dead man, but—as I had been the winter before on Peak Twelve Four Thirty—I am wrong about what I am seeing. It is only a rain suit Dave laid out to attract our attention.

"That was full power coming out of there," Richard says softly as the rotors chop at the meager air and pull us back over Lost Man Creek. Kevin calls Tom—what do you want us to do? Set down and stand by, Tom says. Richard puts the helicopter down in a clearing near the mouth of Lost Man Creek, and we wait, rotor spinning.

> I wasn't sure if I was going to see someone walking through the woods or someone lying down in the woods or someone lying there moaning and groaning. I wasn't really sure what I was looking for, except for a person who could have been miles away. I had so much energy I felt like I was going to create this person if I didn't find him.
> —*Lori Hart*

Mostly what you're looking for is evidence, for signs. It's going to be a coincidence if you run into the person. You need to look for boot tracks in the snow, look for empty pop cans or cigarette wrappers and that sort of thing, just any sign that someone has been there and that that someone is the person you're searching for. Hunters are the worst, because every guy out there is wearing camo. I've found with hunter searches you interview a lot of hunters, and if there are a lot of hunters in the area, they're all wearing Vibram-soled boots. And they're never glad to see you.

    —*Dave Lofland*

To start their search, Dave and Lori split off from the Lost Man Valley and start hiking up through spruce along Jack Creek. There is no trail and the terrain is steep; sometimes they scramble on all fours. After the better part of an hour they break out onto a small, open rib along the north side of the creek. Ahead of them a cliff band rears up. Below and to the left is the creek, a one-step-wide stream burbling down through smooth granite boulders and a fringe of conifers along its banks.

Dave heads right to traverse the base of the cliff band. Lori walks along the rib, looking down into the creek. They have only one radio between them, and agree to keep in voice contact. Every few moments they call Mark's name. As she trudges up the open rib, Lori alternates between watching where she is walking and looking down toward the creek. Suddenly, framed between two trees, down in the shadows of the watercourse, is an incongruity.

"I see this orange hat," Lori recalls. "I'm yelling, 'Mark, Mark, DAVE! DAVE!'"

Dave runs back to Lori, who points to the hat. For a moment neither is sure of what they see in the evening gloam.

> We started to take a couple steps in that direction and I said, "Oh my God, there's a boot, there's a leg, and there's another leg. That's him, Dave." We both just started yelling his name, and there were millions of thoughts, there were light-years of thoughts that went through my mind in the fifty yards that I had to go from that point. You know what it's like to be in a dream when you're trying to run away from somebody, you're trying to run and you can't get anywhere? I wanted to get there, but I really didn't want to get there. I wanted to arrive, but I wasn't sure what I was going to find.
>
>   My legs were moving but my mind was resisting, and I started thinking, "What am I going to find?" All we could see were the boots

and the legs, because he was in camouflage, and I was beginning to come into view of the chest and the short-sleeved shirt. I still couldn't see his face. What was going through my mind at the time was, "Okay, is this person going to be mauled, is he going to be shot, is he going to be dismembered, is he going to be alive, is he going to be moaning and groaning, and am I going to have to save him?" I was scared. I was scared.

—*Lori Hart*

Mark Lobsinger is not alive. His blue eyes are stuck half-open, staring at some place neither Lori nor Dave can see. He is lying on his back by the stream, one foot hooked under a log, tucked between a rock and a tree. If Lori hadn't looked through the gap in the trees when she did, searchers might have wandered for days without finding him. He is stripped down to his white T-shirt, lying on another shirt. His jacket is off and lying nearby, as is his pack.

"At a glance I just knew," Dave recalls. "He just looked dead."

Lori kneels down to check for vital signs, but finds none. She cannot close his eyes. This bothers her immensely. The two of them step away from the body, climbing back up into the sun. Dave keys the radio and calls Sloan at staging, reporting only that they have "made contact." He knows everyone in the field is listening, including Terry Phillips, Mark's hunting partner. He is hiking with Jace and Ron Bracken, taking them up to the camp by Scott Lake. The three men are climbing a steep avalanche path below the camp; they're spread out and searching for clues when Jace hears Dave's radio report.

Jace has spent much of the afternoon with Terry, talking to him on the trail, helping relay questions from Tom about how Mark might behave if he is lost, learning about who these two men are. The hunting trip is an annual high point for Mark and Terry, an opportunity to watch the birds, identify the flowers, and just be together. "As I got to know Terry, I got to know Mark, too—wife, five kids, all that stuff," Jace says. "I liked being with Terry."

Jace wasn't worried about finding a body. "As far as handling bodies, dead people, I'll do it," he grins, mentioning his former job in a mortuary. "I'll pick up the pieces, I'll do anything. I'll handle a thousand bodies. It's not going to bother me." What he hadn't counted on was handling Terry.

I had the only radio, and it came across that they'd found him. When Dave said, "Switch to channel eight," I knew right then he'd found Mark dead, that he was a "Frank." So I switched over and listened in and just confirmed it. I was walking over toward Terry. I yelled out that they've found him and we'll get some stats in a minute. So I turned the volume down and I was walking over toward Terry, and Terry was like, "Well, how is he, what's going on?" So I just listened and confirmed what I had thought. That was the hard part, telling Terry, "I'm sorry, your friend is not alive." He sat down and started to cry, and so Ron and I just sat there with him.

It was hard for me to get those words out. The exact words I said—I said, "I'm sorry, your friend did not make it." Those were the hardest words I've ever had to say.

—*Jace Michael*

The Aspen airport shuts thirty minutes after sunset, and we are burning daylight as the helicopter idles on the ground. After twenty minutes Tom McCabe calls Kevin—fly a team up, get Mark's body onto the helicopter, and get him out. Richard lifts off and flies to the junction of Jack Creek and Lost Man Creek, landing in a small meadow by a stand of old spruce. A half-dozen searchers are congregated there by now, crouched low, backs turned to avoid the rotor wash. As we set down I look at Kevin. Richard, after his earlier passes into the valley, doesn't want to land more than one passenger, and no packs. The air is too thin, the landing zone too small for the little helicopter to carry a full load. "You go up," Kevin says. "I'll take off the packs."

We fly a mile up the valley. After circling twice, Richard settles on a tiny clearing a hundred yards from the creek. A tall spruce marks one side, a dead snag the other. The air is calm, and he carefully settles into the hole between the trees with only a few feet to spare. Three feet off the ground he holds the hover and spins in a slow circle, looking for rocks and uneven spots before touching down. Richard nods to me, and I carefully unclip the seat belt and shoulder harness, open the door, latch it firmly behind me, then crouch and scuttle downhill and away twenty yards. I turn and give him the thumbs-up.

After he lifts off I stand up and find Dave hiking up from the creek. After determining Mark is dead, he set about trying to find some sort of identification, just to make sure this is the man we're seeking. Going through Mark's pack, Dave finds a note, penciled almost illegibly on a topo map of the area.

"Things aren't going so good here," the note begins. Mark explains how he had fallen and broken his hip, trying to get back to his camp. Unable to move, exposed to the snowstorm, Mark knew he was going to die. At the end of the note he listed the names of his five children. "I love you," he concludes. "See you in heaven."

> At that point Dave said, "I can't read this." All of a sudden he [Mark] had this human quality. I knew he had loved ones. Then it was harder, because he was no longer just a body. He had people who loved him out there, he was writing this note as he was dying. You knew he was in pain, you knew he was dying, and that was—that was really hard for both Dave and me. That was when I just wanted to bless his soul. I'm not real religious. I think I just said, "God bless you," and that's about it. I felt like I wanted to say something to him.
> —*Lori Hart*

A whistle lay near Mark's body. He had probably blown it, but there was no one near to hear. His right hand was across his chest, clenched in a fist—but it held nothing. The note answered some questions, but it raised others. Where had he fallen? What had happened to his bow, his black-powder rifle, the poncho and binoculars we knew he carried? How had he come to be here, in this quiet, sheltered spot by a small mountain stream?

There is no time to figure it out. I pull out my radio and call Sloan. The helicopter is flying to the trailhead to pick up gear. Mark weighs 190 pounds, and we need to get him up the slope to the tiny helispot.

"We need a three-hundred-foot rope, uphaul bag, extra webbing, bivvy bag, and a Sked," I tell Sloan.

"Bivvy bag?"

"Large, dark, heavy-duty, long-term bivvy bag."

"Copy that."

In a few minutes Richard is back. Crouching under the rotor wash I pull the gear from the side baskets and begin to rig a simple uphaul system, while Richard ferries first Ray, then Jace to the tiny landing zone. Once Jace arrives, Richard steps out of the helicopter, leaving it running, and walks over. "You've got twenty minutes," he says.

Everyone is sweating, running up and down the hill, getting Mark into the body bag, then lashing the body bag in the Sked, a flexible, plastic sled that wraps around a victim like a taco shell. We tie one end of the haul rope to the Sked. The rope runs through a pulley attached to a tree by the landing zone, then comes back down the hill. Dave and Lori maneuver the Sked around obstacles, while Jace, Ray, and I grab the other end of the rope and, by pulling downhill, haul the Sked uphill.

At the top of the hill we pick up the Sked and heave Mark onto the helicopter's starboard cargo basket. There's a special weight to a body, an unmistakable thickness, that you never forget once you have felt it. We lash the whole package down with bungee cords, avoiding the screaming turbine and hot jet exhaust only a few inches away. As we step back Lori comes running up the hill, out of breath. She has Mark's shirt and pack. Richard puts them on the passenger seat.

We retreat down the hill and listen to the turbine wind up, to the bite of the rotors as Richard changes the pitch and the machine strains against the load. The helicopter lifts off gently and Richard slowly spirals 180 degrees as he climbs to treetop level, his tail rotor passing within five feet of the big spruce. As he flies over us, he waves once. Everyone watches the body on the side of the helicopter, tails of webbing fluttering in the breeze, as the machine, silhouetted against the clear, almost colorless eastern sky, curls with unspeakable beauty down and around the ridge.

Suddenly I am aware of how quiet the wilderness is, how serene this place. People unclip helmet straps, swig from water bottles. There is relief in the air, and laughter. This is a good place.

"It was a beautiful evening," Lori says later. "I was really aware of that. The skies were clear, the stars were starting to come out. I really felt alive."

I THOUGHT about every aspect, over and over again, and I just couldn't sleep. Just the fact that you're going to bed and you have nothing to do but just lie there and think about it is difficult. I just try not to let it change my routine. It does to some degree—I didn't have a very productive day at work the next day.
        —*Dave Lofland*

Lori Hart spends a long time on the phone that night, talking to an old friend in San Francisco. Jace Michael calls his mother, an emergency room nurse. Tom McCabe and David Swersky sit for hours with Mark Lobsinger's hunting partner, Terry Phillips, talking upstairs in the office of the rescue cabin. David offers Terry a bed in his own house, if he wants it.

The next morning, despite rain in the valley and snow up on the peaks, Chris Myers and John Zell take Terry back to Mark's tent. After breaking down the camp they spend hours scrambling over snow-slicked scree fields, searching unsuccessfully for the gun and bow Mark had lost somewhere. Everyone wants to understand, to know what happened. Until they do, Mark Lobsinger's death will haunt these people.

> I got home around ten-thirty, and things were spooky. I was real jumpy, looking behind my back. I called a friend in California—I just had to tell somebody about the whole experience. Then I lay in bed for a long time. I had a hard time getting to sleep because I just kept thinking about the incident over and over and over and over again, from the moment I left work to finding his body.
> —Lori Hart

Two days later three critical incident stress debriefers gather in the front room of the rescue cabin with Lori, Dave Lofland, David Swersky, Scott Messina, Ray Peritz, Marion Berg, me. Initially developed to help combat troops adjust to civilian life, organized critical incident stress debriefings were adapted for civilian purposes in Boston in the 1970s. Greg Mace's death precipitated the first debriefing for Mountain Rescue-Aspen. Since then, debriefings have become standard for team members involved in body recoveries. Indeed, they are offered to any team member who feels he or she needs help after a rescue.

"The first time you go to one, you're kind of like, 'I'm not crazy, I don't need a shrink,'" remembers Bob Zook, who has become a big proponent of debriefings. Bob has learned to handle the stress in a variety of ways, but after thirty or thirty-five body recoveries—he can't remember them all—in a dozen years of rescue work, it still catches up with him sometimes.

In 1988 the famous physicist Heinz Pagels fell almost two thousand feet from Pyramid Peak when a rock gave way under his foot. His body was in an inaccessible, near-vertical location. The only way to reach it was to fly a rescuer in on a cable hanging under a helicopter. Bob, dangling like a fishing lure, was carefully deposited by the pilot on a narrow ledge twenty feet from Heinz's mangled body. After hammering several steel pitons into the rock for an anchor and clipping his rope into them, Bob ventured out into the gully where the body was lodged. He slid a sling under Heinz's armpits, retreated from the deadly rockfall raining intermittently on the body, and waited until the helicopter returned. Then he clipped the sling to the cable dangling beneath the bird and watched as Heinz was lifted from the mountain.

A year later Bob was on his first big wall climb, a multiday undertaking up the side of a Utah canyon called Space Shot. After a day of climbing alone, he anchored himself to the sheer red rock twelve hundred feet above the valley floor. He rigged an artificial ledge the size of a cot and, still in his climbing harness and clipped to his anchors, squirmed into his sleeping bag.

> I was in and out of sleep all night long in a beautiful canyon. Absolutely gorgeous setting. I heard this noise, a very loud noise. It was a rustling, banging sound, kind of like rockfall. But it was in the wrong direction. In my dream I woke up and I heard a voice out there also. I said, "That's not right, there can't be anything out there, because that's space, that's air." I looked over there and it was just like in television, with the eerie lighting and everything, and he [Pagels] floated up to me and grabbed me around the neck and said, "You're coming with me." I reached into my sleeping bag and grabbed my knot that I was tied to the wall with. I held onto that and I said, "No, I'm not, I'm staying here." Then I woke up. The moon had just crested the mountain behind, it lit up the whole other side of the valley, the river and everything. But everything was okay; I had my hand on the knot.
>
> —*Bob Zook*

> You train to do these things. You train to pick up bodies, you train to scrape people off of rocks and out of airplanes and out of burning cars and one thing or another. But in that training you never deal with that. You can't, obviously. You're going to get shocked at some point, and I don't have any idea what it will do to you.
>
> I need recuperative time when I get these nasty ones. You get a summer of twelve dead, and half of them are mangled in one fashion or another, and you deal with the next of kin, the person that watched them die, their sons, their daughters, their moms, their dads—boy, you hope it's a long, slow winter.
>
> —*Tom McCabe*

John Zell learned the rescuer's informal creed the hard way. On his first body recovery, a difficult extrication of a suicide victim from a boulder field, he made the mistake of reading the

two-page note the man had left. A relative of John's had committed suicide when John was small, and the note hit him hard.
"One of the sheriff's deputies saw how upset I got after this, and
he started yelling at me, 'You never, never get involved like that!'
It taught me a lesson," John recalls. "I had nightmares almost
every night for a year. His face would always pop into my mind,
and I had a lot of trouble dealing with that."

"He has nightmares, he talks in his sleep, sometimes he
screams out loud or he sits up in bed," says Mariela, shortly after
she and John are married. "Or he just can't sleep. It bothers him.
And it's weird, because he can talk to some people about those
things, and other people not, and I don't think he can talk to me
about them. I don't know if he thinks that I wouldn't understand
how he feels because I'm not a Mountain Rescue volunteer. But
just by looking at him I can see how he's feeling, so I understand."

Mariela, a small, dark-haired woman who looks a decade
younger than her thirty years, was born in Uruguay but grew up
in New York. It isn't her role, she says, to push John to talk
about something or do something if he doesn't want to. "It does
bother me, because I want him to be able to tell me anything he
wants," she says, "but maybe he feels that it wouldn't help if he
talked to me about it. I don't want to see him get upset, so I just
let him talk to Scott or whoever. Him and Scott talk about things
a lot—a lot—where they both break down. He tells me that, but
he won't go into details."

More than most team volunteers, John is emotionally open.
When he's up, he's way up, and when he's down or angry, he
doesn't hide it. "That's the way he is," Mariela says. "Sometimes
it gets a little obnoxious. But he's one extreme or another.
There's no middle."

John is easily swayed by others, and this, combined with his
strong emotions, leads him to be caught up in the fate of rescue
victims. Some volunteers don't like to deal with the victims
themselves—it is easier, they say, to work on the technical side,
to do logistics or handle ropes or run the radios. But John goes
straight for the litter. That drive, Mariela says, comes from John's
suffering through his mother's painful death from cancer in New
York, which lasted several years.

"He's so far away he really couldn't help her," she explains. "I think maybe that just carries to people on rescues. He wants to help, in the same way he wished he could have helped his mother. He's always willing to help somebody. He'll make a good father that way."

ᛜ   ᛜ

As the last of the commuters drive out of town along Main Street, those team members who have come to the Mark Lobsinger debriefing sit in an uneven circle of chairs and couches. The meeting is an opportunity for people to tell their stories. The debriefers generally sit quietly, letting the team talk: who they are, why they're here, what they did that day. What matters is not what the debriefers have to say, but what the team members have to say.

Debriefing teams include a mental health professional and a couple of people in fields similar to those of the debriefing subjects. On this day a ski patroller and a member of another Mountain Rescue team, both trained in debriefing techniques, have come to Aspen. Their goal is not particularly complex; indeed, these people aren't really necessary. But they catalyze a process that begins with rescuers talking about what happened, who did what, how the pieces fit together. Then rescuers speak about their reactions. Many rescuers, expecting to be able to solve a crisis, are very hard on themselves when they cannot. They may also think they have failed if they have a physical or emotional reaction—if, in their minds, they can't handle it.

Much of what debriefers do is to help people understand that those reactions are normal. They explain how adrenaline gets in the way of accomplishing tasks, how it's acceptable to be upset, how this incident shouldn't eat you alive. Witnessing trauma and handling bodies affects people in various and subtle ways. Sometimes team members don't sleep well, or are irritable with their spouses or girlfriends. They may have nightmares, or can't erase an image from their minds, or are unable to focus on work. They may drink too much, lose interest in sex, withdraw. Or none of these things may happen. But occasionally, after months or years of trying incidents, volunteers will start to show the stress. Some of the most veteran members of the Aspen team have found themselves overwhelmed at debriefing sessions, unexpectedly collapsing in tears as the weight of years of body recoveries and gruesome rescues breaks across them. Sometimes tragedies elsewhere in their lives are the triggers, sometimes it's just a slow deterioration in their lives they can't understand, can't put a finger on.

For the first half hour Ray keeps his Ray-Ban sunglasses on. Eventually he peels them off and, like the others in the room, becomes more voluble. People talk about the sequence of events, not only during the rescue, but prior to and after Mark's fall. I don't speak much. When I talk I am more choked up than I thought I would be. I find it easier to listen. It's not my first body recovery, and it doesn't seem to have affected me too badly. Only the first night, the night we flew Mark's body out. Then I dreamt an old childhood nightmare I had not experienced for twenty-five years. I was struggling from inside a house to extinguish fires someone was lighting against the outside of the house.

This one wasn't too bad, really. Much harder was a body recovery we did earlier in the summer. Jon Campbell, a man in his twenties, had died rescuing a dog from a swift creek. The death didn't bother me at all until Tom McCabe told me the dead man had, in fact, saved the dog. I had to turn away then.

At the Lobsinger debriefing there is an innate need to understand not only who on the team was doing what, but what Mark had done. Preliminary autopsy results suggest he dislocated his hip but didn't break it. He had clearly taken a hard fall—but where? The grassy slope leading down to his body wasn't severe enough to cause that kind of injury. The note he left had cleared up some questions, created others. Had he fallen while trying to climb up something or down something, heading toward his high camp or trying to find his way out to the road?

Although his fall was severe, that wasn't what killed him, Marion says. He apparently died of hypothermia, probably Sunday night. Still, people wonder why Mark hadn't done more to help himself. He had matches, food, water, he was near wood— why not light a fire? The questions are profoundly unsettling.

Part of the need to understand derives from a tendency to identify with the victim. Team members almost universally are most troubled by incidents in which the victim had been doing the sorts of things the rescuers do. "I guess I feel plane wrecks are more to chance," says Debbie Kelly. "It's easy for me to say, 'Well, I wouldn't be there.' Whereas the people that fall off Capitol Peak climbing, that kind of stuff, the people who die doing what I do on a regular basis, it's like, 'Oh, God, that could have been me.'"

One of Dave Lofland's problems was that the incident happened so late in the day that there wasn't much else to do but go home, lie in bed, and think about it. "I tend, on [body] recoveries, to detach myself pretty early," he says. "When I got back to the cabin I didn't want to talk to his friend. I think it's part of the detachment. The more I get involved with the emotions—that's what I'm trying to detach myself from."

Dave, a hunter himself, pondered whether he could have been in Mark's position. In the end he concludes no, that wouldn't have been him. He might have fallen, but he wouldn't have been wearing cotton clothing, which provides little protection in wet weather. Still, he knows he's going to have to work through some unsettled days and nights, as he has before. "Injuries don't get to me nearly as much as fatalities," he says. "Somebody all busted up and still alive doesn't affect me nearly as much as someone who's dead. It's just something about seeing bodies. I don't think I'll ever get used to it. I've learned to deal with it, but that's about it."

After two-and-a-half hours the meeting drifts off the topic. People begin debating rescue techniques, and Scott wanders into the comm room, looking for something. It is clear that the session is over, and everyone, just by talking about their fears, feels better. "I verbalized the story over and over again," says Lori. "I think that helped me work through it. I think that was the real key to closure." She jokes now about "men dying to meet me."

"It really solidified my whole feeling of what the team is all about, why I'm on the team, why I'm involved in this whole thing," Lori says. "It was the quintessential sense of being on the team."

The debriefing is a powerful experience. It is an opportunity for people who have been through a difficult event, something few people will know and one that would seem ludicrous to volunteer for, to talk about themselves and their feelings. It is an organized opportunity to turn your skin inside out, to show deep fears and insecurities. The debriefings serve as group catharsis, but they also cement the relationships developed in the field in moments of stress and crisis and even naked fear.

> I've been a real loner all my life. I've had a few close friends, but I've never had the bonding with so many people. Half the reasons I'm on the team are selfish reasons, because it makes me feel good about myself that I would drop anything to go help someone. And the fact that I'm so close with the people on the team—you may have friends for fifteen years, but you never know whether those people are going to put their life on the line for you. On the team, people that I may not be close to, that I may not associate with except on the team— I'll put my life on the line for them. It's a bond with people that I've never had in my life. Your first really tough rescue, or your first body recovery, you just look into the other person's eyes and you know they're there for you.
> —*John Zell*

Of all the people who worked on Mark's body recovery, Jace is the most upset, and he is surprised. "I'd sit there and cry," he says, "and not know why." Like John Zell before him, Jace has learned what it means to get too close to a victim. Jace is unable to attend the debriefing—he has previously scheduled a trip to Chicago and is out of town. Talking to his mother helped, although not enough.

> I wanted to talk to someone on the team. It just didn't work out. I wanted to talk to someone like David Swersky, or Tom, someone who's been through that stuff and could kind of help me out with it. I didn't know why it was bothering me. I'm still not sure if I understand why it was bothering me. It wasn't like I couldn't sleep—I could sleep fine. If I got to thinking about it, emotionally I would get upset. I talked about it a lot with my girlfriend, Barbara. She's not been through a lot of things like this, but she just tried to help me understand why this was bothering me, because I could not explain it. I could not say, "Well, this is why it's bothering me." I was just more attached to it.
> —*Jace Michael*

Two weeks after Mark's death, Jace takes his dog and hikes back up Lost Man and Jack creeks. Sitting where the helicopter had landed, he raises his binoculars and begins scanning up the valley. Almost immediately he spots a hat on a rock a hundred yards away. Next to it he finds a coin purse, binoculars, and Mark's rifle, still loaded.

"I knew what happened when I found the rifle," Jace says. The firearm lies at the base of the cliff band. Jace climbs forty feet to the top. "I went to the point where he was when he fell. I know I stood right on the spot where he fell, where he slipped off. And it was straight. He might have bounced against a rock, but it was a pretty straight fall. There was nothing to grab."

In his mind, Jace puts the story together as best he can. Caught in an early season storm, Mark—already beset by a bad sense of direction—tried to make it back to camp, perhaps coming up out of Jack Creek. But as he climbed above the timberline he became disoriented. The snow was heavy, the storm blowing hard. His cotton clothes were probably soaking wet, and he was cold. His poncho, whipping in the wind, wasn't doing him much good. He decided to wrap it around his bow and stash them somewhere for later retrieval—he was carrying too much gear, and his situation was getting desperate. Unable to find his camp he stumbled back down, headed for the road a few miles away. Perhaps it was dark, perhaps the snow obscured his vision, perhaps he simply misjudged and slipped off the top of the cliff.

However it happened, when he got to the bottom he thought he had broken his hip. Now his situation truly was desperate. He left his gun and binoculars where he fell. He took a few snacks from his pack and ate them, lucid enough to realize he was going to need the energy, then left the wrappers behind. He started to crawl downhill. He may not even have intended to end up at the creek. He could have slid inadvertently down the last slope to the shelter of the trees and boulders. But there he rested, a little way out of the wind and storm. He found that by hooking the foot of his bad leg under a log and pushing with his other leg he could put some traction on his bad hip and relieve a little of the pain. He drifted in and out of consciousness as the hypothermia got worse. He was able to write his note with a pencil, and perhaps he blew his whistle into the impervious storm.

In the end, just before he died, he felt marvelously warm. Too warm. He pulled off his coat. He tucked his shirt under himself, and he lay back to sleep.

> It made me feel a lot better. And I was doing this for the family, too, you know. They were kind of strapped for money and stuff like that. His rifle was a .300 Mag, it was a six-hundred- or seven-hundred-dollar gun. It helped me. I didn't like the feeling that some of his stuff was still out there, some Joe Blow could just walk by and say, "Oh, here's a rifle," and take something. It just didn't seem right to me that that stuff was still up there.
> —*Jace Michael*

Nine months later, Mark's widow, Denise, and a friend come to Aspen to see the place he died. Linda Koones and David Swersky lead them up Lost Man Creek.

"She mentioned that she had asked him not to go on the hunting trip this year, because at the time they had a seven-month-old daughter," David says. "She just wanted him to stay home with their daughter and maybe go next year. So she had a lot of anger about why he ended up even going on this hunting trip when she had asked him not to. Underneath that anger there was a lot of hurt that she had asked this and he hadn't listened, then he had gone and died. She was pissed. I think it was really good for her. I was perfectly willing to be a sounding board and let her get out whatever she had to and come to a conclusion on this episode."

⋀ ⋀

One of the most rewarding aspects of volunteer rescue is the sense of empowerment. Faced with a crisis, the rescuer is the person able to solve it. Few things in life are clearer or more compelling, and few can be more rewarding in their outcome. The ability to act fulfills a childhood fantasy in which life is black and white, simple: problem, tool, solution, reward. Children often want to solve their problems with toy guns, pulling a trigger to make them vanish. Mountain Rescue-Aspen members behave in a more socially beneficial manner, but are motivated by the same root impulse.

The ability to act is an enormously valuable outlet for energy, an antidote to frustration and powerlessness. Team members have skills, information, tools, mutual support, and a mandate. Those they leave at home—spouses, girlfriends, boyfriends— have none of these things. Possessing little knowledge of what's happening in the field, they often assume the worst, even if their mate is in fact performing a mundane task like baby-sitting a res- cue vehicle at a trailhead. It doesn't help that rescuers often have trouble talking about what they've done. Some team members want to spare their wives or girlfriends the stress of a traumatic incident. Or they just don't want to try to explain what it is they do, what they have done.

"Sometimes I don't think the members realize the stress they're putting on their families," says Julie Mace. "I'm more worried about Scott now, because Scott's out in the field more." Since she lived at the Mace Hut Julie has carried a radio, and she still does, if only to listen. The day Greg died she had to call the rescue cabin—nobody called her—to find out it was her husband who was injured on the Bells.

"It's a hard subject for us to talk about," Julie says of Scott's risks. "I think Scott's pretty good about calling me. He knows it's important for me to get some updates, to know what's going on, that I don't want him out there three days without knowing.

"It's easier for me when I'm working because I'm busier. I certainly will call the cabin once in a while, and I want to know. I want to know if he's coming home. It's hard. I know the reali- ties of what can happen. It's happened to me."

After Scott and Julie eloped they planned a big reception at the Mace Hut. The day of the party a child was lost in the Crystal River, and not a single team member could attend. Even those who had slept at the hut to help prepare the feast departed when the page went out.

"You don't know that you can have an evening without it being interrupted," Julie says. "Go to the ballet and your pager goes off. Go to the movies and your pager goes off. Do you take two cars every time you go out? It's very frustrating."

One ex-spouse of a former team member put it this way: "It was not a positive thing, and you don't want to say that about wonderful Mountain Rescue. You know, 'These people risk their lives.' But for a lot of men it is an escape. It is a mistress."

"I can think of a couple of people that probably use it as an excuse to get away," says Mariela Zell, "maybe because their relationship isn't good, or they're bored with their mates. But I see that a lot. They use it as an excuse to get out of the house."

She and John don't have that problem, she says, but like many women, she worries. "Anytime that pager goes off he gets all excited, he's like, 'Oh, make me a sandwich! Oh, get me some water!' He runs around like a lunatic to make sure he's got everything around the house, and his adrenaline starts pumping.

"I always want to know where he's going, how dangerous it is, you know? 'Cause that's what always makes me think about— every time he goes on a rescue I think about how Julie's first husband died, and that just scares the shit out of me." She is choked up now, speaking fast, as if she wants to spit this thought out and away from her. "One day he's going to go on a rescue and something's going to happen and I'll never see him again."

John promises to call, she says, but he rarely does, and so she is left to her own demons. "I watch TV or call my mother, try to distract myself," Mariela says. "One day I'm going to get an ulcer about it."

⋀⋀ ⋀⋀

When Chris Myers first started dating Katie Gartner, "I was highly impressed," Katie recalls. "I thought he was this big stud Mountain Rescue guy." They met in Colorado's San Juan Mountains. She was visiting from Chicago and hiking with friends, he was on a separate trip, using llamas as pack animals. Their paths crossed, she came over to pet the llamas, and before their trips were finished she was sleeping in Chris's tent.

Katie, a tall, broad-shouldered woman with the clear skin and bright smile of a midwestern American blond, moved to Colorado in 1991. After three years with Chris she has less tolerance for the demands Mountain Rescue work puts on him. "Probably the last year it has strained our relationship the most," she says. "From the start, I just let it be Chris's thing. His pager would go off and he would just be gone. He would always call, but he would say, 'I'm going on a rescue to the Bells, so I'll see you,' and I didn't know what was going on. It was really frustrating, but it just seemed to me it was easier at that point to just let it go and let it be his thing, and he always came back and he was always fine.

"The thing that's different now," she continues, "is that our relationship became more and more serious over time and more and more committed, and he also became more involved, being on the board and being president." There were meetings, trainings, politics, and while those demanded much of Chris, Katie says, she didn't mind the chance to spend time by herself or with other friends.

"The thing that changed a lot was when he would go out on rescues, it would affect me a lot more," she says. "I worry in a weird way. I would keep myself very, very busy, because if I sat down I'd start to think about it, and then I'd be worried, and then I'd be angry. I'd have a lot of anger, especially if I knew it was stupid people out there doing stupid things. That would piss me off, and I would get a little resentful. The practical part of my mind knows that these people absolutely have a right to go out and climb these mountains just as much as we do, and learn—I've only been climbing for four years. But I would still, the emotional side of me would still say, 'This asshole shouldn't have been up there anyway, and now my boyfriend is going to look for him, and if something happens to him, everybody's going to pay.'"

Although she considers Chris to be perceptive and deeply considerate of her, Katie struggles with his tendency to attend to others before himself. On his first Mountain Rescue mission, long before he met Katie, Chris discovered and dug out the body of Teeny Jeung, a woman who had been killed in an avalanche near Pearl Pass. It was profoundly unsettling, and he has never grown immune to the psychological torsion of body recoveries.

"He pretends that he's okay about it," Katie says in mild frustration. The ethic of what David Swersky calls the "me-us-them" rule—look out for me first, team next, victims last—manifests itself in a deep and multifaceted bonding that is impenetrable, sometimes incomprehensible, often frustrating to partners of team members. "It really seems to affect him, but he still won't talk about it," she continues. "Yet he is always the one that's telling everybody else, 'You'd better go to the debriefing, you'd better be there.' He always feels—and he's like this in other areas of his life—he always has to take care of everybody else, make sure everybody else is okay. And when I ask him about it, he'll say, 'It's really okay, I've done it before, no problem.' If I ask him the next day, he might say, 'I hate it, it was really hard.' It usually takes a while."

Chris's tendency to look out for others goes to the heart of the team. "I don't respond for the victim," says Ray Peritz, "so much as for the fact that if I'm taking up space on the roster and I'm not there and you need some other person—you've got to do that kind of stuff. You're there to help the other guys. Your fellow team members rely on you to carry weight."

"Even if it's just driving to the trailhead and hanging out, you start to form a very, very solid friendship with people, working with them like that," says Bob Zook. "And then the first time it's you and that person together on a team, and it's just the two of you, that's when you start to form the brotherhood. I mean, John Zell and I are brothers from what we went through together [on past rescues]. I consider him just as close to me as a brother. There's very little difference between that and a blood brother. It's that strong of a bond that forms when you have to rely on each other in that manner."

What forges this bond is the shared fear and shared horror of what Mountain Rescue members do. Like cops, like soldiers, like firefighters, they work in a world that is largely their own, and they depend on one another not only to survive it, but to understand it, sometimes even to glorify it. More, perhaps, than they should.

"Some of them seem to get off on this," says Katie, "and some of them just do it and it goes to some part of their body that doesn't get dealt with. I see a lot of men—and some of the women—on the team who are either too connected, and it's like their identification, which is scary, or who think it's just this ball-blasting, gutsy, great thing. And I see a lot more sadness in it, in what they do."

IT IS just a few rocks, tumbling down around the corner and onto the snowfield below. The clatter quickly dies away, and the high ridge is quiet again for a few seconds. Then comes a fluttering, guttural sound that Jon Gibans, an emergency room physician, knows and fears in his gut: it is the sound of obstructed breathing.

He shouts for his partner, Eric Scranton, as he turns and tries to find a way back down the steep slope they have been climbing. He scrambles twenty feet down to the horizontal seam between the top of a snowfield and the rock face, and hurries around the corner to where Eric was trying to work his way up the steep ground to a better route. The snow has melted away from the rock, creating a gap and a snow wall several feet high. As he rounds the bend, the first thing Jon sees is a red smear, a foot wide and three feet long, down the snow wall. It ends at Eric's head. He is upside down in the gap between the snow and the rock, propped on his face, moaning.

Things had been going so well. Jon, thirty-five, and Eric, a twenty-nine-year-old bicycle mechanic, had left the trailhead at six-thirty the morning of October 1, heading up Capitol Creek to the forbidding, silver-gray tooth of Capitol Peak, 14,130 feet high. The two men had climbed in the Andes and the Himalayas as well as the Rockies, although never together. This was to have been a relatively easy climb, a one-day summit strike. They covered the six-and-a-half miles to Capitol Lake at a trot in less than two hours, then turned east and climbed 850 feet to Daly Saddle. They crossed over the 12,450-foot saddle and began traversing the east flank of the great ridge that leads to the peak.

Working along the rocky flank of the ridge, they wandered off the best route. At the top of the short, steep snowfield, a remnant of the previous winter, they realized they were too low on the side of the ridge—soon they would run up against an unclimbable cliff face. They decided to scramble uphill to a better route, then traverse up the flank back toward the ridgeline. Just out of sight of each other, they began to climb. It was nine-fifteen in the morning.

When Jon reaches Eric his face is already swelling. He makes Eric wiggle his toes and fingers, to show he hasn't broken his back or neck. Then Jon rolls Eric upright and drags him a few feet to a spot where he can sit on the snow and lean against the rock.

Eric is a mess. He doesn't know what happened. He doesn't know what day it is. He doesn't know what month it is. He doesn't know he is in Colorado. His forehead is gashed, his upper front teeth missing, his lower front teeth protruding through his lip. He is bleeding from the nose and mouth, and when he looks around his eyes don't move in unison. He keeps asking Jon the same questions.

Jon thinks about his options as he changes Eric out of his sweat-soaked clothes into dry gear. They have a hundred-foot length of rope with them. Perhaps he can lower Eric seventy-five feet down the forty-degree snowfield to the boulder slope below. But then what? Eric clearly has a head injury, and the two men would have to walk across the boulders, down the valley to Moon Lake, then from there down to Snowmass Creek and out to the Snowmass Creek trailhead—a seven-mile trip, descending four thousand feet. Eric is strong, but is he that strong?

So as Jon wraps Eric in clothes and puts more clothes under him to insulate him from the snow, he tells his amnesiac friend the same thing again and again: I'm going for help, you stay here; I'm going for help, you stay here. He ties Eric loosely with the rope to the rocks behind him. He wants to keep him from sliding down the snow, but he doesn't want to strangle him if he slips. Lastly, he takes a big brown garbage bag he carries as emergency shelter and places Eric in it for protection from the weather.

After forty-five minutes, Jon starts down the mountain. Eric's head injury doesn't seem to be getting any worse, but it isn't getting any better. If his brain swells severely, Jon won't be able to do anything about it even if he stays on the mountain. What worries him more is Eric's ability to breathe. His face has swollen enormously—if his throat does, too, he will suffocate.

Jon starts to run down the trail, seven-and-a-half miles back to his car. Perched at the top of a snow slope at 12,600 feet, Eric Scranton dozes off.

⋀ ⋀

Debbie Kelly isn't far from the cabin when the page goes out at 11:45 A.M.

"This could be the big one!" she yells as she throws open the locks to the cabin doors and turns on the radio. She has a nasty head cold, but she'll cover for Chris Myers, the 501, until he can get to the cabin.

> I knew it was a fast response. As soon as I called the sheriff's department they said, "We have a climber with serious head injuries on Capitol." Immediately you know the urgency. You don't have to sit down and calculate your urgency—age of victim, experience—none of that. Because it's a rescue, not a search, the revs get pretty high.
> —*Chris Myers*

Chris clambers into his blue Isuzu Trooper and roars up Highway 82 from his home in Basalt, nineteen miles from Aspen.

Jeff Lumsden comes over from the sheriff's office to supervise the rescue. Quickly, the decision is made to call in a helicopter.

The only machine available is a Bell Long Ranger from DBS Air.
The helicopter is based in Glenwood Springs, only forty miles
away—but nobody on the team has yet flown with the pilot,
who just recently completed the necessary paperwork with the
Pitkin County sheriff's office so he could be employed by Mountain Rescue-Aspen.

Soon the front room is cluttered with gear and shouting people. Dr. Marion Berg arrives from the hospital with an extensive
emergency pack and begins suiting up. He'll do a field tracheos-
tomy if necessary, cutting a hole in Eric's throat to enable him to
breathe. Ron Bracken and Vicki Chavka scramble to find crampons that will fit. Chris shows up, along with Scott Messina and
Dave Brown. All three get ready to go in the field, even though
Chris or Scott, the 502, normally would stay in the cabin to run
the mission.

At 1:10 P.M. the helicopter lands at Aspen Airport. Drew
Dolan and Bert Fingerhut head to the Capitol Peak trailhead to
start hiking, a backup team in case the helicopter operation
fails.

The helicopter team crowds into the comm room, all anxious
faces and rustling Gore-Tex. Debbie Kelly looks grim. She usually
exudes an easy confidence, an attractive lack of self-consciousness
and quick sense of humor that make her amiable and person-
able. But she can drive severe, commanding authority into her
voice, and she does so now. The room is quiet as she gives a
quick rundown on where Eric is, what to expect. Jon Gibans,
who has come to the cabin, stands behind the group and listens.
He will become a Mountain Rescue support member in a few
months, but now he has nothing more to offer.

Jeff Lumsden speaks up. Although he's willing to let Debbie
run the show, as deputy in charge he is going to exert at least a
little authority. Six feet tall, stocky, and baby-faced, he tucks in
his chin and looks at the group through square-rim glasses.
"Marion, you and Ron are medical," he says. He points to Chris
and Scott. "You're safety, you're air ops. You guys go in first. If
this LZ doesn't work," he says, gesturing at the map stuck to the
wall, "try this one down here. He's a new pilot. Don't push it."

The team tumbles out of the room and into Rescue 1, headed for the airport. Tom McCabe, who has been listening quietly, leans over to Debbie. "Let's hope," he says softly, "this doesn't go to shit."

/Λ\ /Λ\

Rick and Landon Deane get their Cessna, One Five Charlie, in the air at one-thirty. A veteran pilot with Pitkin County Air Rescue, a horse-packer for decades, Rick knows every bump in the Elk Mountains. Twenty-two minutes after takeoff, Landon spots Eric, sitting in a brown bag by the brown rock atop the snowfield. A three-foot-wide pool of blood stains the snow beside him, but he waves. A few minutes later the blue Long Ranger, Eagle Star Three, clatters into the big bowl on the east flank of Capitol. Rick circles his plane above Eric, trying to show Chris and Scott, the helicopter's passengers, where Eric is sitting. After a couple of unsuccessful passes they tell the helicopter pilot to set it down—they'll find him on foot.

They land gently in an open patch of alpine tundra, just beyond the boulder field and a mile from where Eric sits. Scott stays to direct the helicopter on subsequent flights. Chris grabs the Sked and his pack, and humps it up the boulders toward the snowfield, still talking by radio to Landon circling overhead. She guides him to the base of the snowfield. "He should be right above you, right on that snowfield," Landon tells Chris as he stands where the snowmelt drips into the rocks.

> I yelled up, "Eric!" and all of a sudden this bloody face looked over the snow, then faded back. So I knew he was alive. I said, "Hold on, I'll be right there, Eric," slapped on the crampons and ice axe and started up. I'm not an EMT [Emergency Medical Technician]—that was probably a mistake. I probably should have let Scott go ahead of me. But I got to him and I just started talking to him. Marion is five minutes behind me, so I talked to this guy. I didn't do any vital [signs] on him. He seemed so stable from his discussion, he wasn't passing out.
>
> I said, "What happened, Eric?" In a nice way, I said, "Do you do this every day?" Some light conversation. He couldn't see himself.

He said that somehow he looked up and a rock was falling. He heard some noise and a rock caught him right in the head, and then he just went over and fell on his face. Double jeopardy.
—*Chris Myers*

The second helicopter run brings Marion and Ron, an Emergency Medical Technician, to the landing zone. Ron carries nearly eighty pounds of gear: a rope, a brake bag, his personal pack, and an oxygen tank. Marion is loaded with other medical gear. They don't know if they're going to have to save Eric's life in the field or not, but they're ready to. "I like that," Ron says. "It excites me. I don't want anybody to be hurt so bad they're going to die or anything, but I would like the chance to do that."

They struggle with their loads to the base of the snowfield. Ron helps Marion strap the unfamiliar crampons onto his boots. Chris, sitting above with Eric, is getting impatient, and yells down to them to hurry up. "Doing the Chris thing," Ron says, shrugging it off.

"In terms of preparing myself mentally, I'm pretty methodical," says Chris, who believes he has mellowed after the better part of a decade on the team. "I'm thinking, 'If we're going to do this right, we're going to do A, we're going to do B, we're going to do C. If you forget any one of those, we're in big trouble. Some people are like, 'The guy is in trouble, we've got to go!' People running off half-cocked and they get there and all they've got is a water bottle."

Chris has more than a water bottle, but he has beaten the medical team to the scene, and now is left to urge them on and make small talk with Eric. "So we just talked about the hike and what he thought had happened," Chris recalls. "He was very philosophical. He said, 'You know, it's a beautiful day. I've just been sitting up here watching the day go by, but God, it's really nice to see you guys. Glad you're here.'"

Thirty-five minutes after Chris reaches Eric, Marion and Ron climb up to him.

It was kind of funny, because I got to the top of the snowfield there, I stuck my axe in and I looked over the edge, and he says, "Hi, how ya doing?" I said, "Fine, how are you?" He was very coherent, asked me to find his teeth. I looked for two seconds—we were busy trying to get set up. He said he wanted to frame them. He had a good sense of humor.

  —*Ron Bracken*

Marion gives Eric a thorough head-to-toe exam. His damage appears limited to his face, where many bones are broken. But everything else seems good, and Eric feels strong. The sun has moved behind the ridge and the air is chilling fast—everyone wants to get out of the bloody spot where Eric has waited for seven hours. Once the sun sets, the helicopter won't be able to fly safely. Quickly, Marion, Ron, and Chris strap Eric into the Sked. They drive ice axes and snow pickets—broad, two-foot-long aluminum stakes—into the hard snow for anchors. By now the helicopter has made a third run, bringing in Vicki and Dave Brown. Together with Scott, they climb to the base of the snow-field. Dave continues up, clips his harness onto the Sked, and be-gins to back down the slope with Eric. The rope from the Sked runs through the anchor at the top and back down the slope to Vicki and Scott, who counterbalance the weight of the rescue load with their own weight, controlling the descent.

Once the Sked reaches the snowfield, Marion does something that surprises the rest of the team: he asks Eric if he can walk. It's the better part of a mile across the boulder field to the land-ing zone, and time is running short. Eric feels okay, and walking will be a lot easier than carrying him in the Sked. His balance isn't good, however, nor his eyesight—he has broken an eye socket, which means his eyeballs don't track together. Dave and Ron get on either side of their patient, who puts his arms on their shoulders and proceeds to race to the landing zone.

"He dragged us down the mountain all the way," Ron says later, chuckling. "We didn't stop to rest. He was ready to get out of there."

It takes less than thirty minutes to reach the landing zone. The team has moved so quickly they catch the helicopter pilot unawares, refueling at the airport. Ron, Marion, and Dave wait with Eric for a few minutes until Eagle Star Three lands. The helicopter takes Marion and Eric to the airport, where Jon Gibans picks his friend up and drives him to the hospital. There he will face nearly six hours of reconstructive surgery and several days of painful hospitalization. His jaw will be wired shut, and his girlfriend will spend weeks pureeing meals into milk shakes.

Eric's mobility means the helicopter pilot has enough daylight left to fly everyone off the mountain; no one has to hike out in the dark. How much weight can the helicopter carry? Chris asks Debbie on the radio. He wants to get everyone out in as few flights as possible. Dave and Ron are the last out, bringing with them everyone else's backpacks. Before boarding, Dave calls the cabin: "I'm going on a diet tomorrow," he promises. The load is a little heavy, and the pilot struggles to get enough altitude to clear a small lip on the downhill side of the landing zone.

Down at the airport, Marion is pumped. "That was fantastic!" he exults, grinning. After the last flight the team loads gear into Rescue 1 and drives slowly back to the cabin. Flushed and triumphant, they wander into the comm room at six o'clock to find Debbie sucking on a cough drop and doing a slow burn. She is angry at Chris, and she isn't afraid to tell him. As he walks into the room she turns in her seat and stares deliberately at him. "I'm not even the goddamn 501," she says. "You're out in the field, and I'm stuck here. I'm not even supposed to be doing this."

⋀ ⋀

Three days later, at the monthly meeting, Marion pulls out a brown manila envelope and withdraws a handful of images—CT scans of Eric Scranton's face. Nearly every bone is broken. It would have been possible, the doctor says, to grab Eric's nose and move his whole face. It is the worst facial fracture he has ever seen in his practice as an emergency room physician. To top it off, Eric had fractured the base of his skull, too.

"Eric's a really incredible individual," Marion tells the crowded meeting room. "He's a tough son of a bitch."

LINDA KOONES brings her aging, faded Irish setter, Carrie, and her bright-eyed, fine-boned black mutt, Sam, to the board meeting. The dark air outside is thick with the damp scent of decay and a brooding expectation of winter. The dogs gently sniff the board members, watching them as they wander in and drop their four-inch-thick binders on the table upstairs. Then Carrie and Sam lie down near Linda's feet, moving only when someone gets up or inadvertently skids a chair into them.

Ray Peritz comes by to get a sense of the work the board is doing. The December election for board seats is two months away, but he expects to be sitting at this table soon. He wears his "Aspen Businessman" outfit: Dockers, loafers, wool socks, J. Crew shirt. As he eases back in his plastic chair he looks rangy and fit, although the gray is coming into his mahogany mustache. Kevin Hagerty comes by too, filthy with grease and dirt from a day of readying the ski lifts at Aspen Highlands. His face is sunburned, blond hair tangled, mustache damp.

"Let's order the pizza now," Kevin says as he plops into a chair.

"You guys might as well decide what you want, and I'll order it," Debbie Kelly answers.

"Lauretta's," Dave Lofland says, "because we all know what's on the menu."

After she phones the Mexican restaurant Debbie begins to read from the minutes of the last meeting, as she does every month. There is little discussion. Kevin, without saying anything, gets up to leave.

"Kevin," Debbie says tensely, "what did you come here for?"

"I just came for the pizza and beer," Kevin laughs. "I'm leaving."

Debbie laughs too, as does the rest of the board. Everyone is nervous. Everyone is expecting Tom McCabe. At the last general meeting Debbie passed out draft copies of the new team bylaws, the product of eighteen months of work by two successive boards of directors. They will be voted upon at the October general meeting. Although few team members bother to read them, the changes they incorporate are significant, especially to Tom; the board effectively has written him out of formal authority.

Nobody sitting at the white table tonight expects that to go down without a fight.

⋀ ⋀

In the mid-1980s Tom and Greg Mace created the 501/502 program. The idea was to develop a layer of middle management, to get the team away from depending on one person—Greg—as the only one capable of running rescues. In the years after Greg's death Tom became the rescue coordinator, responsible for training, scheduling, and managing the rescue leaders. It was a position of authority and one in which he took great pride. Tom's radio call sign became "500," the first in the Mountain Rescue call series. In an organization with few official badges of leadership, that call sign is one. It put Tom, in some ways, at the top of the heap.

In the past two years, ever since Tom stepped down as president, this has not sat well with the board.

> We wrote him out of the 500 position because during that whole "Miracle on the Mountain" thing we had some discussions about the fact that the accountability in the team didn't run linearly. We had the board and the people under the board, and we had this other leader over here that wasn't really under the board, that was separate from the board, out to the side. So what we did was we took away all his powers and gave them to the board, so he couldn't make decisions that would affect the way the team was running without board approval.
> —*Debbie Kelly*

The board also eliminated the requirement that prospective members take two Mountain Rescue classes taught by Tom each year at the local community college. Board members say they will still require the classes—they just want to remove that requirement from the bylaws. Tom is rankled. The course teaches everyone the basics of rescue work: knots, radio protocol, where the equipment is stored. It eliminates, he says, a lot of on-the-job training and reduces mistakes made under pressure.

"They think there's no value to that [class], because they don't know," Tom grumbles. "And I'm tired of preaching, because they're not listening. What I'm willing to do—and it ticks me off—I'm willing to let them flush it down the toilet, because then they'll have to rebuild it."

Tom does not come to the board meeting on this night.

⋏⋏ ⋏⋏

"There aren't many opportunities for live comedy in this town," Lori Hart says a week later as team members crowd into October's general meeting, a congregation that sounds like a fraternity party, "but these meetings sure do the trick."

The gathering is small—only about twenty-five people—because so many have left town for the traditional long, low-season vacation between summer and winter. Still, it is loud and raucous. Debbie hoots when, flipping through photos of Eric

Scranton's rescue, she comes to a picture of Chris Myers standing on a snowfield in shorts.

"Look at those legs!" she hollers. "Look at those legs!"

Hunting season is under way, someone says—carry orange gear and be ready.

"Carry a gun to shoot back," someone else mumbles from the back of the room.

"Be sure you wear your regulation brown suede jacket," adds a third voice.

"And an antler cap," cracks a fourth, not missing a beat.

Almost immediately Debbie plunges into the bylaws discussion, flipping back and forth in her notebook between the old and the new versions. "You guys can't say yes to what you haven't even read," she says by way of explaining why she's going to summarize the changes before calling a vote. "I know for a fact only one person even read them."

"We sat through a lot of meetings," Chris snaps when the group refuses to stop wisecracking. "You can sit through one."

"We're going to vote on all the changes at once, so listen up and shut up," Debbie says.

"Ooooo," responds the room, but it quiets down.

Debbie moves fast, explaining changes in wording, modifications to accommodate the Americans with Disabilities Act, the philosophy behind it all. The board has tried to alter the bylaws so that, in the event of a catastrophic failure, it will be more difficult for a hostile attorney to seize on one small failing and make an issue of it. Thus, requirements regarding, for example, the gear carried on rescues, have become suggestions.

She blows quickly through the sixteen pages, drawing only a few questions. The changes to Tom's position are not mentioned. But in the course of the discussion about 501/502 training, Debbie gives Tom an opening. She does not, she says, know how to turn on the landing lights at the airport—a task previously handled by 501s but now the responsibility of sheriff's deputies. Nor does she think she needs to know it, she says.

Tom speaks up. "I think that everything that is happening is to the good of the group," he says benignly before slipping in a shiv. "For those of you too young to know," he continues, "that comes from a time when all of us used to go out and turn on the airport lights and run rescues from the airport, and you were all just too lazy to take advantage of it when it was offered at the last 501 training." By now his voice drips sarcasm. It is as if Tom is challenging the board: You have pushed me out; who is going to pick up the ball? Who knows what I know?

Nobody rises to the bait, and in a few minutes the changes are approved unanimously. Tom knows there's no point in casting a dissenting vote. Someone asks about Tom's rescue class, slated to begin in a few weeks. Tom is vague. Maybe he'll teach, maybe that responsibility will fall on the backs of other rescue leaders. Tonight, though, he seems to be leaning toward undertaking the class.

"It includes," he intones to the room, "how to change the batteries in the secret decoder ring."

ʎ ʎ

The bylaws are finally signed and sealed a few weeks after the general meeting at the late October board meeting. Chris walks in at the beginning of the evening and, bursting with pride, announces he has become engaged to Katie. Chris proposed to her in a tent in New Hampshire's White Mountains during an early season snowstorm, after carrying the ring around loose in his shorts pocket for two weeks.

"If she said no, I was going to throw her out of the tent," he grins as Debbie leans over and whispers in Scott Messina's ear.

The meeting starts, as usual, with a dinner order—this time to Paesano's—and then Debbie begins to read through the minutes. Scott's cell phone rings, and as he gets up from the table, answering "Aspen Alpine Guides," he steps out of the room. When Debbie notes that the board authorized Chris to ask a local foundation for eight thousand dollars toward a new rescue vehicle to replace the Unimog, he interrupts to say he asked for ten thousand. Debbie reads on, taking nearly forty minutes, what with the meandering discussion, to approve the minutes.

This vote coincides with the arrival of lasagna and cannelloni, Caesar salad, and cheesecake, and people quickly push their binders away. Suddenly Scott—who has been gone a long time—

walks back into the room, bearing two bottles of red wine and a handful of plastic cups.

Chris looks bewildered, and his gaze settles on Debbie.

"We figured if you could make a ten-thousand-dollar request without board approval," she smiles, "we could do this without board approval."

Ray walks in and someone tells him of Chris's engagement. "To Chris," they say, and all the cups are tapped together.

"First prerequisite for divorce," Ray says out of the side of his mouth before sipping.

Scott is typically fidgety—the class-clown aspects of his character quickly surface in formal settings. Suddenly he steps across the room to the second-floor French doors and flings one open. On the far side of the alley a light burns in the window of a small house; someone is working there.

"Howdy!" Scott yells.

He closes the door without waiting for a response and looks back at the rest of the board. "Keeping the neighbors happy," he says, deadpan, and picks up his wine cup again.

"JESUS CHRIST," Ray Peritz wheezes, "we're going to be here all night!"

His headlamp beam swings unevenly through the crisp, dark air, coursing across a small hell of fallen aspen trees, loose scree, and early snow, all angling steeply toward an unseen ridge. If ever there was a place to break an ankle, this is it.

Ray catches his breath, picks up his end of the orange, plastic Thompson litter, and stumbles up the hill, cursing. I follow with my end, echoing him. Above us, other headlamps wave feebly through the trees amid the sound of dead wood breaking. Overhead, through a scrim of leafless aspen branches, stars glitter with the adamantine clarity unique to dark, cold, high places far from man's light.

"Chris, which way?" John Zell's voice crackles over the radio on my chest. "We're at the top of the meadow."

"Keep following the flagging," Chris Myers says as Ray stumbles and slips.

"Where is the flagging?" John asks with slow exasperation. "We can't see anything up here."

"Just keep coming up. Up and left. Look for the flagging."

"Shit," Ray says, stopping again to catch his breath and watch the dim beams fifty yards ahead probe tentatively left. "We're going to be here until four o'clock."

∧∧ ∧∧

The call went out just after 6:00 P.M. for "a short carryout up the Frying Pan." The response to the cabin is quick but thin, which isn't surprising. The Frying Pan Valley is long, lonely, and distant. We will have to drive fifty miles before we even start walking.

Upstairs, Tom McCabe teaches the first session of his fall rescue class to would-be members. Down in the front room four people cram gear into their packs: Ray, John, Scott Messina, and Ron Bracken. Kevin Hagerty is in the comm room, talking to the 501, Bob Zook, who is still at home. Dave Lofland and Chris Herrera step in the front door. They can help, but will have to stop home and pick up gear, then follow in Dave's truck. Chris Myers and Dave Brown have already headed out from their downvalley homes as the hasty team; they have a twenty-mile head start.

Kevin sticks his head out of the comm room. "What do you guys need?"

"Get us a pizza," Ray says as he hops on one leg, trying to slide Gore-Tex pants over his hiking boots. "I've got to eat."

Kevin dials Peppino's in Basalt. A few late stragglers for Tom's class wander in and look very lost. Somebody shoos them upstairs. We clatter out the back door in Rescue 1. While I drive, John reaches over and turns on a new device that Chris Herrera recently installed: flashers, known as Wig-Wag lights, that rapidly switch the headlights on and off in a left-right sequence. Since the sheriff doesn't let Mountain Rescue employ the flashing red lights on the roof, ever, this small alteration has been made without asking anyone whether it is legitimate.

"We're not running code," John says, as much to himself as anyone else. "All the fire department guys have this. This works better, because it's right in their mirrors. And we're *not* running code."

It does work. As I pull the big Chevy up behind vehicles, they ease off to the side of the highway. Several times I charge up behind pickups full of orange-clad hunters—some of whom drive a little unsteadily and perhaps think it is a state trooper on their tail, interested in discussing that beer in the cab.

We make the winding nineteen miles to Basalt in twenty minutes. The tires squeal as I pull into the parking lot shared by 7-Eleven and Peppino's. On the way John gets a briefing via radio from Bob. The information is very sketchy; all we have is a report of a possible broken tibia and fibula on a hunter. We are to meet a deputy, Randy Smith, at Thomasville. He'll be with the hunter who reported the accident, and they will guide us from there.

"Who's got money?" John asks as he scrambles out of the truck into the humming, ghastly 7-Eleven glare. Only Scott has brought his wallet: he has a five and a fifty. He gives the fifty to John for pizza, the five to Ron for Gatorade from 7-Eleven. Each immediately begins running into the wrong store until the yelling and laughing turn them around.

By the time I have the truck pointed up the river they are back, piling in with the smell of mushrooms and pepperoni and sloshing around the sticky, sweet Gatorade, which seems to be the unofficial drink of Mountain Rescue-Aspen. The road up the Frying Pan River runs east toward the Continental Divide from Basalt, a three-block town that once served as a junction stop for the Midland and Denver & Rio Grande railroads. As soon as we pass the last mercury lamp on Main Street, the valley—narrow red rock, piñon and juniper, hushing river down below the road—goes dark and still. The two-lane road twists twelve miles to the base of Ruedi Dam. Cresting that, we drive another thirteen, now high above the reservoir on a slope of sage and yellow dust, until we reach Thomasville, a single store at the eastern end of the lake but still twenty miles from the Divide.

In the glow of the sole streetlight there—visible and alone for miles—Randy Smith sits in his patrol car with a sixtyish hunter. As we approach, Chris comes over the radio. Another hunter is showing him and Dave Brown the way up to the victim and has requested that we carry extra water for all of them.

"Fuck that," John snaps at the radio.

"We don't carry water for any fucking hunters," Scott adds from the backseat.

"You don't give any liquids unless a doctor says so," says John as Ray and Ron make acknowledging sounds in the dark.

I park in front of Randy's car, and everyone gets out to stretch. Randy and the hunter step into the light. He is a lumpy orange man wearing an earflap hat and a Day-Glo cotton sweatshirt. Scott stands by the front right tire of the truck, urinating in the dirt and interviewing the hunter over his shoulder.

The hunter doesn't know much more than we do about the victim's injuries, but he tells Scott where to start hiking, which is enough. John drives, slowly now, for the road has turned to dirt, and the steady passage of hunters' trucks has packed the debris of an early November storm a few nights past into fat spaghetti lines of ice. The road cuts a defile through thick stands of Engelmann spruce and alpine fir. We curl five miles up the Cunningham Creek drainage, finally parking behind the dark bulk of Dave Brown's pickup. No one is here. The tracks don't even clarify whether we should start climbing to the left or right. While the rest of the team pulls the guts of the truck's compartments out into the snow, Scott and I call Chris, who directs us to a strip of flagging on the left side of the road.

"You guys look like a Chinese fire drill," Randy says as he pulls up. Chris starts calling for gear: Thompson sled, a couple of brake bags, a three-hundred-foot rope, and the pulse oxymeter, a device used to measure a victim's pulse and blood oxygen saturation level.

We dump the contents of the brake bags on tarps, selecting only the necessary equipment—two brake tubes, a handful of carabiners, anchor ropes, webbing—to stuff into our packs. Everyone pulls unnecessary personal gear from their packs. Food, bivvy sacks, sleeping bags, extra socks, stoves, and fuel are tossed into a dark jumble in the back of the truck.

"This is gorgeous," John exults, throwing his head back and staring at the moonless sky, then grinning around him. "I'm out here with my friends, on this beautiful night, and we get to go for a hike." He is genuinely elated.

As we prepare to head out, Dave Lofland and Chris Herrera pull up in Dave's truck. They'll be a few minutes behind us on the trail. Scott and John take the point and plunge into the forest past the yard of orange tape Chris Myers left dangling from a stump. There is no moon, and there are boot tracks everywhere in the desiccated snow. Within fifty feet we are lost, and the back-and-forth begins with Chris on the radio. For a long time Chris keeps insisting "follow the flagging, follow the flagging," like an American in Europe who believes if he just speaks loud enough, these people will understand English.

After 150 yards we break out into a clearing, a meadow that rises several hundred feet up the south face of the ridge. The snow has melted out here, but the grass is slick and tufted. Scott, Ron, and John scramble ahead as Ray and I stumble up with the seven-foot-long Thompson litter, sometimes putting a hand on the steep ground for balance. At the top of the meadow the trio spends a long time wandering before Chris convinces them to move left into a Dantean agglomeration of rock, logs, and snow that leads only upward, and from which there seems to be no escaping.

The route probably would not seem half so bad or so long in the day, but wrapped in darkness, stripped down to little more than long underwear in the fifteen-degree night and still sweating, guided only by radioed admonitions to keep heading up, it is phenomenally demoralizing. Chris says he has a big fire going, but we can see nothing, not even a glow through the trees when we turn off our headlamps and stop in the darkness, breathing heavily, trying to let our eyes adjust. Finally, in the distance, John hears Chris blowing his whistle and heads for the sound. Soon we come upon another hunter, standing with his headlamp facing downhill, ready to direct us the last hundred yards. In all we've gone only about a mile and climbed six hundred feet, but we have taken the better part of an hour.

Across a small clearing, uphill from the huge, rotting, silver-brown hulk of an ancient Engelmann spruce, three small fires burn on the ground around a man who lies in the fetal position. Several more hunters stand quietly in a half-circle among the fires, their faces in shadow, their orange garb reflecting the fire-light in a surreal glow.

Dave Brown sits just uphill from the injured hunter, Marty Langenburg, a middle-aged man from Colorado Springs who stepped on a rock the wrong way, felt it roll, heard the sickening snap and crunch just above his ankle, went down in a heap. From under a blanket Marty extends his gloved right hand along the ground and over his head, as if he is raising it. Dave, sitting quietly, holds Marty's hand in his own. John Zell, his face flushed from exertion, leans close to Marty, talking softly, all his energy directed to a pale man old enough to be his father.

Chris steps back and walks to the edge of the clearing.

> He was a military man. He was in pain. That was hard. We cut his boot off with a hunting knife. I've never done first medical on scene before. It was good—I really enjoyed it. It was fun having that rapport and talking to the guy, saying to him, "Okay, we're here, we're here to help you and we need your cooperation, and this is what we're doing. We're going to get your respiration and pulse, and relay that, talk to a doctor, and he's going to guide us in terms of what he'd like us to do."
> —*Chris Myers*

Chris and Scott shake into jackets to ward off the chill and walk across the clearing to scout a better route down. They find a small, timbered rib that begins a hundred yards east of where Marty lies. It runs, generally rock free, down to the top of the big, grassy meadow. We can lower Marty down the steep slope the same way we took Evelyn Hoffman down the Ute Trail, affixing a series of brakes to trees, then running a long rope tail off the litter and through the brakes. The problem now is we don't have a rope. Chris Herrera is bringing one up and somehow thinks somebody ahead has another, so he doesn't hurry.

Chris Myers has appointed himself team leader, and he is getting frustrated. The rope isn't here, the first anchor isn't set where he wants it. "Break it down and move it over here," he tells the brake team, "just drag it over there, come on, come on!"

With the help of the hunters, John—who has taken over the medical responsibilities—gets Marty loaded into the Thompson, wrapped in blankets and strapped in. Marty weighs nearly two hundred pounds, and normally six people would clip their climbing harnesses onto the litter rail to carry him. But we only have nine on the hill, so just four men pick up the load: John, Dave Brown, Ron, and Dave Lofland. They scuttle awkwardly across the clearing to the first brake, then tie in on the rope, which has finally arrived.

Chris Myers runs back and forth, directing the pair of two-man brake teams on where to set up anchors as he scouts a route down the rib. The brake teams leapfrog down the hill. The four hunters wander along the periphery, trying to illuminate the route as best they can with headlamps. As the operation runs on, Chris's demands and barked directions begin to wear on everyone. He falls into a tone of voice that, though unconscious, sounds condescending, and it festers in the volunteers stumbling down the hill, grunting under the weight of the victim, tripping across logs and rocks. He snaps at Scott and Ray when he doesn't think they are moving fast enough. He accuses John of "whining" on the litter and eventually takes over for him.

> It's tough doing a night operation, not being able to see six feet ahead of you. I thought it went a bit slowly at times, like, "Come on, let's speed this up." His buddies were kind of following along but getting in the way, because you couldn't tell them from rescuers [in the dark]. There was also some confusion as to the route—go this way, or go this way? Why are we going this way? That is just something where somebody needs to take charge and say, "Okay, we're going this way, let's do it." I thought there was a lot of bickering. It was like, "Come on guys, we're all on a team, let's work together."
>
> Tom McCabe always felt you should stand back and let people do it and make the mistakes. Sometimes you can do that, but there are some times that's inappropriate. We are on a real-life mission, and we have a job to do. We need to do our job, and you can't often let people make all the mistakes.
> —*Chris Myers*

John is scouting the route when Chris snaps at him about making a poor choice. The outburst surprises John and leaves him grinding his teeth.

I was too upset, really, really upset. It had happened before, and I was really afraid that it would get physical, so I just didn't do anything. Chris and I had had a few problems before that. He lashes out very harshly. It's just not fair. We're all trying to do our best. If somebody screws up, then you can politely say, "Hey, John, we need to do this or we need to do that or you're doing that wrong." You don't need to lash out at somebody. You can't talk to people like that, especially in a volunteer situation where everybody's trying their best.
—*John Zell*

After taking John's spot at the head of the litter, Chris leans over Marty. "Hang in there, Marty," he says loudly. "Are you in pain?"

"Yes," Marty says quietly.

"Hey!" Chris says, straightening up and looking around. "He's in pain!"

"He's been in pain the whole time, Chris," John says wearily.

By now the litter team is at the fifth brake station, at the top of the meadow. They begin backing slowly down against the friction of the brake. Chris Herrera, manning the brake, pays rope out, but the litter team isn't moving. Suddenly they lurch down and backwards, sitting down hard, and the rope snaps taut against the brake. The rope had hung up on an unseen snag between the litter and the brake, which suddenly broke. Everyone is surprised, but no one is hurt.

The cold has killed all the radio batteries. We are reduced to shouting directions from the scout to the litter team and the litter team to the brake. By the time we reach the bottom of the meadow, John's water bottle is beginning to freeze. After the seventh brake station the litter team continues on flat ground, crashing through the trees toward the road. Ron, Dave Lofland, and Dave Brown have carried the litter now for an hour and a quarter. Ron's legs nearly buckle as they walk the last few yards to the light pooling around the ambulance. The rest of us straggle in behind, carrying the brakes, dim headlamps, and dead radios. As Marty is loaded into the bright interior of Medic Four, not long before midnight, Chris solemnly shakes hands with everyone. "Good job," he declares.

"He loves to help people and he loves to be in control," says Katie Gartner, Chris's fiancée. "He was so proud to be president of the team. He loves to lead. He would be the last person to admit it, but he enjoys having some power. It's hard for him to delegate and to let things go. I think part of being a leader, especially of Mountain Rescue, is you're educating new people and you're building a team with consensus, teamwork. It's too hard for him to accept other people's styles of management or other people's styles of learning. That's what took a toll on him, because he could not believe that somebody would be doing something a certain way. He just believed that it was not right. And the few times I'd say to him, 'Well, that's probably just the way they do it, that's their style,' he would say, 'But it's not right, it's not the most efficient way.' I would say, 'Well, you can control some of that, but you're not going to be able to control all of it,' and he would get really pissed off at me.

"Each year I've known him," she continues, "he's been able to let down a little bit more on that, and I think as he gets older that's going to keep going."

Ʌʌ Ʌʌ

Nobody repacks anything. Dogs have never been this tired. Backpacks, uncoiled ropes, the litter are crammed in the back of Rescue 1. As Ray starts the fifty-mile drive back to Aspen, Chris radios good-bye from Dave Brown's truck.

"I wonder if Myers will come to the cabin and show us how to repack this stuff," Scott snorts, "since he's shown us how to use it."

"I don't know what it is," John says. "We used to be friends, but now all our relationship is is him yelling at me.

"I talk about how upset I am with Chris half the time," he adds later, reflecting on the mission. "But I would risk my life for him. Absolutely."

THE TRAIL leads nearly straight downhill into thick timber and chest-deep snow. As I lash snowshoes onto my boots, Joe Mincberg steps close and lowers his voice.

"Listen, if they're dead, bring out their collars, would you?"

I try to say something reassuring. With Ron Bracken behind I plunge over the side of the hill, following the track in the snow.

⋀ ⋀

The night before, Chris Myers had called. Doing anything tomorrow? he asked. Want to go for a hike? Soon I was on the phone to other team members, trying to round up a few volunteers for an unofficial rescue mission.

Joe and his girlfriend, Georgia Jessup, had taken their dogs for a February afternoon walk on a quiet road along an uninhabited ridge near Snowmass Village. The area had received a yard of fresh snow during the previous week, and the snowbanks along the small road are five or six feet high. Joe let the dogs—Flo-Jo, a beagle; Streeter, a Jack Russell terrier; Bubba, a bulldog; and Yogi, a yellow Lab—off their leashes. They cavorted up and down the road until they came to a hairpin turn. Here the snow-plow driver had pushed the snow down the hill, and the dogs were able to escape over the snowbanks that had walled them in. Well ahead of Joe and Georgia, they dove over the side, plunging down into the timber and out of sight. By the time the owners caught up, all they found was a single, furrowed track. There was no sign of the dogs, despite much pleading and call-ing. Joe tried to follow the track, but without snowshoes sank to his shoulders and had to retreat to the road after a few feet.

With darkness approaching, the frantic couple called the sher-iff's office. Nobody there was going to page the rescue team out for a dog search, but somebody passed on Scott Messina's phone number. Scott and Jace Michael agreed to drive up to the dogs' escape site and have a look, but they found nothing new as dark-ness settled into the valley. By the time Chris called me, the own-ers were panicking.

"It's not an official mission," Chris said, but he thought we might be able to help out. He gave me Joe's phone number. A woman answered on the second ring. As soon as I introduced myself, she blurted, "We're going to pay five hundred dollars a day for every person who comes out and searches." Her voice was taut and not a little desperate.

Ah, I thought, the New Aspen. "You don't need to do that," I said. We made plans to rendezvous early in the morning.

I called Chris back. It will be cold tonight, we agreed. In the teens. Those dogs are probably coyote bait.

Ron and I wait in the parking lot of the Snowmass Village Conoco until Joe drives up. It is a glorious late winter morning, deep blue sky arching over ridges and valleys softened by fresh snow. A year has passed since Ken Torp and his friends under-took their infamous ski trip up Express Creek. The ski lifts are humming over nearby runs. Wisps of smoke and steam curl from the chimneys and vents of the hotels and condominiums scaling the slopes. Joe is in his late forties or early fifties, big-chested, loud. He has a dark, graying ponytail tucked through the back of his woolen Dodgers baseball cap. He drives a new red Toyota 4runner, in which he keeps an oft-used cellular phone.

He is in a surprisingly good mood.

"Streeter showed up last night!" Joe says by way of introduction. The terrier was found wandering around Snowmass Village, a mile from where the dogs were last seen. Chris and Jace arrive in Chris's truck, and Joe leads us a mile to where the dogs disappeared. The road twists along a ridge separating Brush Creek from Snowmass Creek. The ski village is on the Brush Creek side; timber and a few scattered houses lie on the Snowmass Creek side.

Jace and Chris drive down toward Snowmass Creek to an irrigation ditch that traverses the lower slopes of the ridge. They'll ski in along the ditch and look for tracks. Ron and I park where the dogs vanished and head down, leaving Joe with a radio and a promise to find them.

The slope is so steep at first I can almost ski on my snowshoes, but blowdowns under the surface make that risky. Ron's snowshoes are smaller than mine, and he has trouble in the deep powder, sinking in to his hips and falling over every few steps. We move slowly. He is working especially hard, pulling himself out of the snow time and again.

We follow the track down through spruce and aspen, a deep half-pipe punctuated by leg holes. We can surmise what happened. The Lab had bulled his way down through the snow, aided by gravity. The other, smaller dogs had followed in his wake. Once down, they couldn't get back up: the snow was too deep for them to reach the ground and gain decent footholds. Only Streeter had been able to climb back up to the ridge. He is so small and light he could walk in the track left by the other dogs without sinking in.

"Flo-Jo!" I shout. "Bubba! Yogi!"

The snow soaks up the sound.

"Flo-Jo!" Ron calls. "Bubba—shit!" He falls over again. His plastic-rim glasses steam up from the exertion.

After a few hundred yards we come to an old jeep road. The track turns onto this, and we can see how, on this more gentle slope down and across the hill, the dogs had been able to pace back and forth in their footsteps.

Waiting for Ron, I catch my breath and call again, gazing idly around the woods.

"Flo-Jo!"

I look down the track and see a little toy dog there: ears perked, head cocked. It takes a moment to register that this is what I'm out here for.

"Ron, I've got the beagle!"

I turn back to the dog, still watching from forty yards away.

"Flo-Jo! Come on! Come here!"

The dog puts her head back and howls. Barks, and howls again. She looks hard at me, then turns and runs down the trail and out of sight.

"Flo-Jo!"

"Let's get our hands on her before we call it in," Ron says as he catches up.

Suddenly Flo-Jo is back. She stops for a second—I can see her deep brown eyes watching me intently—then howls and scampers again down the trail. This time I can watch her as I follow. She runs to a large hump in the snow, an old woodpile left from when the jeep trail was cleared. She looks up the trail at me and howls again. Her tail wags furiously.

As we near the pile Flo-Jo runs up to us. She is a small beagle, skinny and fine-boned with a thin coat. She shivers from the cold, or perhaps excitement. Then she runs back to the woodpile. We're only twenty yards away now, and I can see what's there. Bubba, the bulldog, is struggling, up to his slobbering chin in the snow. Cream-colored with brown and black splotches, he is the size of a pony keg of beer, a good forty pounds. His short, old legs are nearly useless. He struggles up out of the hole by the woodpile and flounders onto the front of my snowshoes, desperate for something to stand on. His lower teeth jut unevenly out over his upper lip, and he is shaking. He makes snorting noises as I bend down to rub him. Flo-Jo is everywhere, running to Bubba, then to Ron, then to me, vibrating with excitement, wagging like a fish, nuzzling and licking our hands and faces.

I key the mike and raise Chris. "We've got the beagle and the bulldog, and boy, are they glad to see us," I tell him. "The track keeps going downhill. You might find something."

"We're following a track on the ditch," Chris says. "Try to bring them down to us."

Ron and I shed our packs for a quick break. This is our first live find on a search, and we are as delighted as our four-footed victims. Ron digs out a crumbled granola bar and gives half to each dog, who lick the crumbs out of his hand. Bubba snorts softly. They are thirsty, too, but we have nothing here they can drink from.

"Okay guys, let's go," I say, shouldering my pack. Stomping hard, I lead, trying to pack a trail over the dogs' track so they won't sink in so far. Ron follows, herding the two dogs along. Flo-Jo is solicitous, running back and forth between us. Soon I come across an old barbed-wire fence buried in the snow, and I understand the traces of blood along the track; Flo-Jo cut her pad here sometime in the night. I stand on the wire while Ron leads the dogs past, then bring up the rear.

Bubba is bogging down badly, sinking deeply every few steps. I settle down on my knees next to him, wrap my arms around his thick rib cage, then lift him as I roll forward, trying to get him on firmer snow. He seems grateful for the help, and he is determined to keep moving. The trail angles downhill, and in about ten minutes we reach the ditch, a dry, ten-foot-wide aqueduct dug along the contour of the hill. Chris calls on the radio—he and Jace have found Yogi huddled under a spruce tree. After fifteen minutes of stumbling and grunting through the snow in the ditch, we round a corner and Flo-Jo lets out a howl, scampering ahead to greet Yogi, Chris, and Jace.

"He wouldn't let us near him at first," Jace says, laughing and slapping the big, wagging Lab on the back. "He put up a good show of barking. But he was barking and wagging his tail. I fed him half my turkey sandwich, and then we were buds."

We trace the route back to the road, a mile more along the ditch. Chris and Jace move faster on their skis, and Bubba does better in their track. Flo-Jo wants to be up front, and soon all four are out of sight. Ron and I stay back with Yogi, the Lab, who is perhaps the most tired of all. He is clearly the one who did the heaviest work the day before, pushing through the snow in one direction, then another, seeking an escape while the other dogs stumbled behind. He is distraught at having lost track of the others, but he is tired, too, and he stops often, sometimes raising a quivering leg up out of the snow.

I sink down to look for ice in between his toes, but find none. All around us we hear the *whumpf* of settling snow as the weight of the fresh powder collapses the rotten, brittle snowpack below—the same snowpack into which the dogs sink and flounder. In steeper terrain an avalanche would have killed us or the dogs by now, for when the pack collapses like this it often slides. But here the slope is too gentle to form a danger.

I snap a snowshoe binding a half-mile from the road. Ron waits while Yogi and I lie in the snow together; the only way for me to make the repair without sinking is by lying on my back. Then I help Yogi along as I did with Bubba, picking him up and heaving him forward while Ron packs the trail.

We are hungry for lunch when we round a corner and see the road ahead. Joe is there, along with Jace and Chris. The battery in Joe's radio had been weak, but he heard enough to know to meet us here. Bubba and Flo-Jo are already asleep in the back of his open truck.

"Come on, buddy," he yells, slapping his thigh and grinning. "Come on Yogi, you asshole!"

Yogi wags his tail feebly and tries a little harder. It is only twenty yards to the road.

"Don't push him," Ron says in a steady voice. "He's exhausted. We don't want to lose him here."

Joe is quiet until Yogi clambers down the plowed snowbank and walks slowly over to him, looking a little sheepish. He drinks from a pan of water as Joe pats him. The day has turned warm, and all the dogs seem fine. But it is clear to us they would have died without our help. Yogi and Bubba were too tired to move on, and Flo-Jo was probably too loyal to leave, even though she could have followed the track with little trouble. Their biggest problem, after a day and a night of hard work, was dehydration. That, more than the cold, would have killed them in another night or two.

I catch a ride back to my car with Jace and Chris. Ron rides with Joe. As he drives, Joe flips out a roll of hundred-dollar bills.

"No amount of money can pay you guys for bringing my dogs back," he tells Ron, steering with one hand, "but I want to pay you anyway."

Later, telling me the story as we drive back to Aspen, Ron shakes his head. "It was hard to look at that fat roll of hundreds in my face," he says, gazing out the car window, "but I don't want to start getting into taking money for this stuff."

Then he brightens up, grinning from behind his glasses. His face is pink from the morning outside and the elation of finding the dogs alive. Blond curls stick out from under his hat.

"I feel great," he says. "I feel really good about this." At dawn his girlfriend, Terri, had telephoned him. She is working for the winter in Florida, and today is Valentine's Day. Ron was rushing around the house, trying to pull his rescue gear together, when the phone rang.

"She was all weepy about our not being together today," he says, "and I was like, 'Honey, I gotta go.' She loves animals, though—loves them. I think she would have kicked my ass if I hadn't come out and saved these dogs."

"THE DIFFERENCE between Crockett and Christ," says Randy Smith, sighing heavily, "is Christ only came back from the dead once."

Randy is not smiling. The deputy slumps in a white plastic chair by the table in the cabin's upstairs meeting room. He is working graveyard shifts this month at the sheriff's office, and he is exhausted. More than that, however, he is demoralized.

Before him lies a wrinkled sheet of lined yellow paper on which Bob Braudis has scrawled a barely legible note. Randy has just read the note to Mountain Rescue's helicopter committee—Scott Messina, Tom McCabe, Donna Rowlands, Dave Lofland, Dave Brown—and they are stunned. The sheriff is ordering the team to "cease and desist" all its efforts at developing policy for using helicopters. That is precisely the work this group ("the Whirlybird Committee," as Dave Brown calls it) has been doing. That project will be taken over by Steve Crockett, who will "entertain" any of Mountain Rescue's concerns.

Only two weeks earlier, Randy had reported to the same group that Bob had promised that Steve would not be involved at all. The committee has been working hard, making real progress at developing a set of safety rules under which the team can use helicopters, one of the most treasured, expensive, and controversial tools Mountain Rescue-Aspen employs. Since the beginning of 1994 Steve and Bob have been harping on how dangerous helicopters are. The formation of the committee has been an attempt to try to make both men more comfortable with the team's use of a machine that costs between several hundred and several thousand dollars an hour, a machine Steve defines as "twenty thousand parts flying in close formation."

"The idea," Tom had said at the first Whirlybird Committee meeting in February, "is every time Crockett throws an obstacle in our face to overwhelm it with compliance." Now, in late May, Steve has prevented even that: he's going to draw up the rules. Mountain Rescue can't even help unless he asks.

"I don't know what Crockett's got on him," Tom says after listening to Randy. He is astounded that Bob has put Steve in the breach yet again.

"Caught him with a sheep," someone quips, drawing a few chuckles.

Randy reads the note aloud again: "Please cease and desist until you touch base with Crockett."

Tom starts gathering his things from the table. "I'm done," he says angrily. "As long as that stands, I'm no longer a player."

/\\   /\\

"When Fred Braun was the head of Mountain Rescue years ago," Bob Braudis says, leaning back in the wide, worn leather chair by his oak desk and lighting a Marlboro, "ordering a helicopter was almost unheard of. Everything was done on carryouts, maybe horseback, maybe snowmobile. It's my belief that in this terrain there's no more useful piece of equipment, so we were seeing a large increase in helicopter utilization. I'd let them pick and choose who they flew with. That was important—they wanted to be intimately familiar with the pilot and his aircraft."

Bob and Steve believe the team has hired "inadequate" airships for the work it has done, and used pilots who—although they may be good—don't have their bona fides documented on paper to the degree or in the manner the sheriff would like. This sort of thing makes Bob—who is very worried about being sued—nervous. Nor does Bob have complete confidence in all of the pilots the team has been flying with, and Mountain Rescue's choices about helicopter missions have done nothing to reinforce the sheriff's trust in their judgment.

Although Bob Zook's old Honda bears a bumper sticker proclaiming, "Helicopters Save Lives," everyone, especially Bob Braudis, thinks they are dangerous. On one mission in the early 1990s the weather was so bad the pilot was able to fly only two rescuers to the site of a fatal plane crash, and even that was hairy. The victims were known to be dead—why, Bob and Steve wondered, did Mountain Rescue's leaders put volunteers at such risk for bodies?

"We aren't going to trade live ones for dead ones," Bob tells the team's leadership.

What rankles the sheriff most, though, is flying rescuers outside of helicopters, dangling them on a "long-line" cable or in a "Billy Pugh" net in order to swing them onto a cliff face or narrow ridge where landing isn't possible. The Federal Aviation Administration (FAA) prohibits such operations with single-engine helicopters—the only kind generally available near Aspen. If the helicopter engine fails, the pilot may—through an emergency landing technique called autorotation—be able to save either himself or the man on the line, but not both. Bob is mortified at the personal legal liability such operations hold for him.

"I stuck my head in the sand," Bob says, "saying that saving a life was worth risking a life. Now I don't believe that anymore. We don't spend lives to save lives. Putting Zook in a rope net hanging from a cable in a single-engine helicopter is wrong. Totally wrong."

Attempting to address the sheriff's concerns, the team creates the Whirlybird Committee in early 1994. In mid-May Mountain Rescue hosts the helispot manager course Steve had canceled a year earlier. A third of the team attends the three-day course, which teaches the Incident Command System protocols for managing helicopters during rescue operations. Steve does not appear. Committee members meeting the following week feel they are close to having a useful set of rules in hand. They'll blend together the best practices used in the Grand Canyon, the Tetons, and Denali national parks to develop procedures that should make Bob feel much more comfortable. It is at this point that Steve is thrust back into the picture.

> What we need to do is manage that very expensive, dangerous resource, and we need to bring it from the unacceptable risk category to an acceptable risk category through good management, and the way to do that is we need to train people how to manage it.
>
> What I hear in the context of Mountain Rescue is, "We didn't sign up to do that, we didn't sign up to manage incidents, we didn't sign up to fill out the paperwork, we didn't sign up to do two-day carry-outs when we can do it in twenty minutes in a helicopter." And I say, "Yes, you did. They just didn't tell you that." That's leadership. That's what I'm talking about. That organization is screaming, crying, begging for good leadership, and what I say to them is, "Do not seek shelter behind being a volunteer. You volunteered to do the whole thing. You didn't just volunteer to fly around in helicopters. You volunteered to work for the public without getting paid for it."
>
> I hear people fucking whining about this and whining about that, and at this point in time I've got a very low tolerance for that. This is the way the bear shits in the fucking buckwheat, people. This is the way it's going to be. These are the laws, and the last time I checked, everybody agreed to play by the laws. This is the world you've fucking chosen to live in. Change the laws or leave the world.
>
> —*Steve Crockett*

Mountain Rescue, Steve charges, is "in a state of arrested development." He wants the team to "grow up, turn pro."

Such talk, not surprisingly, infuriates team members. "Braudis is saying the wave of the future for rescue teams is professional—not paid professional, but he sees us getting our standards up to professional standards," says Scott Messina. "Who the fuck's standards is he comparing us to? We have the National Mountain Rescue standards that we adhere to and we're accredited by, and we meet or exceed the standards. What other standards?"

/\\ /\\

Steve comes to the helicopter committee meeting on June 1, a week after Randy reads Bob's note, wandering in from the spring evening wearing a faded pink Izod shirt with the collar turned up, sandals, amber-lens Ray-Bans. For two hours he dominates the conversation. His message is simple: Bob Braudis is going to get his way.

"What that sounds like in negotiations is 'Let's do it my way,'" he says, "and Mountain Rescue needs to understand that. Either way, one way or the other, the sheriff is the man. You want to take on the most popular elected official in Pitkin County? You're going to go up against that? Good luck. Maybe, maybe you'll get a punch in. But you're going to get your fucking butt kicked."

Later, he says it is his goal to "de-autonomize" Mountain Rescue-Aspen. "Because of changing times, increased demand for service, the sheriff's department and Mountain Rescue are bumping into each other," Steve explains. "That's what the tax-payers are demanding out there. And the mating dance is what we're having trouble with. You've got to get out there and step on each other's toes and sniff each other's assholes and do your whole mating dance routine."

Steve takes away a list of concerns from the committee, things they want him to consider as he develops a helicopter policy: what kind of fireproof clothing should members wear, can the team get an FAA exemption to fly people outside the helicopter, what gear goes into a helispot kit. He promises to have a draft for the committee to read by June 14. The sheriff wants a proto-col in place by July 4.

Despite Steve's bombast, the meeting is generally cordial. Tom, in fact, is the most cordial of all, thinking the best thing he can do is give Steve rope. Bob has sent a letter to Scott restating Steve's authority to develop rules and manage rescue aircraft. That document is a small relief to the committee members. It means if something screws up, if somebody dies because a heli-copter wasn't used where it could have been, it's the sheriff's fault, not Mountain Rescue's. In private conversations team members have wondered if someone is, indeed, going to have to die before Steve is pulled off the job.

"I think that what we're going through right now is a cycle," says Bob Zook, "and it's driven by Bob Braudis and Steve Crockett. Everybody wants a degree of control over air operations, and that's fine, but the severity of what's going on could eventually get somebody killed. We could lose a victim we might not otherwise."

Nobody wants that, but there's a feeling that might be what it takes. At least with Sheriff Braudis's letter on file there's a sense that the team has its tail covered. The blood won't be on Mountain Rescue's hands.

A few days later Steve meets again, this time with the 501s. He makes three points that ring in their ears. First, he says, the sheriff is responsible for rescues, even if Mountain Rescue members think the sheriff's department doesn't know what it's doing. "It is the sheriff's prerogative," Steve declares, leaning forward across the table, "to fuck up incidents."

Second, use of helicopters will be approved only by Steve or, if he's not in town, by the sheriff. Make your case, he says, and if it's a good one, we will approve helicopter missions.

Last, he says, Mountain Rescue doesn't go anywhere or do anything without being told to by the sheriff. Period.

⋀ ⋀

"He is not a team player," Chris Myers says of Steve, "and I think it is doomed to fail because he is not a team player. He needs to have absolute control, and if he doesn't have absolute respect and control, he falls apart. I don't think he's a person who can see the faults in himself. He's still a little kid in many respects, in the way he deals with others. It doesn't make it easy."

Chris is frustrated. Everyone is frustrated. For six weeks team members have been trying to find the body of Mark Tozer, a climber killed by lightning April 23 on the summit of Capitol Peak. Steve's directive means no one, officially, can go look for Mark unless the sheriff asks, and come June the sheriff isn't asking.

Mark, thirty-four, a father of five from Colorado Springs, had climbed the technically demanding northwest buttress of Capitol with Alex Carlson, eighteen, and Darren Greve, nineteen. As they reached the summit a winter thunderstorm blew in and Mark took a direct, instantly fatal lightning strike to the top of the head. Alex and Darren managed to climb down and ski out a day late, just as rescue team members were heading up Capitol Creek to search for them. But Mark's body remained hidden somewhere on the half-mile-high north face of the peak.

In the days following Mark's death several feet of snow fall on Capitol. Throughout the month of May, as the weather warms and the snow clears, Mountain Rescue begins searching for his fallen body, an effort the sheriff's office makes no attempt to stop. Four times team members go up in aircraft, flying sometimes within a few yards of the face, trying to spot something, anything, among the crevices and gullies and ribs of gray rock. Others hike or ride horses up the valley, then ski the last two miles to Capitol Lake. They glass the face with binoculars and spotting scopes, work along the bases of the cliffs, look for anomalies among the rock and ice and water and lichen. Until Mark's body is recovered he cannot be declared dead, and until he is declared dead his widow and children can receive no Social Security benefits. The situation weighs heavily on the team.

On June 14 Marion Berg and Sallie Shatz hike and ski the seven miles to the lake. They are looking for Mark, but in deference to Steve's early June prohibition of unauthorized searching they go as private individuals, not as part of an organized Mountain Rescue mission. As soon as they crest the last rise and scan the broad apron of snow along the base of the north face, they know Mark is there. After six weeks of staring at the reconnaissance photos piling up on the comm room counters and tacked to its wooden walls, they recognize nearly every rock in the area. On this day there is a new, dark object in the middle of the snowfield.

The mountain has finally relinquished Mark's badly battered body. A series of warm days has released the body from where it had lain frozen. It scraped down a damp gully, carrying moss with it, before landing on the snow.

"Finally, it ends," Scott says as he stands in the comm room the next day, looking at Sallie's photographs.

But it doesn't end that easily. Bob Zook, the 501, wants to use a helicopter to carry the body out of the valley. A few team members can hike in to package the body, then hike out again, he says. If they can just sling the body on a cable under the bird rather than carrying it out, everything will be quicker and easier. He can accomplish an operation like that in a day with four people. Otherwise, fifteen people will need two days to carry it out, since there are no horses available right now from outfitters.

"You don't ever want to be in a position where you have critical dependence on a single individual," Steve had admonished in late May. "That's bad management." Yet that is what has happened. Steve is out of town. So is Bob Braudis, who is at a Denver hospital with his ill wife. Neither has delegated decision-making power to those left in Aspen. Steve, reached by phone, quickly nixes Bob's plan.

The deputies who now must manage the body recovery are angry and frustrated. Nearly everyone in the sheriff's office agrees a helicopter would be appropriate, but neither Steve nor Bob is available to hear the arguments in person. In the end, twenty people recover Mark's body over two days with the help of horses supplied at the last moment by Rick and Landon Deane. The operation goes well, but the deputies who have been working for the past few months with Mountain Rescue—Joe Disalvo and Tom Grady—say they've had it. They don't want to have to go through this kind of brain damage and frustration at Steve's hands again.

⋀ ⋀

Three weeks later, on the tail of Independence Day weekend, a late afternoon page goes out for a hasty team. A girl has injured her ankle four miles up Willow Creek, a rough drainage just west of T-Lazy-7 Ranch in the Snowmass-Maroon Bells Wilderness. There are only a few hours of daylight left, and the team will need to hike fast to reach her before dark.

Steve has maps spread on the hood of his white Pitkin County Jeep when I arrive at the trailhead with Scott, Jace Michael, and Josh Landis, a new support member. David Swersky, the 501, is there. The team crowds around to get a quick briefing on the mission, but Steve waves people away.

"I'm going to brief David, and David will brief you," Steve says.

"He doesn't need to pull this shit with us," says Scott as he scuffs around the dirt parking lot. He has learned the communications center paged Steve about this rescue at five-fifteen, but the 501 page didn't go out for another thirty-three minutes, even after Scott telephoned the dispatcher to ask that the 501 be paged immediately. Now the hasty team is standing around instead of hitting the trail. In all, Scott estimates Steve has cost the team an hour of precious daylight.

When Steve beckons the hasty team members back, Scott lines them up and marches them smartly up to the Jeep, then salutes.

"Don't you fuck with me," Steve says, although he thinks the prank is funny. He explains that he's sending an assistant fire chief from Carbondale in with the hasty team. The assistant fire chief, in his late thirties and sporting a fledgling beer belly, is a few yards away at his white pickup truck, packing his blue frame pack. His job is to be a helispot manager, Steve says; the plan is to fly the girl out via helicopter in the morning. The lower two miles of the valley are full of blown-down trees, making a carry-out very difficult.

"Does he have food for forty-eight hours?" Jace asks belligerently, glaring from behind his Vuarnet sunglasses, almost nose-to-nose with Steve.

"He has food for forty-eight hours," Steve answers, gazing evenly from behind his yellow Ray-Bans.

"Does he have gear?"

"He has everything he needs. He's going to be part of your team."

"He's not part of our team," Jace says acidly, turning on his heel in disgust.

The assistant fire chief drags on the hike, and the Mountain Rescue members wait for him repeatedly. They reach the girl, Joelene Liperind, on a steep hillside, arriving just before dark and just behind Rick and Landon Deane, who have ridden ahead on horses. Jace splints Joelene's ankle by the light of his head-lamp, and the team moves her down to a flat spot in the valley to sleep. As the group prepares to camp for the night, the assistant fire chief collapses into sleep without even eating dinner. The rest of the team stays up past midnight, preparing for the next day.

That night Scott learns via radio that Joelene will have to be carried out. Steve has had a long talk with the local forest super-visor, Sonny LaSalle, who has decided the team cannot use a heli-copter in the wilderness area unless the injury is life-threatening.

The next morning Scott hefts the assistant fire chief's pack—it weighs only a third as much as the Mountain Rescue packs and holds little more than a few PowerBars and a sleeping bag. No rain gear, no warm clothing. "If it rained," Scott says later, his voice contemptuous, "he was fucked. If we had to do anything, he didn't have the energy. He came in and passed out. I guaran-tee he won't go in again. We kicked his ass."

The assistant fire chief hikes out by himself early the next morning, not even bothering to sign out with Scott. Twenty-one Mountain Rescue members hike in and join the hasty team to carry the litter over hundreds of blown-down aspen trees. It takes the group seven hours to cover four miles. Not only is the unmaintained trail difficult, but Joelene is large, weighing well over two hundred pounds.

Joelene handles the ordeal well, and as her boyfriend drives her off to the hospital for X rays, Steve arrives at the trailhead with a paper bag full of vanilla Haagen-Dazs ice-cream bars. After he leaves, Debbie Kelly holds a Budweiser in one hand, an ice-cream bar in the other in the afternoon sun. "You know," she says, "now we're going to have to say, 'That guy sure is a jerk, but he did bring us ice-cream bars that one time.'"

⋀⋀ ⋀⋀

The ice cream doesn't mollify team members for long. At the July 11 general meeting people hash over what they see as Steve's meddling in Mountain Rescue operations, and in the course of the conversation they grow increasingly frustrated.

"What are we doing to get him out?" Drew Dolan asks the board.

"It would be good to document the sheriff's department screw-ups, which are replete," Tom adds.

"Tom, I don't have time," Scott replies. Every time the conversation in a meeting turns to Steve or the sheriff, Scott looks as if he has just aged ten years. His smile vanishes, the bags under his eyes seem more pronounced. He looks exhausted. He is exhausted. The post of board president is "the biggest baby-sitting job I've ever had," he says, and his guide service is busier than ever. He doesn't have time for meeting after meeting with Steve and Bob, then with the board and the team. Yet that is what is being demanded of him. Soon he will be in the woods, guiding. "After next week," he says, "I disappear."

Scott and the board find themselves able to do little more than react in the face of a bureaucracy that seems committed to eroding the team's resistance, its independence, its will. Nobody has the energy to get ahead of the curve in the team's dealings with the sheriff's office or many other areas, all crying for attention. The one attempt to do that, the Whirlybird Committee, has been shut down. At each board meeting, at each general meeting, people say they will do something the team needs done—design a new brochure, write a fund-raising letter—but then don't follow through for months. The problem is endemic to volunteer organizations, and it puts Mountain Rescue at a distinct disadvantage vis-à-vis the sheriff's office.

Steve, on the other hand, is paid every day to watch and criticize the team. "I think Crockett is almost heaping demands on the team so at a point they're going to say we can't handle it anymore," says Chris Myers. "He's going to go to Braudis, 'See, they can't handle it, let's do this professionally.'"

Board members and the rest of the team feel they have no ability to counter Steve's nay-saying, and are convinced Steve wants to be put in charge of the team and paid for it. Nobody has the energy or the stomach for a political mud fight with Steve; even the day-to-day needs of the team aren't being attended to. No one, for instance, has been appointed to Tom's former role of managing the 501s and 502s. The board has taken the responsibility of managing the rescue leaders, but in practice lets them drift. Monthly meetings of rescue leaders become sporadic; their cohesion and training starts to erode. Nobody has the time to do what they know must be done.

Scott looks out at the team gathered in the cabin. "What does the board want me to do?" he asks wearily. "What does the team want me to do?"

"Get him out of there," Jace says.

/\/\   /\/\

I'm trying to delegate this to the right person. Crockett may not be the right person. I want to delegate this to someone in my organization who can make it happen, and Steve and I have had hours of real hard, heart-to-heart communication, and I don't know if he can make it happen. I know I could make it happen. If I dropped everything else I could spend a lot of time really getting to know the decision makers at MRA and saying, "Guys, is there any argument that we should do better in these areas? No? Okay, how are we going to get there?"

Steve is the most complex psychological person I've ever worked with. We're good friends, but our friendship has pretty much evaporated. We have a very strained personal relationship. I don't know what the resolution's going to be. Steve is by far the most highly trained and intelligent person to bring order from this chaos. But he may be doomed.

 —Sheriff Bob Braudis

"You always negotiate from a position of strength. That's what responsibility and authority and support is," Steve says. "If I can be given that by the sheriff, then my opportunity to succeed is obviously increased tremendously.

"I told Bob it's really hard for me to do my work as disaster coordinator, which is Incident Command System, and separate search and rescue, and separate aviation. They're joined at the hip. If I am going to succeed at ICS there's a search-and-rescue component to that and there's an aviation component to that, and I have to have the authority and the responsibility for all of those things to do my job. It isn't empire building."

Deputies and rescue leaders alike complain to the sheriff about Steve's behavior in the wake of the Mark Tozer body recovery and Joelene Liperind carryout. But unlike July a year ago, when Steve lost Bob's support, something different happens. Just as Mountain Rescue's board members draft a letter of complaint about Steve to the sheriff, Bob circulates a memo detailing Steve's new job as "emergency management coordinator." He puts Steve in charge of the twenty-eight thousand dollars Mountain Rescue receives annually from Pitkin County. He puts him in charge of rescues. He gives him the authority to play any role he wants on a rescue. The memo reads like a job description Steve wrote for himself. The significance is clear: Steve has been reappointed SAR czar, and this time Bob seems to mean it.

"What's this?" asks Ray Peritz when Scott hands him a copy of the two-page memo.

"The first page is about Crockett," Scott says. "The second is my resignation."

Ray looks horrified. Scott waits three beats and breaks into a grin. "Did I get you?"

Ray rolls his eyes and gives Scott a very hard look, glaring at him from under lowered eyebrows. That, says Ray's brown-eyed stare, was not funny.

FOURTH OF JULY weekend is hot, dry, dusty. The air palls with smoke from distant wildfires spawned by the hottest June on record. The last decent rainstorm was in mid-June, the last before that, Memorial Day weekend. The cloudless days linger upon us, and begin to make us uneasy. The mountains are not supposed to be like this.

At ten thousand feet the forest duff crackles beneath my feet like steel wool. The moss under alpine firs is split like a desert mud flat. Every morning now I get up and look out the window, wondering if it will rain. Saturday, two days before the holiday, I hike up the Ute Trail. The dust powders the little bushes and flowers along the ground. At the top I hear the bump and rumble of thunder, but the storm is twenty miles downvalley. It will miss us, I think, or pass by with a tease of virga, curtains of rain draping toward the ground but evaporating before they can touch, driven off by a fierce shimmering.

Rain, I say to myself, believing the gods can hear me. Come on, baby, rain. Get me wet.

It does a little, just enough of a sprinkle to create a double rainbow under dark clouds in the east end of the valley. That seems to be all, but as I arrive home, the wind picks up. The western storm has grown and run, and the gust front before it is strong. It flips all the fat aspen leaves belly up and strips petals from the red geraniums on my deck. The cottonwoods across the road hiss and roar, and then the first drops come, fat plops slapping down on the deck, a sprinkle of bouncing hail, then huge, cutting sheets of water running up the valley, slashing into the windows, washing a froth of dust down the tarmac. Lightning flashes and snicks onto the ridges, even striking twice downtown. I stand in the open sliding glass door, feel the air turn cool and damp, draw deep the sweetness of rain.

We need a storm like this every day for a month, but Sunday is hot and hazy again. I spend the late afternoon sitting in the grass outside the Aspen Music Tent, listening with two thousand other people as Britten and Chopin and Debussy filter through the canvas. I drink Anchor Steam ale and serenely spit cherry pits. On the way home my pager goes off.

"501, respond to the courthouse to meet with seven-nine and Steve Crockett about a climber who has fallen in an ice field on the Maroon Bells."

I have often wanted to pull the emergency brake and throw the wheel hard, skidding the car around in a one-eighty like James Garner used to do in *The Rockford Files*. I think about it for a moment, but just make a fast U-turn and hit the flashers instead.

The cabin is open. Chris Herrera is out back, ripping gear out of a giant duffel in his old Saab and cramming it in his pack. Tom McCabe walks in, wearing a yellow Mountain Rescue T-shirt, three days' gray stubble, and a worried look. He's the 502, and David Swersky, the 501, hasn't responded.

I grab the ringing phone. It's Scott Messina, on his way to the courthouse. "I just kind of want to be able to help in case something comes down," Scott says, "and to try to help shepherd along the sheriff–Mountain Rescue relationship, to make it work. I'm just going over to be available—to keep the peace, basically."

Scott doesn't want to be in the sheriff's basement conference room, the command post. He'd much rather be in the field. But he knows he has to represent the team. He has had long discussions in recent weeks with other board members and the 501s about the potential for conflict with Steve over deploying helicopters on rescues. Steve was supposed to have developed a set of rules for when helicopters will be used and under what restrictions. But, burdened by an outbreak of regional wildfires that has monopolized his time, he has not. This rescue sounds bad, and it is in dangerous terrain, treacherous for rescuers as well as victims. If Steve quashes a helicopter request and the only remaining option is protracted, dangerous work by ground teams, somebody may have to say no. The Bells are a roll of the dice not just because they are high and steep, but because they are loose, the geologic equivalent of a fourteen-thousand-foot pile of broken crockery. Add fifteen or twenty people on a slope or in a couloir, kicking rocks down on each other, trying to keep a victim alive and get him off the mountain; it is a recipe for disaster.

Scott knows the rescue now facing the team could be difficult and risky. Maybe too risky. Nobody wants to walk away. A major problem rescue leaders face is keeping people reined in. Team members cringe at the idea of letting somebody die because the operation is judged too dangerous. That has happened before, although not for years. On the other hand, nobody wants to lower an injured party down twenty-five hundred feet of rotten rock, either, rock where you can't find a solid anchor if your life depended on it—and it does. Scott has known for many weeks that it may come to this, a big Bells rescue with Steve saying, "no chopper," and if the team is going to halt an operation because it is too dangerous, Scott wants to be the one to make that call. He feels it's his responsibility. He doesn't make a big deal about it in the team's "what if" discussions, and he doesn't now, driving over to the sheriff's office conference room. But the rescue leaders know why he's there.

/\\ /\\

Our information was very sketchy. It was very third-, sometimes fourth-hand that somebody had told somebody that somebody had

fallen, that they were going to go look for them, please go tell the forest ranger. So by the time the forest ranger called us, I was the fifth party. It was just like, do we really have anything here?
—*David Swersky*

"These are great," Debbie Kelly laughs as she turns on the Wig-Wag lights. Cars pull off the road. Jace Michael sits in the front seat, laughing and joking, amped up at the prospect of a rescue. The Maroon Creek Valley floor is already in shadow as Debbie speeds the nine miles up to the trailhead at Maroon Lake. Every summer more than two hundred thousand people drive or take the bus to the two parking lots and campground beside Maroon Lake, two miles from the foot of the Bells. On clear days the meadow around Maroon Lake and the broad trail to Crater Lake, a mile farther up the valley, are sclerotic with tourists. It is a region many Aspen locals avoid, an unofficially designated Tourist Sacrifice Zone.

By the time we arrive, most of the tourists are gone for the day. A few linger, all potbellies and white legs, black socks and Bermuda shorts. Some shoot video of the rescue staging area.

"Everybody sign in!" yells Randy Smith. He has maps spread on the hood of his sheriff's department Jeep and is talking to a young girl who works for the Forest Service, trying to determine where the missing climber's friends are located on the valley trail. Rick and Landon Deane pull up with several wranglers and a long horse trailer. In a few minutes they have seven saddled horses out and lined up. Debbie, Jace, and Chris pull apart brake bags and medical packs, taking what they want, leaving the rest. The object is to go light, move fast, locate and stabilize the victim. We cram extra equipment into our packs: oxygen bottle, crash pack, half-body splint, heat packs, trauma pack. I clip a dozen carabiners onto the outside of my pack, along with an avalanche shovel and crampons. I stuff an ice axe inside. Somebody else grabs a three-hundred-foot rope. Chris takes a brake rack and a couple of pulleys.

I put the pack on and climb into the saddle, barely managing to heave myself up. This doesn't feel like going light. My horse is actually named Trigger. The tourists part, and we start down the trail at a walk, following Landon. Shannon, a quiet, tall, pretty ranch hand, and Rick come along with Jace, Debbie, Chris, and me. "Hey," Chris yells from the back. "Where's the throttle on this thing?"

The horses are tired from a day of carrying tourists, but they walk at a steady clip, faster than we could hike. The valley is achingly beautiful in the early evening. Most of the hikers are gone, and the place is quiet despite its Wagnerian presence. We head south up the valley. The sun cutting across the west ridge lights up the upper half of the valley wall on our left, making the red rock and green trees luminescent. We climb the packed, rocky trail toward Crater Lake and the base of the Bells, past blue spruce bearing clusters of tight, fat, purple cones. Where the sides of the trail are damp the ground is rich with cow parsnip, bluebells and harebells, larkspur and monkshood. In drier areas there is the magenta flourish of Indian paintbrush, and among the rocks the eggshell blue and white of columbine.

Landon is in a good mood, her white teeth flashing under the dirty cream of her cowboy hat as she turns around to check on us. She leads the group as if this is a nature ride, pointing out the flowers by the horses' hooves.

"That's snowball," she tells Jace, "and this is yarrow. It looks a lot like Queen Anne's lace. That purple one is elephant head, and those little blue ones are gentian."

The two lakes, Crater and Maroon, are stacked one above the other in the rising valley. At Crater, along the foot of North Maroon, Minnehaha Gulch drains in, pouring down in a rush through the firs from a high, unseen bowl. The horses stop briefly to water and snatch a few mouthfuls of grass. As we pass the lake and come under the flank of South Maroon, a stream emerges from the base of a long talus slope, launches off a tall cliff, fades into drifting curtains of mist, then disappears into another talus slope.

Pyramid Peak passes slowly in a welter of glimpsed minarets and crumbling walls, the ruins of some Tolkienesque fortress. From a bowl behind Len Shoemaker Ridge, a great curling flank of Pyramid, an unnamed stream falls in rotund white swells down to the valley.

A mile above Crater Lake, the valley almost dark now, only a hint of pink left in the sky, Landon takes off her hat. "I smell smoke," she says, before slapping it back on her head and riding into a dark grove of spruce. On the far side she finds a climber, Stuart Knapp, standing in the trail. Just behind him is a United States Forest Service ranger, wearing a wide, silver hard hat and a worried expression. In a tiny meadow by the trees, a tent has been set up and a small fire burns. Two people sit by it, hugging each other, rocking gently.

> The report was they were descending some steep snow and his friend slipped and went down. The slope went down and doglegged to the right, and his buddy was unable to get to him. And that's when Tom and I said, "The Grand Couloir." Tom and I looked at each other and said, "It's Greg's couloir." We figured he's fucked. You go down there, and bam, you hit the wall.
> —*Scott Messina*

Stuart Knapp, Kris Wallack, and Bob Olson do not know about Greg Mace or the couloir in which he died. They are members of the Colorado Mountain Club, here from the Denver area to climb this peak, and their day has gone from bad to worse. They had attempted South Maroon the long way. Their route was a giant hairpin that involves walking south up the valley, then climbing west to the ridge that comes off the south side of the peak, turning north and following it up. They took so long just to make the ridge, at about thirteen thousand feet, that Kris and Bob turned back. John Wallack, Kris's husband, continued with Stuart. They summited late, around two-thirty. After a quick lunch the two men started down, chased by a small, threatening storm. They considered the first snow-filled couloir they came to as a quick route back to Crater Lake and their camp, but decided it was too steep. A short while later, after climbing over a hump, they came to another couloir. This looked better, and the weather didn't. John stepped off the ridge and onto the snow. The day was warm—too warm to be on the snow that late—and a small dish of the soft corn snow gave out underneath him. He rolled onto his chest to self-arrest with his ice axe and planted the spike in the snow. But nothing happened. John kept digging the spike in, but he was gaining speed now, sliding down over the runnels and sun-cups in the uneven surface, crying and grunting from the impact, flying up into the air, back onto the snow again.

Then Stuart couldn't see John anymore. He was alone on the top of the ridge, scared, his friend gone, a storm bearing down on him. He shouted, he blew his whistle. He started to climb down the snow but was terrified. So he turned south back to the long ridge he had come up, hurrying as much as he could, afraid of how the mountain had taken his friend so swiftly. Afraid of what he would have to say to Kris.

Stuart didn't hike all the way down to the valley floor, but hairpinned back north after descending fifteen hundred feet and traversed along the flank of the ridge for a while. Perhaps, he thought as he struggled with exhaustion and the shortage of oxygen, he could intercept the couloir lower down and look for John there.

⋀ ⋀

The ranger pulls out a careful drawing he has made in a small, spiral-bound notebook. He points up to the edge of the ridge to the southwest. Two thousand five hundred feet up, just visible in the fading light, are two couloirs. The upper one, perhaps two hundred feet long, is shaped like a dagger, tip down. Immediately left and contiguous with it is another, a right-facing monkey-wrench shape that connects to the bottom of the first. Contrary to Scott and Tom's expectations, this is not Greg Mace's couloir but a much smaller gully a mile south from where he died.

"They were descending the first couloir when John fell," the ranger tells Debbie, pointing to the drawing of the couloirs he made in his notebook. "He was wearing red gaiters, periwinkle pants, a gray pack. The corner where he lost sight of him is the top of the monkey wrench, where it joins the first couloir. The last time Stuart saw him he had lost his ice axe and was in a tumbling, uncontrolled fall."

The woman by the campfire, Kris, starts sobbing quietly. A breeze from the south fans the flames of the little fire, sending sparks out into the grass. Blackness looms over the pass to the south: another storm.

We leave the climbers and retreat to the trees where Landon is tying up the horses. "He didn't have to describe what sounds like an unsurvivable fall in front of them," Debbie says, shaking her head. She pulls out her radio and looks at us. Nobody is willing to climb a vertical half-mile in the dark to search for a missing man who's probably dead. "It's steep, it's loose, and we're not even sure where we're going," she radios David Swersky. "We can't go up there tonight."

Kris, Bob, Stuart, and the ranger head out to the trailhead and to the rescue leaders waiting there. They are funereal in their rain ponchos, shuffling down the trail. We dig out rain gear, stoves, and food, pooling the emergency supplies from our packs: instant rice, a can or two of tuna, black bean soup, chicken soup, freeze-dried chicken and rice. As we cook, Tom McCabe and Chris Myers walk into camp, accompanied by Rick and Shannon, who had returned to the trailhead to carry the two men's packs on their horses.

"Damn!" says Chris Herrera. "We wanted to eat everything before you got here."

There's jollity in the camp, little talk of what we will do tomorrow, no discussion of death or injury. The half-dozen people here are not consciously avoiding the topic—rather, they're simply enjoying the opportunity to be together, camped in this gorgeous valley, telling lies and swapping stories. Once, though, the talk drifts to the task at hand. Tom is standing with his back to the group, scanning the ridge with night vision goggles that make every detail hum and pop in a luminous, electric green, looking for clues. Chris Myers, squatting by the wind-whipped fire, pauses from scooping up rice and tuna. He is to be married in two weeks.

"Oh, man," he sighs. "I don't want any critical stress incident stuff in my life right now."

We kick out the fire and move down into the trees to sleep. No one on the hasty team has brought a sleeping bag. Chris carried an extra, which Debbie claims. "Who wants to sleep with me?" she asks brightly. "I'll just add another name to the list of Mountain Rescue members I've slept with." She and Tom spread a black body bag out on the fir needles as a ground cloth, then lay the open sleeping bag over themselves and a poncho over that. Before going to sleep we gather in a circle of headlamps and make a plan over the map. Debbie calls David Swersky and relays it to him. Then we turn off the radios and lie down in the dark. It is eleven o'clock.

I take off my boots and slide into my bivouac sack, a big, zippered Gore-Tex–treated nylon bag. For padding I spread out a tiny four-foot-square foam pad I keep stuffed in the bottom of my pack. The gear I carry isn't supposed to make me comfortable, just keep me alive. Comfort weighs too much. I lie on my back and look up through the fir boughs to the stars and the black bulk of the ridge where a fallen climber waits. I am warm, I am comfortable, but I cannot sleep. Occasionally I hear a rustling that tells me the others can't either. I lie there for a long time. If he's up there in pain, how can I sleep down here? Better he's dead, I think, than dying.

I drift in and out until the sky seems a little lighter. My watch reads 4:44. I hear the chirping of someone's wristwatch alarm. In a few moments we are standing around a stove, wearing headlamps, picking the jokes up where we left off the night before. Everyone has packets of instant oatmeal. Landon shares two blackened bananas. Chris adds hot chocolate to his oatmeal and mixes it all together. "I've never had a meal that tasted bad while camping," he proclaims evangelically, but others decline to taste. Tom has enough instant coffee for one cup, which he passes around.

By the time the light touches the peaks we are ready to go. Rick, Shannon, and Landon lead the horses back down the trail while Debbie tries to raise Scott at the trailhead. Chris Myers and Jace are impatient. They want to hike upstream, cross the creek, and try to climb the opposite slope to look for John with binoculars.

"Let's just wait until I can check with staging and they can okay that," Debbie says, but they head up the trail anyway with long, ground-gobbling strides. Tom and Debbie exchange a knowing look, frustrated but relieved to be rid of them.

"You can be sure," Chris Herrera proclaims as the pair disappears up the trail, "if you go with Myers he'll have a plan. He may not have the right plan, but he'll have a plan."

Debbie, Tom, Chris, and I start traversing up the west side of the valley toward the two couloirs a little after six o'clock. The open slopes are dotted with wildflowers, and as we rise out of the valley the view expands dramatically. But the gentlest slope lies at thirty degrees, and the going is slow. Each person carries at least thirty pounds. We trade off the rope, which adds another fifteen or twenty. After an hour I look up, then down. We are not even halfway to the couloirs.

In the distance a small plane approaches, high and silver. Edgar Boyles is flying Navajo Nine Five Three Charlie with two spotters. He has trouble locating our team, and Debbie can't seem to contact him on the radio. Then Chris Myers comes on the air, calling for the plane. Tom looks at Debbie.

"Who died and appointed him 501?" he asks.

Chris and Jace hike back across the valley and start up the slope. They travel faster than we do, and by eight o'clock Jace is at the base of the first couloir. Like Chris, he is headstrong and excitable. Both men are anxious. Debbie has to remind them more than once to stay together, to work as a team. They are high enough that Scott, down at the trailhead by Maroon Lake, can see them through a spotting scope. He calls Debbie.

"What do you need up there for a lowering? Do you need any technical gear? Do you have any BFRs?"

In fact, there are no BFRs—"big fucking rocks," a climber's favorite anchor. There are piles of little rocks. There are small outcroppings of shattered, crosshatched sedimentary rock. There are acres and acres of broken, loose rock. There are no trees. There isn't even enough hard snow to sink a picket into. There is nothing worth hanging your life on. The only thing that comes to mind is finding an anchor on the ridge and tying together a half-mile of rope to try to lower a litter.

"I thought," Debbie says later, "about telling him to just dump out the truck and bring everything up."

The question of a helicopter evacuation had been settled the night before. If John is alive and in critical condition, the team will get a helicopter. But by eight-thirty the decision is moot, for the wind has come up to gusts of forty miles per hour, too strong for a small bird to operate close to the ground. Five Three Charlie makes several passes as the spotters search for signs of John, the plane bucking and yawing into the wind, but finally the pilot has to retreat to the airport because of the turbulence.

"What we need up here," Tom says, "is a Chinook with a long line."

No one wants to think about what will happen if we find John dying and can't create a way to move him. To go out to rescue a man and then watch him suffer or die because the team can't do the job—the thought alone is anguishing. "I almost hope we don't find him alive," Debbie says, "because if he is, we aren't going to be able to do much for him."

More teams are coming up the valley. Soon almost thirty people will be in the field or ready to go. Crested Butte and Vail Mountain Rescue teams have been put on alert for possible mutual aid. Without air support, even if we can find anchors, getting John out, alive or dead, will take all day, much of the night, and dozens of people.

Jace and Chris scramble up into the couloirs. By nine-fifteen Jace is at the corner where the dagger and the monkey wrench come together. He finds nothing. No footprints, no skid marks, no gear. No body. No sign anyone has been here.

Scott and David Swersky confer. They had interviewed Stuart, Bob, and Kris the night before, around midnight. They had been assured these couloirs are where John fell.

> They were really fatigued, very dehydrated, and extremely depressed, and my job was to interview them. Unfortunately, I think they were led a little bit by the forest ranger, who gave us a very accurate drawing of those two snowfields, the one we called the monkey wrench and the thin sliver above that. And they were so positive. He had taken these big bounces, and then boom, he turned around the corner. Well, that's exactly Greg's fall.
> —*David Swersky*

What started out as a rescue has become a search. Jace and Chris Myers top out on the ridge at about thirteen thousand feet.

Debbie, Chris Herrera, Tom, and I slowly begin traversing north along the flank. Several hundred yards away is another couloir in a notch. Perhaps John is here. We kick rock off constantly as we work our way across the folds and gullies of the slope.

Someone screams, "Rock!" and we look, scatter, watch it bounce by. Tom and I get ahead. Sometimes we cannot see where Debbie and Chris are below us. When a head-size boulder goes bounding down the slope I grab the radio. "Kelly, rock!" It is nerve-racking for us and for the teams monitoring their radios elsewhere in the valley.

Below, from the valley floor, Dave Lofland uses binoculars and a radio to direct us to the couloir we cannot see. As I work along a small outcrop I come upon a bumblebee as big as my thumb, happily crawling over a palm-size patch of moss campion, reveling in the dozens of tiny pink flowers. He is oblivious to the whipping wind. The incongruity of his presence makes me smile.

The couloir is narrow, an ice-filled slot in the rock that opens out to a thirty-yard-long fan of snow. In the neck at the top of the fan I see something dark, perhaps a tangle of legs and boots. Tom comes over slowly, breathing hard. It has been six hours since breakfast, and he is dragging. "That's certainly a good place for him to hang up," he says, squinting up the snow fan. "Looks like something."

He begins climbing up the rock. I start straight up the fan. The snow lies at a forty-degree angle, soft and rotten. I kick steps and plunge the shaft of my ice axe in to the hilt. Every few steps I look up, and my conviction grows. This is him, I think. This is him. My heart races from the exertion, the altitude, the find. As I get closer I see something flickering in the wind—clothing, perhaps. I want to look up at every step. I make myself take ten steps, then look. I want this to be him because I want to be out of here.

Ten yards away I look up again and see that my victim is a pile of wet rocks. The flicker is a ribbon of water caught in the wind. By the time Tom reaches me he is moving even more slowly. We stop for water and the last of my snacks, a handful of dried apricots. Debbie and Chris have stopped below, out of sight, waiting for us to make progress. We can hear Chris Myers and Jace on the radio, trying to figure out how to traverse over to this couloir from above.

Tom leads up through the neck of the couloir, into the main body. Here the slope steepens to fifty degrees, and the rock walls rise twenty feet on either side. If a rock comes down there is no place to go. The snow is rotten, collapsing every few steps. This is a very bad place to be. The whole couloir could avalanche. Thirty yards above us a five-foot-high rock dam runs across the gully. We want to check beyond it, but neither of us likes it in here.

Down at the parking lot, Scott and Steve Crockett, watching through a spotting scope, try to figure out what to do. Stuart Knapp, John's climbing partner, is starting to waver in his conviction that where we are searching is where John fell. Moreover, two different campers staying nearby have walked up to Scott this morning and mentioned that they saw flashing lights the night before up on the Bells. They had told a forest ranger, they said, but he dismissed the reports and didn't pass them on to Scott or David. Scott, too, dismisses the first report.

"I didn't let it register," he says. "He was pointing way off. It really didn't match up. But then another couple came up later on Monday, saying that, 'We saw three lights.' And it really sparked my interest that they said it was three flashes, three specific flashes. I drew a drawing, sketched out North [Maroon], South [Maroon], here's the snow. They drew a circle right where it was."

It was Greg's couloir, a mile north of the search teams.

"I said, 'Steve'—I showed him my sketch—'look up in this area. They saw three distinct flashes.' He looked in there [with a spotting scope], and he called right back, 'Hey, I see somebody up there,'" Scott says. "I looked at it and this guy was descending, you could watch him very methodically kicking steps, frontpointing down. He was kicking steps, moving real slow. First thought was maybe he was just descending, because we'd heard reports a lot of people had been going up and down. Maybe he was just coming down, some of the first people climbing. Knowing the terrain up there I'm going, 'Boy, that's not very steep to be kicking steps, for him to be facing in.' So that's what kicked it off to me. Let's keep an eye on this guy."

⋀⋀   ⋀⋀

Up in the notch couloir, Tom and I have ground to a halt. I radio Dave Lofland, who is watching from below. "We have a fatigue problem, and we have no tracks," I say.

"Get out of there," Dave orders.

"I know it's early in the day," Debbie cuts in, "but we've been going hard for six hours."

"Let's have everybody pull back," says David Swersky, who has been listening. "We need to pull back and replan."

As we start back down out of the couloir, the snow gives out under my feet and I fall. I roll over to self-arrest but don't get much purchase in the soft snow with my axe. I'm not going too fast, though, and within a few yards I manage to guide myself into the *bergschrund*. There, in the gap between the rock and the ice, I stop. Near the bottom of the snow fan Tom falls, and he, too, finds it hard to stop. We are both very happy to be back on rock, even if it is loose rock.

Tom gazes down at the valley floor, more than two thousand steep feet below. "Time for four Advil," he says, popping open a bottle. He hands me the vial full of mixed pills, saying, "You've got to fish around in there."

⋀⋀   ⋀⋀

Ray Peritz had walked downtown to the Cantina the night before. When the first page went out he'd just finished his third margarita and ordered a beer. He paid his bill, stepped out of the bar, and approached a motorcyclist waiting at a stoplight. "I said, 'Excuse me, do you mind giving me a hand? I'm with Mountain Rescue, I've got a rescue going.' I hop on the back. This guy was going to the Hickory House to have dinner." He dropped Ray off on the way.

After a sobering evening of lingering at the trailhead, Ray went back home for a few hours' sleep. Marion Berg, who lives twenty-five miles downvalley, slept on Ray's couch. Or tried to sleep, after three cups of coffee. Both men were back at the staging area beside Maroon Lake at 6:00 A.M. By 10:45 Ray, Linda, Kevin, Rick, and Landon are halfway up the trail to the previous night's camp, near the head of Crater Lake. Landon sets up a second spotting scope to get a better look at the climber descending the Grand Couloir.

"He did have red gaiters on, that was a positive," Ray recalls. "He had blue pants on, that was a positive identification. But she still couldn't tell. Maybe he had a gray pack on, but she couldn't be sure."

More and more people watch the lone climber descending the Grand Couloir. He is a mile north of where Stuart said John fell, and both Scott and David Swersky are reluctant to send a team up to meet him in case he is just another climber on the mountain. At eleven David drives from the courthouse to the trailhead with Stuart. He has been keeping John's wife and climbing partners down in town because he doesn't want them to be standing at the trailhead if the news comes over the radio that John has been found dead. Now, however, David wants Stuart to look through the spotting scope at the climber. At eleven-thirty Stuart walks up to the spotting scope on the tripod in the parking lot and puts his eye to it.

"That's him," Stuart says.

⋀ ⋀

Ray and Linda start working up the steep slope at the base of the Grand Couloir. The descending climber could follow any of three gullies out, and Ray is not sure which route to take up to intercept him. Ray sees two men climbing toward him and Linda, and waits until they catch up. They are brothers, camped across the valley. They have been watching the climber with binoculars. He looks like he has a limp, they say, and he sits down every ten feet.

"I have a keen sense of the obvious," Ray says. "This must be our man. How many people are down-climbing alone with a limp and sitting down every ten feet? We've got somebody who probably beat the shit out of himself."

Ray sends the two brothers to the right. He goes up a gully to the left. Linda takes the center. The brothers reach the climber

before Ray does. He backtracks to their side, leaving Linda behind. "This is him," they yell, and Ray keys the microphone.
"We have a confirmation!" he says breathlessly into the radio,
and everyone in the valley can hear the smile in his voice.

> I was pumped—this guy was alive. What more could you ask? Based
> on the information we had, I thought we were going to fill a body
> bag. I mean, what else would you think? Particularly when you guys
> [the first team] couldn't find any tracks. The way it was described,
> this guy was tumbling out of sight, had gone a long way. Then we
> had a little bit of rain. I figured if he was up there he probably got
> wet in the rain, and if nothing else killed him the hypothermia might
> if he was at all shocky. It was real exciting to find the guy alive and
> doing as well as he was.
>
> I sort of checked him out as he walked over to me. He looked a
> little unsteady. I sat him down, said, "Sit down and calm yourself
> down for a minute." He said, "I've got a double life," and I said,
> "You bet your ass you do. There's a lot of people worried about you.
> You're going to have one happy wife."
> —*Ray Peritz*

John tells Ray he had tried to self-arrest when he fell, but the
snow was so soft when he put the ice axe into it that "it was
like going through grain." He had fought all the way down, trying to stay on his stomach, but he was bounced around hard before he lost consciousness. When he awoke he was sitting
upright, four hundred feet below where he began his slide. His
back was against the snow, his legs resting on rock. He opened
his eyes and found he was facing Pyramid Peak, across the valley. Of the fifty-four peaks above fourteen thousand feet in Colorado, John had climbed fifty-three. Only Pyramid, which swam a
little as he tried to shake the dizziness from his head, remained
on his list.

Below him, John realized, was nothing but sheer cliff and
space. The edge was only a few feet away. He turned around and
looked up the slope. In the snow were several large, fresh, widely
spaced divots—his track as he tumbled down.

The capriciousness of mountains was written in that track.
The difference between John Wallack and Greg Mace was a
lucky bounce.

John had heard Stuart calling, but he was too dazed to respond. As night fell he rationed his food and water. He had lost his ice axe, but he still had his headlamp, and with that he flashed signals toward the parking lot. He didn't sleep. At first light he started climbing down, resting often. He had injured his left hand and left ankle—maybe sprained, maybe broken—and strained muscles in his neck and back, but he got within a thousand feet of the valley floor before Ray reached him.

Rick and Landon wait on the trail with horses, and once Ray and Linda have walked John down and have him safely in the saddle, Ray hikes out ahead.

"I think the most exciting part of it was talking to his wife," says Ray. "That was really exciting. It was just wonderful. Here was this woman who'd been scared to death and she probably thought the worst, like the rest of us did, and it was fun to tell her, because I was the first one that she'd had the opportunity to talk to. I got stoked."

Two days later John writes a thank-you letter to Mountain Rescue. "I have spent the day resting, looking at the blue sky and the trees with an appreciation I will not attempt to describe," he writes. "The support given to the four of us when we truly needed it will never be forgotten." He encloses a check for a thousand dollars.

⋀ ⋀

On the slow climb down from the two couloirs on the south ridge, Debbie tires of carrying her pack. She takes it off. She heaves it down the slope. It rolls and bounces in a mesmerizing way, and everyone watches until it comes to rest in a gully five hundred feet below. Debbie thrusts her arms in the air as if she has scored a touchdown, and grins. That's five hundred feet she doesn't have to carry it.

Jace and Chris Myers come down a different route and soon find themselves above a loose, exposed cliff band. Chris Herrera and Debbie both yell at them to climb back up a few yards and come around into a gully.

"We just want to check this out," Jace radios. Soon he and Chris are climbing down the loose rock. If they slip they will fall

150 feet. They kick off a steady rain of rockfall onto the snow-field below. Tom shakes his head.

"I don't like to go out in the field with Chris," he says. "He's a loose cannon, and he doesn't listen."

Near the bottom of the slope Chris takes a short fall, sitting down hard on a sharp rock. He gashes his upper hamstring just above the hem of his shorts, a cut that requires eight stitches later that afternoon. Chris's injury, impending wedding, and honeymoon will take him away from rescue work for five weeks.

On the hike back to the trailhead, Tom stops below the Grand Couloir to point up to where Greg Mace died. "My least favorite place in the world," he says softly.

ᴧᴧ ᴧᴧ

Somebody goes down the street to Carl's Pharmacy and returns with several twelve-packs of beer. A few people sit on the couch in the darkened meeting room, boots off, hot feet up on chairs. As the light filters through the lilacs outside and the day drifts toward evening, the room fills with laughter and stories, an informal debriefing. Debbie flops backwards across the couch, grinning at the ceiling.

Sucking on their Budweisers and Millers, team members piece together the explanation for why they ended up searching an area a mile from where John fell. Stuart had told Scott the night before that they hiked down from the summit for only twenty minutes before turning into the couloir, and Scott knew they couldn't have reached the monkey-wrench couloir in that time. "Looking back at it," he says, "that's where I should have trusted my knowledge of the area and my knowledge of the time and distance, which would have pinpointed where they came down."

Stuart and John had not understood how close they were to the summit of South Maroon when they decided to descend the couloir, nor did Stuart realize how far south down the ridge he went after John fell—more than a mile. When he hairpinned back to the north along the flank of the ridge, he believed he was still quite near the couloir where John disappeared, and he convinced himself that the first couloir he came to, the monkey wrench, was it. The forest ranger helped solidify that conviction, and Scott and David Swersky were not ready to disbelieve it until a number of other clues suggested Stuart was wrong.

Nobody slept well the night before, and the beer quickly goes to people's heads. Everyone needs a shower. No one really wants to leave. Everyone is exhausted, but these little parties are the best part. And so the beer is spread around and the talk gets louder.

"He didn't sleep," Debbie says, lying on her back and looking at the ceiling, "and we didn't sleep either. It's like there was something going on there."

THIS IS the rescue that I think affected him the most since the "Miracle in the Mountains." I was gone in Denver Saturday and Sunday on a bachelorette party. I got back about seven-thirty at night and was just really ready to see him. It's only a couple weeks to the wedding, and he had talked about pulling back with work and pulling back with rescues and not going out for everything like he almost always does. And I came back and he wasn't there. It looked like he had left in a hurry. He had left a scrawled note that said, "Went on a rescue, it's 6:40 P.M." Every time that happens I don't know. Sometimes I see him in an hour, sometimes I don't see him for three days, which is what happened with "Miracle in the Mountains."

That night at ten-thirty I had a call from the sheriff's office that said he's out on a rescue on the Maroon Bells, he's going to be out all night, and hopefully they'll be back tomorrow.

I shut it off. I'm pretty good at shutting it off, because I'll sit there and imagine the worst if I don't shut it off. So I just have to keep remembering he's good at what he does and he's working with the team and he's probably going to be okay. But it's harder the closer it keeps getting to the wedding, and I keep saying, "Chris, do you mind just not doing this, for my own sanity?" And I think if I would have been there, he wouldn't have gone. I could have talked him out of it.

—*Katie Gartner*

Jace Michael tapes up the gash in Chris Myers's leg and he is able to hike out of the West Maroon Creek Valley without a problem, but Marion Berg tells him to come down to Aspen Valley Hospital for some stitches. When he arrives at the emergency room Chris calls Katie in Basalt.

"It's great to hear from you," Katie says. "Is everything okay?"

"Yeah, yeah, fine."

"God, at least you're not calling from the hospital."

"Well," Chris tells Katie, "I am."

Her first reaction is to get angry—angry at everybody. It is a reaction she does not understand. Then she tells Chris she is heading up to Aspen.

"You don't need to come up. It doesn't matter," Chris tells Katie.

"I don't care. I'd like to come now."

"Well, I might not get stitched up for another hour or two, so don't come up for a while."

"I'm coming up anyway. I don't care."

"Well," Chris says, showing more emotion than he usually does, "I'd really like that if you did."

Katie's first view of Chris at the hospital is of his exposed hind end, where Marion is finishing up his stitching job. Katie is worried and sad and angry all together, and thrilled to see Chris. She desperately wants him not to go out on any more rescues. But all she says is, "I'm really glad you're okay."

The two of them drive over to the rescue cabin, where team members have congregated to drink a little beer and where Chris endures a number of jokes about his butt. Katie sits quietly in the back, not saying much, and after a while they head home. They stop for dinner at the Woody Creek Tavern, a small bar halfway to Basalt.

"You guys, you do great work," the waitress tells him as she hands Chris and Katie menus. Chris is still wearing his Mountain Rescue T-shirt. "I'll buy you a round of drinks."

She looks at Katie. "I'd like to buy you one, too, because you have a hard job, too. You have to sit around and worry about him."

After they get their drinks a man rises from his seat at the bar and walks over to their table. He bows. With a British accent he explains that he, too, would like to buy the table a round of drinks. "I can't believe what you do," he tells Chris, noting he's visiting the area. "It's amazing work. Thank you so much. It's so important."

As the visitor heads back to the bar, Katie looks at Chris and sees his eyes brimming with tears. She has never seen him cry about rescues. Never seen him cry over body recoveries. Never even heard of him doing this.

"I'm getting a lot of signs about this rescue," Chris says, "but it's hard when you get this kind of reward from the public.

"Goddamn it, the politics, I'm sick of it," he continues. "Sometimes it's rewarding. But I'm getting married and we're going to have a family, and I tell you, I don't get the rush out of it that I did when I was single and I didn't give a crap about anything."

Chris talks for half an hour, pouring out his conflicting emotions to Katie. Finally he says, "I'm sorry, I'm blabbing."

"It's okay," Katie says. "You're supposed to be blabbing."

I'm ready for him to be off the team now, because I feel like he's ready and he just needs a push. This is another thing—he admitted to me he was thinking about me up there on that mountain. That worries me. I don't want that to go on. I don't want him to worry about me or think about me up there, in case he makes a mistake. He kind of mentioned that that could have had something to do with it [his injury]. He had his mind on other things and he might not have been paying attention fully to what he was doing. I do not want that going on at all. Not at all. Yeah, I'm ready for him to be off the team now.
—*Katie Gartner*

RESCUE 1 is parked at the edge of the swelling crowd, beside the small awning set up as a medical tent. A half-dozen team members lounge in low chairs in the shade, watching girls walk by. Some are working on sixteen-ounce Miller drafts, free to the team from the stand just up the fence line. Mariela Zell labors as a volunteer in the smoke and heat of the food tent. She has already seen to it that her husband and anybody else who wants one has had a burger or a chicken sandwich, courtesy of the Hard Rock Cafe.

Since five o'clock in the morning the team has been at the Buttermilk ski area, working on the Hard Rock & Roll Run & Ride, a benefit staged by John Zell's employer for Mountain Rescue and the Aspen Valley Ski Club. Team members have marshaled the five-mile footrace and seven-mile mountain bike race. They have tended to the scrapes and cuts of those who crashed or fell. They have directed cars and checked tickets as hundreds of locals paid ten dollars each this hot, hazy day to hear three bands perform on the stage set up at the base of the ski mountain, to eat burgers and drink beer and check out a little skin.

When the pagers go off shortly before one o'clock, announcing "an injured climber below Capitol Lake," John leaps up and begins rearranging gear in the truck, which has been serving as the medical cache. He pulls out supplies to leave with those volunteers staying at the benefit. He rearranges the hasty team members' packs lying inside the back door. Van Kyzar, the 501, has already headed the three miles into town to meet with Steve Crockett in the sheriff's office and begin planning the rescue. A dozen team members churn around the truck in the noise and the dust, ready to go, waiting for direction.

"We're wasting time," John says to no one in particular. "I've got to go to the cabin. I've got to get boots and overnight gear, and we've got to get fresh radio batteries." The hasty team Van Kyzar designated ahead of time—John, Josh Landis, Carl Ellerbrook, Kevin Hagerty, Judd Anders—is supposed to be ready to leave from the benefit and go straight to a rescue. But rarely does everyone have everything as organized as they could, and John, thinking an operation at Capitol Lake could easily run into the night, wants more gear.

Dave Brown, on his rookie shift as the 502, can't be found. Nobody wants to leave for the cabin—the opposite direction from Capitol Lake—without approval from Van or Dave Brown, but they seem to have disappeared. What the hasty team doesn't know is that Van is arguing with Steve Crockett. Van wants to get the hasty team on the road. By the time they reach the trailhead, a thirty-minute drive, he will have things organized. Steve wants everything organized before the hasty team leaves the concert.

John climbs in and out of the truck, organizing and rearranging, telling anyone who will listen he really needs to go to the cabin. Finally Tom McCabe, standing by the driver's door, says, "Go."

John starts the truck. He gets no farther than the parking lot at the base of the ski area, however, before he runs into Dave Brown, who stops him. John makes his case to Dave. "We're dicking around here," he says as Dave tries to reach Van on the radio. "This is bullshit."

Finally Dave tells John to go to the cabin, and he does. On the drive to town Van reports by radio what he knows: the victim is a climber with a knee injury. Immediately, everyone slows down. In their minds each member of the hasty team has a vision of a hiker who has twisted his knee. It's still a rescue, but it's not a life-threatening situation. On the drive back out of town from the cabin John is almost sedate, cruising down Highway 82 at a steady sixty-five.

Rescue 1 reaches the trailhead to Capitol Lake, a clearing on a ridge with a long view up the Capitol Creek Valley to the steel-gray spike of Capitol Peak, at about two-thirty. The last mile of road is steep, uneven dirt, and when the truck gets to the top Josh realizes the back door has been jolted open. Several packs have escaped, but they are retrieved from the dust.

Gear is added to packs, gear is subtracted. Should we bring overnight gear or plan on working through the dark? Who's going to carry the Stokes litter, broken down and lashed to a backpack frame? Who will hump "The Wheel"? Are we waiting for Marion Berg or going without him? Here, add these extra water bottles. Is anybody bringing a stove? Do we need a stove?

Dave Brown is characteristically laconic at the trailhead, letting the hasty team that arrived in Rescue 1 spread their gear out in the dirt and mess with it for the better part of thirty minutes. Nobody is in a rush now, and the hasty team has, in fact, been beaten to the trailhead by Scott Messina and Debbie Kelly. Those two now are the first team on the trail, hiking the six-and-a-half miles up to the lake.

We hit the trail at three o'clock: Kevin Hagerty, John Zell, Judd Anders, Josh Landis, Carl Ellerbrook, Chris Herrera, and I, forty minutes behind Scott and Debbie. The trail is busy with hikers coming down from day trips or from camping at Capitol Lake, a popular jumping-off point for trips to Capitol Peak. Scott and Debbie stop and talk to everyone, trying to learn more about the injured climber.

"We ran into four guys that said, 'Yeah, there were some people coming off the peak, making a commotion about eleven-thirty, twelve o'clock last night,'" Scott recalls. "There was talk, they said, of somebody injured. At first I thought maybe somebody was just hiking around near Capitol Lake and got injured because it [the initial report] was so early in the day. Then after we talked to these guys, we get that information that this guy's been injured for a while. Why hasn't he moved?"

The afternoon is hot, the sky high and thin and silver. Dust powders our boots as we hike along an old irrigation ditch contouring the side of the valley. After a mile-and-a-half we break out into an open hillside of scattered aspens and sere grasses. The raspberry leaves along the trail are turning brown around the edges, and except for some scraggly purple asters the wildflowers have all gone to seed. At the top of a rise, two miles into the hike, John drops his pack in the dust for a break.

"I guess I didn't get enough sleep last night," he says, his face glistening with sweat. "We're busting our humps, and we don't need to. I want to save myself. I don't want to burn up before we've even gotten there. We're going to be out here all night, and he's just got a bad knee."

The team is starting to string out—Chris and Carl are steady but slower than Kevin, John, and Josh, a new support member on his second hasty team assignment. A native Coloradan with the heavy upper body of a kayaker, Josh scrapes by as a limousine driver and carpenter. Twenty-four years old, he is smoothly tan, with a shy, easy smile beneath brown eyes and dark, tousled hair. He was going to have dinner with his girlfriend, Dustin, tonight, he says: black bean soup. He shrugs.

Judd, the other new support member in the group, is slowest of all. He struggles up the hill with "The Wheel" lashed onto the back of his small pack. Not long out of Louisiana State University, twenty-four years old, Judd talks often about his fraternity, Sigma Nu. A onetime oil-rig roughneck, he now works security at the Ritz-Carlton. He finds it difficult to keep up with the team today, for although he is full of energy he has about thirty extra pounds on his fleshy, five-eleven frame.

"Let's trade," Josh offers as Judd drops his load. "You take my pack."

After a few minutes the group shoulders up and starts off again, trudging a rolling trail that cuts along the open side of the valley. Josh leads, leaving the radio in his chest pack turned on. Kevin, the team leader, walks behind and listens to the traffic as Scott calls back to Dave Brown.

"We have just spoken to some people who have seen the victim," Scott says, breathing hard and hiking as he speaks. "They report a possible open compound fracture of the femur, massive blood loss, and he may be shocky."

> We encountered a group of five to six people. They went into a lot more detail about the accident, how this guy fell, how the rock fell on him, how he pulled a piece of bone out of his leg, and how the other leg was really damaged by another rockfall. So that really amped us up. We said, "Yeah, we're from Mountain Rescue." A guy looked at us, he kind of snickers at us, "Huh, you're going to have fun moving him. You're not going to be able to move him. This guy's bad." At this point the guy's [reportedly] got bone sticking out, there's bone exposed. Figuring it's a compound fracture of his femur, something like that. They were saying he's going down bad, fast, there's no way you're going to move him. So that switched us 180 degrees mentally and energy-wise. It was like, oh, here we go.
> —*Scott Messina*

Kevin doesn't say much, but he takes the radio from Josh and walks with it in his hand, listening. Everyone starts hiking faster. The entire tenor of the afternoon has changed. No longer are we on a long walk to help a guy who twisted his knee. Now we're racing time, trying to reach a man who may be dying.

A femur fracture of any kind is a rescuer's nightmare. The shock and pain of a broken thigh bone, the massive blood loss into the surrounding muscle, can be enough to kill a hiker or climber who doesn't reach a hospital quickly. A compound fracture—a break where the skin and muscle either are opened down to the bone, or the bone projects through the skin—is even worse, for it introduces the very real possibility of infection. Bone infections are notoriously difficult to treat. They take limbs. Sometimes they exact lives.

Scott puts his head down and plows up the trail, hiking with ski poles for balance and speed, putting his arms into it. Debbie isn't quite able to stay with him and tells him to push on. Alone now, Scott tries to dredge up some of his EMT training, to remember how to handle this.

"Open compound fracture," he says to himself. "What the hell do I do?"

/\\\ /\\\

Marion Berg is hiking up the trail alone, behind Kevin's group. He has detoured to Aspen Valley Hospital to pick up the physician's pack, a forty-pound backpack stuffed with intravenous fluids, intubating equipment, injectable and intravenous painkillers and antibiotics. After talking to Dave Brown at the trailhead he pulls a loaf-size bag from inside the physician's pack and stuffs it into his own backpack. It contains painkillers and injectable antibiotics. The rest of the physician's pack he leaves locked in his charcoal Toyota 4runner.

Marion, who was out on a late date the night before and is operating on two hours of sleep, has been hiking for about an hour when he hears Scott's breathless report.

> Now everything changes. I'm expecting a guy with an ACL [anterior cruciate ligament], an MCL [medial collateral ligament]. I got back to Dave Brown [on the radio] and said, "Just to let you guys know, this is an emergent situation, which means helicopter. We'll just have to see."
> —*Marion Berg*

Marion digs through the drug kit he has in his pack, knowing that if the climber is in bad shape he will have to give him painkillers and antibiotics intravenously. He has the drugs but not the IV fluid. That's with a third team that has just left the trailhead, led by Jace Michael. By now fifteen people are in the field, launched with an all-night carryout in mind. If the climber's condition is bad, however, a carryout may take too long.

"I really wish I'd known that information before," Marion thinks, "because I would have fine-tuned my kit going in. I would have wanted to have more IV fluid. I'm going to feel like a shithead if I get up there and say, 'Well, I'd like to give you this antibiotic, like to do this stuff, but guess what, it's thirty minutes behind me.'"

If the climber's condition is as bad as Scott's report suggests, time is critical. The teams pound up the trail under high clouds, but they know a carryout is not the answer. This is a situation that calls for a helicopter, if one can be found and brought in before dark—and if the sheriff's department will approve it.

Van Kyzar, sitting at an oak conference table in the sheriff's office, listens to the radio reports and tries some reverse psychology on Steve Crockett. "Well, it still isn't a helicopter," he offers.

"No," Steve agrees, "we're not getting a helicopter."

"Well," Van says slyly, "I wouldn't mind hearing the reasons why Marion wants a helicopter. I'm in no position to sit here and say no helicopter if my highest medical authority is in the field and he wants a helicopter."

⋀ ⋀

Scott and Marion each turn the situation over in their heads. Scott has learned from hikers that the climber, Chuck Pine, forty-three years old, was injured the previous afternoon while climbing Capitol Peak. If he truly has a bad femur fracture, he should be dead. He certainly shouldn't have been able to hobble back to the lake, as he apparently did. And if the injury is so bad, why did his partners take almost twenty-four hours to call the sheriff's office? Some things aren't adding up.

A half-mile from the lake, Scott, hiking alone now, encounters a descending hiker who says he is in Chuck's party. He's hiking out to make some phone calls. Nobody in Chuck's group hiked out this morning to call for a rescue, he explains; they waited until another group left and asked them to call the sheriff. He tells a very different story from the one Scott heard thirty minutes earlier.

I said, "He has a compound fracture," and he said, "No, he pulled a piece of bone out of his leg. He's not so bad, he's doing okay." I kind of knocked back the urgency meter a little bit. There was apparently a lot of blood loss, according to everybody we heard. He said, "No, he bled a lot, but it wasn't an inordinate amount of blood." I'm thinking, "Well, he bled a lot, but he hasn't bled out yet. It happened at three o'clock in the afternoon, we are twenty-four hours plus into it. It can't be that bad."

—Scott Messina

David Swersky arrives at the trailhead and begins talking via radio to Marion. Because a shoulder of the Elk Mountains lies between the Capitol Creek Valley and Aspen, rescuers in the field cannot speak directly with Van Kyzar and Steve Crockett at the sheriff's office. David grills Marion on why a helicopter evacuation might be medically necessary, relaying the doctor's answers by cellular phone to the command post in town.

Marion listens to Scott's report of the most recent description—that Chuck isn't in such dire shape after all—and sits down on a rock to talk with David. Everyone on the trail throttles back a little bit. Josh, Kevin, and I have dropped the balance of the second team but are still a good forty minutes from the lake. All the way down the valley, rescuers are strung out along the trail, listening to Marion's discussion with David.

The most disturbing piece of information is that Chuck says he pulled a sliver of bone or cartilage from the wound, a puncture caused by a falling rock. "By definition, if that's true that they have pulled something out, it's an open fracture," Marion says. "This is not as important as if the bone was sticking out, but you have to remember you still have potential for bone infection."

"Is this life threatening?" David asks.

"It's potentially limb threatening, and I suppose you could say it may be life threatening."

Scott reaches a broad, sloping meadow above the timberline, just shy of the lake that lies at the foot of Capitol Peak's sheer, two-thousand-foot-high north face. A thick green carpet dotted with alpine buttercups, pale orange Indian paintbrush, and pink elephant head spreads before him for several acres. On his left are two small, rocky knolls encrusted with krummholz. At the first knoll he finds several tents, but no one who knows anything about an injured climber. Scott walks a hundred yards south to the second knoll. Two men are sitting in the open, near a brook as precise and beautiful as a Japanese garden. The water seeps out from beneath the meadow in a broad, shallow band and flows across green-gray pebbles. Small islands of lime-green moss scatter across the waterway. Elephant heads and wild irises grow amid the moss.

"Hey," Scott shouts. "How's it going? Anybody over there named Chuck?"

One of the men, dressed in blue rain pants and a blue rain jacket, waves. Scott strides over, flicking his hiking poles in the dense, ankle-high vegetation.

"My name's Scott," he says. "I'm from Mountain Rescue. How's it going?"

"Pretty good," says Chuck. He looks relaxed. He's certainly not about to die. As Scott examines Chuck, the climber tells his story.

Saturday he and two partners, all from near Buena Vista, Colorado, had set out to climb Capitol Peak via the northwest buttress. It is the same route on which Mark Tozer was killed by lightning in April. Near the top of the two-thousand-foot climb Chuck was belaying another climber, holding the rope as the second man climbed above him. The rope snagged a softball-size rock and pulled it loose. The rock crashed into Chuck's leg just above the right knee. He was wearing long pants, and although they were not torn the rock left a two-inch-deep puncture, broad as a nickel, in his leg. Chuck tied a bandana around the wound and kept climbing. They were too close to the summit to retreat safely, and they could walk down an easier route, the northeast ridge, once they topped out.

Chuck began climbing as his partner pulled up the rope. He grabbed a rock, a big slab three feet on a side. As he pulled up he felt it loosen. He swung right to get out of the way, hanging on the rope now, but the rock slammed into his chest and left thigh, leaving what had been his good leg with a huge, darkening bruise. Despite this second mishap the trio made the summit, where Chuck unwrapped the bandana and examined the puncture above his knee. Lying on top of the bleeding wound he found a white sliver, one centimeter by three. He put it in his mouth. It wasn't hard like bone. Maybe it was cartilage. Whatever it was, he still had to get down off the peak.

A previous climber had left a hiking stick near the summit, and Chuck used that to begin hobbling down. It took eight hours for the group to make it back to camp. On the way Chuck stumbled, hyperextending his left knee. He thought he might have blown a ligament in there, but he still made it down, scrambling across the jumbled blocks and slabs of the long northeastern ridge, sitting down and scooting along the precarious Knife Edge, traversing slowly off Daly Saddle back to the lakeside camp.

He spent the night rolling over in his tent, trying to get comfortable, popping Advil, drinking water.

"Holy shit," Scott thinks to himself as he feels along Chuck's chest and back for other injuries, listening to the story. "This guy is tough."

An hour behind on the trail, Marion ponders what to do. Steve and Van are relying on him to assess the significance of Chuck's injuries, and he's frustrated. Chuck is stable, he's alert, he's comfortable. The situation clearly is not as bad as the first group of hikers had portrayed it to Scott. But Chuck may have pulled a piece of bone or cartilage from the wound, which means there's still a risk of bone or joint infection. It is close to six o'clock. By the time Marion reaches and examines Chuck, it will be after seven—possibly too late to bring a helicopter in safely, should he decide one is warranted. Without an X-ray machine, he won't be able to determine what came out of the wound.

Marion's tired. He's starting to fade, and he knows everyone else on the trail has been up and working since 5:00 A.M. Carrying Chuck out on the trail will be an all-night operation, and he doesn't relish the prospect.

"Why not call a helicopter?" Marion asks himself. "Because I'm worried about some political bullshit that's going on within the county? My job is not to make the call whether it is safe to land or not, it's not to deal with the administrative aspect of flying a helicopter into a wilderness area. The way I see it is whether this is medically indicated or not. Other people make those decisions."

At the courthouse, Steve Crockett agrees that a helicopter evacuation may be necessary. Steve is wary, however. He doesn't want Mountain Rescue setting him up to take the fall if he fails to call for a bird when one is needed, but he doesn't want to bring one into the wilderness area unnecessarily, either. He and Van find Scott Thompson, the deputy who is overseeing the rescue, and tell him what they know.

"Life is limb," Scott Thompson says. "We have to cover a lost limb in this. We don't want to risk it. It's a definite helicopter situation."

"The second Thompson said yes," Van recalls, "you just got out of Steve's way, boy. That helicopter was coming."

Soon David Swersky is on the radio to Debbie, who has joined Scott.

"We need the following information from you," he says. "Elevation of a one-hundred-by-one-hundred-foot helispot, with slope not greater than six degrees or 10 percent. Wind speed and direction. Cloud cover. Gust spread. Precipitation. Visibility, temperature, and aerial hazards."

A few minutes later Debbie radios back. "We have a helispot just north of the lake at eleven-six. Temperature is fifty-five, wind is calm with gusts coming up the valley at five to ten. Cloud cover, partly to mostly cloudy. The ceiling is well above the fourteen-thousand-foot peak near here. No precipitation. Visibility is good."

"Okay," David says. "And we'll need to designate a helispot manager."

"That," Debbie says in a clipped voice, "will be me."

⋀ ⋀

When John Zell reaches Chuck's camp he drops his pack and walks over to the tent in the krummholz. He expects to find somebody in pain, probably wrapped in a sleeping bag in the big yellow tent. There is nobody there. Finally he looks at Chuck, who is relaxing on a nearby rock, still in his rain suit, legs stretched out before him, hands clasped in his lap. He looks perfectly comfortable.

John looks at him. He hates to have to ask the question, but he does.

"Are you the patient?"

As the second team straggles in people pull on warm gear, drain water bottles. The radios are quiet. "Take off your wet shirts," Debbie orders the men around her. Then she smiles. "I'll watch."

John sets about getting something to eat, and he's not content with a PowerBar. Chuck and his climbing partner, Rick, offer the use of their Whisperlite gas stove. John salivates at the prospect of a hot meal—even freeze-dried food pulled from the emergency stash in the bottom of his pack—when Debbie shouts from the other side of a clump of trees.

"Helicopter arriving in twelve minutes!"

John stops, disappointment written on his face. "I guess," he says, beginning to fold up the stove, "I won't be having dinner now."

The helicopter comes in high the first time, the pilot misunderstanding the group's location, thinking the landing zone is closer to the lake. Debbie stands in the middle of the flattest section of the meadow, a white helmet on her head. She is wearing a fuchsia pile pullover, holding a yard-long strip of plastic orange flagging in each hand for makeshift wind indicators. As the orange and yellow Aerospatiale A-Star whines overhead, the pilot comes across the radio. He sounds professional, cheerful, distant.

"Okay, now I see you," he tells Kevin, who is talking him in. "We were looking at a tent up by the lake. Now I see your guy."

"Actually," Kevin radios, "that's a girl."

The pilot breaks right and circles around the southern knoll, then comes in just over the krummholz of the northern knoll. This is the dangerous part, when the aircraft is close to the ground, with little room to maneuver, susceptible to a gust of wind, working near people who won't have time to duck if anything goes wrong. A few weeks earlier another helicopter run by this same air ambulance service crashed on a rescue in an adjacent county as it maneuvered into position to receive a patient. Both the pilot and the nurse aboard were killed when the pilot, in trouble, chose to sacrifice the helicopter rather than hit rescuers on the ground.

The bird seems too low but clears the stunted spruce, vaguely predatory as it eases toward Debbie. She holds her arms straight out, then begins to bring them down as if she is slowly flapping wings, waving the helicopter toward the ground. The wash from the three blades beats the elk spinach and Indian paintbrush into a flat circle. The pilot touches down and eases off the power. But he doesn't like the way the bird is sitting and so the turbine spins up again to a high whine. He picks the bird up a few feet, turns ninety degrees, hops right and downhill five yards, finds a spot he likes, and shuts down the aircraft.

As the rotors slow and droop, Scott keys his radio. "502, helicopter Foxtrot Charlie Three is at the Capitol Lake helispot and shut down."

Everyone takes a deep breath. We get up from where we have been squatting in the flowers and gather around Chuck, who is lying in the plants by the edge of the helispot. He is shaking now, his body sensing that he will be okay. In critically injured patients this can be the most dangerous time. The body's fight-or-flight mechanism has been keeping the victim alive, fighting shock. It has been constricting the blood vessels in the limbs, reserving blood for the critical organs in the torso. Perceiving salvation—rescuers, an ambulance, arrival in the emergency room, or a helicopter flight out of the wilderness—the victim may uncontrollably relax the adrenaline response. Blood pressure can drop and the victim can go into life-threatening stages of shock.

Chuck is not so critically injured that this is a problem. But the rescuers sitting with him notice as he begins to lose his composure a little, as he begins to shake.

A male nurse hops out of the helicopter. He wears dark Ray-Bans, a blue jumpsuit, white surgical gloves. He is very pale. He carries a large black bag up through the flowers to Chuck. As he introduces himself he betrays an overly solicitous manner. He seems to have come from the how-may-I-help-you, thank-you-for-the-opportunity-to-be-of-service school of air ambulance nursing.

After a few questions and a cursory look at Chuck's legs, he stands up. "Well," he announces, as if he's offering a treat to a small child, "I think we're going to end your mountain adventure now."

Four men carry Chuck down to the helicopter and set him on the stretcher. In a few moments he is secure inside the machine. The pilot, a small, balding man with matching jumpsuit and glasses, isn't sure if he can take the weight of Chuck's forty-pound pack in the bird.

"Well, we can put it in and try it," he tells Kevin. "I'll take off and take a power check, and if it doesn't work you'll know, because we'll kick it out."

He turns to Debbie. "Where's the hospital?"

"Go down this valley and take a right, then go up the valley until you see the Prince of Peace Church," she says. "It's just past that."

As the pilot prepares to take off Judd trudges up the trail, looking green. He is an hour behind Josh and Kevin. He pushed so hard to keep up he has spent part of that time vomiting up a hamburger by the side of the path. He takes little interest in the proceedings at the landing zone. He staggers over to where the packs are piled, flops on his back, and begins nursing a water bottle.

The rotors wind up slowly, the flowers bend down again, the machine lifts gently into the air. The pilot hovers for a moment, checking his power. Then the aircraft pitches forward and spills down the hillside, gaining speed, arcing out over the trees. In a moment it is gone.

/\\ /\\

John Zell is beginning to unfold the stove again when word comes over the radio that another rescue may be getting under way. There's a report of a woman who has fallen and injured her head near Grizzly Lake, forty miles away.

"Don't let that helicopter get away," Chris Herrera says.

"I guess maybe I'm not cooking dinner," John says, disappointed again.

"I don't want to cook," Debbie says, shouldering her pack. "I'll eat a PowerBar. I want to hike out while it's light."

In a few moments she and Scott are gone with Chuck's climbing partner, Rick. Then Kevin, then John and Chris. In a matter of minutes the team is humping back down the trail. Marion and the third team are already turned around and hiking back out.

After a couple of miles the ache starts in the soles of my feet. Over the course of ninety minutes it seeps up into my calves, the back of my knees, my thighs, as high as my hip joints—a blunt, osmotic pain. Now there is nothing to do but put my head down and walk, and we do—Chris, John, and I—walking fast, the sooner to be done with it.

"I hate this part, because you think you're there, but you're not," John says. Even though the rescuers at Capitol Lake won't get out for hours and will have hiked thirteen hard miles by the time they reach the trailhead, even though they understand in their heads they probably will play no part in the Grizzly incident being handled by the balance of the team, they cannot bring themselves in their hearts to rest, to sit still while another rescue is under way. And so we hike out faster than we hiked in.

It is almost 9:00 P.M. We reach the old irrigation ditch trail. The path is nearly pitch black, thanks to clouds and the hillside of aspen trees, but we don't bother to use lights. The trail is smooth and flat and so we march by feel, an arm's length apart on the track. As we fatigue we start to lose our balance. The little trim-tab muscles that keep us upright are weak. When I look up for the moon I stagger. When Chris stutter-steps to scratch his calf we stumble into each other.

Finally we break into the clearing of the parking lot.

"Honey," John calls brightly. "I'm home!"

Dave Brown is there, waiting until everyone is out of the field. Scott and Debbie are waiting, too. John abandons his pack and eases up onto the open tailgate of Dave's red-and-white Ford pickup, eager to get the weight off his feet. Debbie appears out of the dark and begins unlacing John's boots and peeling off his socks.

"What is this?" John asks incredulously. "This is not the Debbie Kelly I know! Oh, my god, this feels great. This is fantastic!" John is moaning now, nearly orgasmic. "Oh my god! Oh, Debbie, I'll do anything for you!"

Debbie smiles softly in the dim glow of the truck's dome light. "We take care of each other," she says quietly, explanation enough. In a few minutes she is having her feet rubbed by John, her back by Scott.

A white Cherokee drives into the trailhead parking lot. Two men are inside: the victim, Chuck Pine, and his third climbing partner, coming back to pick up Rick, who has hiked out with Scott and Debbie.

"Oh, shit," Scott says to himself when he sees Chuck. "Did we really screw up?"

Scott and the others stand in the open door of the Jeep as Chuck explains why he has already been released from the hospital. The first rock, he says, hit no bone or cartilage in his right leg. The white object he removed was apparently a piece of fascia, a tough, fibrous muscle sheath. His left knee is too swollen to examine, but he'll go to see an orthopedist in the next few days. The helicopter, because it was an air ambulance, will be paid for by his insurance.

Everyone at the trailhead is happy for Chuck but quietly mortified. Chuck was not that badly injured. He could have been carried out.

⋀⋀ ⋀⋀

Steve Crockett puts the phone down and looks across the room at Van Kyzar, busy on the radio with the Grizzly rescue. He smirks.

"You know that guy that went to the hospital?"

"Yeah?"

"He just walked out."

"You're kidding."

"He walked out of the hospital." Steve isn't smiling now.

"You're kidding?"

"No. He walked right out of there."

"Oh, shit."

It's a real roller-coaster ride, and it's all driven by that information. We had information coming to us all through the course of the incident. It wasn't like he was out there, you guys go find him and then you get to him. And Van was in the same roller-coaster compartment that I was. We all were in the same little buggy going up and down the roller coaster. It went from, "This isn't going to need a helicopter evacuation," to "Yeah, man, it looks like this guy is in trouble," to "We got some more information, it isn't as bad as we thought." I would characterize it not as Van and I being pitted against each other—we were both in the same vacuum of information.

I brought forward the issue immediately—did you manipulate the information to do this? Got that issue out on the table, and we discussed it. He was as shocked by the outcome of it as we were.

—*Steve Crockett*

⋀ ⋀

Marion never even sees Chuck. As soon as he gets back to the trailhead the doctor drives to the hospital, but by the time he arrives Chuck has been treated and released. Marion lies on the couch in the front room of the Mountain Rescue cabin, staring at the ceiling, exhausted.

I was really bummed. For one, I hate being wrong. I was sitting there, really hard on myself. "Damn, it wasn't an open fracture." So I was pissed at myself about that. I kind of, in a certain sense, felt maybe I'd let the whole team down. I was worried about the politics of things, because next time if we really do need a helicopter for whatever reason, here it is, Marion's crying wolf again. I feel bad because of the political situation, and I feel bad because I'm letting that enter my judgment.

I somehow felt I let the team down, or the team was not going to be trusting my judgment again. I don't know why I do that. I'm very hard on myself when I'm wrong. I shouldn't even say "wrong" —when I'm not right. But looking back at this in hindsight again, would I do the same thing? Probably. When somebody says, "I pulled something out of the wound," I may question them about it. But I think I'll do the same thing again.

—*Marion Berg*

"OH, MY GOD," says Scott Messina, leaning back in his chair and rubbing his face with his hands. "I haven't eaten for two days."

He orders a huge plate of veggie lasagna and a side of mashed potatoes with gravy from Debbie Kelly, who phones the board's order to Little Annie's. Then Scott twists the cap off a bottle of Buffalo Gold beer as the meeting gets under way. Scott has been guiding for two weeks straight, returning to town only long enough to grab a shower and a new batch of clients every few days. The work has caught up to him. Until the food is delivered to the cabin he is tired to the point of being sullen.

When the brown paper bags arrive Scott eats ravenously as the others talk, wolfing down lasagna, rolls and butter, salad. Another six-pack makes the rounds of the meeting table. Scott leans back, his belly distended like a leprechaun's, a fresh beer in his hand.

"What's for dessert?" he asks, smiling.

Ron Bracken, new to the board, has been quiet. He has been appointed to the training officer's position held by Dave Lofland, who has left town for several months to help build a house in another county. Ron, a nondrinker, surveys the growing population of empty bottles at his first board meeting.

"Did you guys ask me to be on the board," he ventures, "just so I can drive you home?"

Scott responds by picking up a bottle cap and flipping it across the room with a snap of his fingers. The cap buzzes through the air and clatters into a locker at the far end. The food has changed Scott's personality. He sticks his thumbs under wide, red suspenders adorned with Mickey Mouse faces, stretches the elastic out to arm's length, and proclaims, "This ain't no fucking Mickey Mouse show here!" before dissolving into laughter.

Over the next three hours Scott fidgets constantly, snapping bottle caps across the room, getting up to collect them and doing it again, opening more bottles for everyone. At one point he opens the French doors and practices parade waves—cupped hand, rotating wrist—to the dark and empty alley. He snaps bottle caps down toward the Dumpster hidden in the darkness behind the building. He even thinks about lobbing his mashed potatoes, which he couldn't finish. But he doesn't.

The board drifts through the usual topics: fund-raising, budget balance, new equipment, upcoming trainings. Scott's good mood is dampened only by the perennial discussion of Steve Crockett and Bob Braudis and their latest demands upon the team. In the aftermath of Chuck Pine's rescue from Capitol Lake, Debbie and Scott spoke with Steve. They reassured him the team wasn't consciously trying to obtain a helicopter for a rescue where one wasn't considered medically necessary. Steve was mollified, and there is a sense on the board that everything turned out all right. But dealing with Steve will be a fact of life for the foreseeable future. More than worrying about the fate of victims now, the board seems preoccupied with learning to live with the sheriff and his

control of the team. It is a reality that can't be avoided.
It is almost universally depressing to team members.

⋀ ⋀

> What I think they've lost, if they've lost it, is the free-spirit personal-
> ity that makes a person leave his family and go volunteer, go do this.
> And if it continues the same way, there're going to be rescue unions,
> you're going to have to get paid, there're going to be certain required
> minimums of training like a fire department, and we—we as a whole
> community—we will have lost the flavor, clearly, and that extra
> sense of duty that we all brought to Mountain Rescue. It's still being
> brought at this time to Mountain Rescue, but if you stop and project
> ahead, and you're a sheriff's deputy and you do this, it's, "Hey, I'm
> not on today, it's Friday and I'm going to go play golf. It's not my
> job." Instead of saying, "How many guys do you have? Two? Shit, I'll
> be right there. I was going to go to a wedding and go play golf, but
> I'm not going to see Rick Deane and somebody else, just the two of
> them by themselves in a snowstorm, no, I'll be right there."
> You'll lose it. It'll be gone.
> —*Dick Arnold*

> The old ways are gone. Tradition is dying here. I don't like going
> around tradition. In my personal life I'm a cultural survivalist. But in
> my professional life, hey man, if I've got to kill it to get the job done,
> I'll kill it. The end justifies the means, because we work for the tax-
> payer out there.
> —*Steve Crockett*

Chris Myers once observed that you can't make a rescue what
you want it to be. That sentiment could encompass Mountain
Rescue work as a whole in the 1990s. Whatever the past was,
whatever the pains of change the present encompasses, the future is certain to be different for the team. As the summer of
1994 draws to a close, team members have come around to the
idea that things will change. What form that change will take,
when, and how drastically remain unknown. Not surprisingly,
such an evolution is causing a number of team members to re-
think their involvement. If the team is going to evolve, it is probably going to shed, too.

At Greg Mace's memorial service, David Swersky vowed to himself that he would do more for the team, that he would pick up the ball and carry on what Greg had done. He became a rescue leader and incorporated the disruption and uncertainty of rescue work into his life. When he is the 501 he doesn't know if he'll be home for dinner. He gets phone calls at strange hours. He has missed too many appointments and parties and more work than he can begin to remember. He stuck with it until a few years ago, when his two daughters were in high school. He decided to quit then; he wanted to spend more time with them. But when he told the girls of his decision they insisted he stay on. Mountain Rescue is important, they told their father. Keep doing it.

"I'm going to retire at some point," David says on a rainy afternoon, sitting in his office after a day of battling tooth decay and gum disease. "It's got too complicated. The bureaucracy has gotten oppressive—the amount of trainings, the amount of meetings. There were four or five trainings a year. Now it seems like there are four or five trainings a month.

"I could go up the Bells. I've climbed the Bells. I've climbed them all. But you don't want me banging around up there anymore. I'm almost fifty years old. There are young, strong people.

"Hopefully, the new people will be able to accept the new bureaucracy more," he continues. "We know we know our stuff. We have a great track record, and the implication is—this was verbalized directly by Crockett—'We don't trust you anymore.' They don't, and the reasons they don't trust us are so bogus, they have no bearing on reality. But that's what's come down. That's the way it is."

Insisting on safer behavior by rescuers, the sheriff seems to have caught himself and Mountain Rescue in an unreconcilable set of demands. Bob Braudis maintains that he and Steve have clamped down because they believe the team was operating unsafely. But he warns that if a rescue leader scrubs a mission, calls it off because it's too dangerous, then Bob will cease to use the team. It will have no raison d'être.

"It will be the last time Mountain Rescue's called," Bob says. "If Mountain Rescue is mutinous I will—I have to—find a non-mutinous resource in the rescue arena."

In 1992 Colorado voters amended the state's constitution to sharply limit the ability of local governments to raise taxes. Amendment 1 has had the practical effect of freezing government budgets at 1992 levels, which actually reduces spending power as inflation takes its annual bite. In Pitkin County, which has boomed for decades and continues to boom, sheriff's deputies are stretched to the limit just handling law enforcement calls and trying to keep up with all their mandated trainings. The sheriff's office consequently has no capacity to field two or three dozen people on a search or rescue, particularly one requiring technical rope work. Without the local volunteers, Bob readily admits, the sheriff's ability to help people in the backcountry would be sharply limited.

Pitkin County can't afford a paid rescue team—that much is agreed by everyone involved. Yet paid rescue seems to lie inevitably in the future. Every month sees new training requirements, new demands placed upon the volunteers. At some point, if the trend continues, the demands will become too much. Bob says he would like to see Mountain Rescue members trained to a high enough level in the Incident Command System to run their own missions. But it is difficult to imagine how many people will volunteer to take the 128-hour Incident Commander Course, plus long weekends for courses in planning, logistics, managing searches, operations, air operations, and every other box on the ICS management chart.

"You don't get paid to sit through trainings, you don't get paid to sit through meetings if you're a volunteer," Bob observes. "My staff does, and because of that, and because of the resources we have, you're going to see a chasm developing between the professionals and the volunteers."

"When we invest in training and equipment," adds Steve, "we need to do that with some assurance we are going to get a return on that investment. We can't do that with a volunteer group." The future, Steve says, will see more deputies taking over the management of incidents, controlling the team's actions in the field, making the critical decisions. They'll run the rescues because they'll know how. "Over the years this mysticism about Mountain Rescue-Aspen developed," Steve says. "You know, smoke and mirrors. Magic. The Mountain Rescue magic. Well, I think a lot of that is being dispelled. It really isn't as complex and complicated as perhaps the sheriff's department let itself be led to believe."

Since Bob again bestowed him with the "SAR czar" mantle, Steve has been thinking about a contract between the team and the sheriff's department. It will spell out training and proficiency requirements. It will sharply define what Mountain Rescue can do and what it can't. It will be Steve's final and definitive salvo in his effort to "de-autonomize" the team.

"The overall objective is de-autonomizing Mountain Rescue-Aspen," Steve says. "I don't think that's an admirable objective. It's unfortunate that we're faced with that.

"The battle over helicopters," he continues, "really isn't over helicopters. It's over autonomy. And the helicopter is the symptom of that. That's where we're going to draw the line in the sand, and we're going to make our stand over this. It's really over who works for whom and who gets the final say and how it's going to be. That's autonomy."

When asked about the future of Mountain Rescue-Aspen, the sheriff mentions money as the only constraint keeping him from going to a paid team. He believes that if he refuses to call Mountain Rescue and forms his own rescue team around a core of deputies, four out of five current rescue volunteers will join up. They are the ground-pounders, he says, the people who want to go out in the storm, walk fast, carry heavy loads, help someone, and go home. Declare a team, Bob says, and they'll come.

It's hard to imagine volunteers growing enthused about a job like that. Where is the joy in volunteering for a team in which the core is comprised of paid personnel? What real responsibility will a volunteer ever get out of that, what ability to learn and to grow, if the decisions and the authority rest with the people on payroll? It would be like taking a post as an intern—or a Sherpa. The characteristic that makes the forty-five people in Mountain Rescue-Aspen's roster function as a team is the sense that everyone is on a level playing field. Rick Deane owns a ranch. Marion Berg has a doctor's sheepskin. Debbie Kelly is a woman in a world dominated by men. Scott Messina is president of the board. But all of them stuff ropes back into their bags, clean the cabin, wash the truck, fill out the paperwork, work at the fund-raisers, carry the litter, debate the decisions, vote at the meetings.

/\\ /\\

Chris Myers returns from three weeks in Hawaii newly wed and seemingly rejuvenated. The gash he sustained on his leg has healed, and the time away from home with his bride has been good for his soul. Within a few days of his return he is on 501 duty. Between a Saturday morning and a Tuesday night he spends twenty hours managing a pair of rescues, and his new-found energy quickly dissipates.

"I can't take this," he says. "I can't take being jerked away from whatever I'm involved in. It used to be easier when I was single, and maybe just a little bit younger. It's not hard on the body—it's just harder on the mind."

He had considered taking a leave from the team before getting married but decided against it. When he fell during the rescue of John Wallack, cutting his leg, "it was just a little reminder that, hey, I am mortal, and even on a mission in territory where you feel comfortable and you've been in hundreds of times, it can bite. And that's why you're in Mountain Rescue, because it can bite hard sometimes.

"So I'm stuck right now," he says, swinging his hand like a pendulum over his beer. "I'm right here, swinging back and forth, because it's harder to drop everything and give it your all—and you need to give it your all when you're there."

Chris tells in great detail a story about a recent sidewalk encounter with a team member who quit several years ago.

This volunteer felt terrible because so many times, when the pager went off, he was busy at work and unable to get away, unable to respond and carry his fair share for the teammates who were depending on him. When he did go on a rescue, he tells Chris, he felt he was letting down the people in his office. Every time the pager sang, he was conflicted, and he couldn't win. In the end, he gave up volunteer work in favor of his livelihood.

The story clearly has settled upon Chris.

/\\ /\\

"I love the organization," says Tom McCabe. "Whether I'm dead or alive the organization goes forward, and things will change from time to time, some of which I won't be able to tolerate. I either have to make an accommodation or I have to go away."

The dissolution of Tom's marriage to Jody has had a profound, almost calming effect on him. He evinces a sort of relief, as if the inevitable, now here, is no longer to be feared, only managed. In the turmoil of his divorce he has come to realize that he needs to devote more time and energy to his daughter, Merrin. That fact, combined with the slights and frustration that drove him to pull back from the team a year earlier, have had a salubrious effect on Tom's perspective about Mountain Rescue. He has given himself distance and a lower profile, put his involvement on a sustainable simmer and tried to step back from the day-to-day irritations.

"You get so aggravated you stop thinking," Tom says reflectively. "I've been in that place frequently enough that I can cop to being guilty about saying lots of things that at the moment felt good to say, but were venting more than they were a constructive look at what the organization needs to do in the future.

"I've been trying to get back and say, 'What am I really about, what are the big issues?' Not 'What are my issues personally?' but 'What's the job we're trying to do and why are we trying to do it?' If there's any truth about what we're trying to do for the community and the service we're trying to provide, then I've got to be able to recognize my own shit and try to put it aside, or at least manage it.

"The reason you're there—take away those selfish reasons that are good for you personally—and when you look back at it, you're doing this for the community. You're doing it because the people that get in trouble in the backcountry are the same kind of people you are. If they've taken the trouble to go backpacking or rock climbing or something else, then at some level they're the kind of people you'd like to be around, more than somebody smoking a cigarette, sitting in a bingo hall drinking a beer. And you hope that perhaps if you're ever in that position that level of expertise will be there for you."

Tom remains aggravated by Steve and his manipulations, the way Steve personalizes problems in the team and denigrates individuals. But, despite his reputation as a mossback, Tom has done something unexpected: he has changed. In the late summer he spends a lot of time talking to Bob, and he comes around to a much more sympathetic understanding of the sheriff's point of view. Part of that derives from the fact that Tom has decided he'd like to be a deputy—for the opportunity to learn and to be challenged, he says. He has applied for a job under Bob. But Tom is smart enough to recognize and step back from that conflict of interest, and putting it aside, he has, simply, mellowed. He is quietly working his way into a wise old man's role on the team. He is even willing to try to help Steve succeed.

"He's a cramp in the ass," Tom says. "He's making me nuts, but I've kind of understood where that comes from in my own personality. I don't think he's worthless. I don't think too many people are worthless. It's just having the patience and the ability to put up with him when he's being such an asshole to other people.

"If you help them [people like Steve], perhaps they will be more effective sooner than if you hinder them or just stand back and let them fall on their nose," he continues, "and I'm beginning to think I can do that with Crockett. I don't know how proactive I'll be. I don't think that I'll help him fail. I used to preach that I would."

Tom's conversion, as it were, is not complete. He promises to fight for the team's interests, to drag his heels occasionally. But he seems to have adopted the attitude of joining if you're not winning, of trying to manage change from a moderately cooperative rather than a wholly confrontational stance. For all that, he still thinks a paid rescue team lies somewhere in the future— maybe in five years, maybe in fifteen. The bureaucrats will see to that, he says. They feed upon each other, beating the relatively simple task of rescue work into increasingly complex shapes. If Bob retires and a sheriff with a more hands-off management style, a sheriff less worried about liability, comes into office, that eventuality may be postponed. Tom doesn't think he can alter the trend, and he doesn't worry about it. On the verge of his fifti-eth birthday, newly single and possibly facing a career change, he realizes that trying to carve a new place for himself on the team takes all the energy he has left.

> If anybody bothers to listen to me, and anybody bothers to ask my opinion, perhaps as time goes on, instead of them reinventing the wheel, perhaps I can give them a little jump on that. Because Scott and Debbie and some of those people on the board are pretty politi-cally naive. They're learning. They're smart people. It doesn't take them too long to look closer. But I think, like me, they're by and large autonomous people who have done their own things and they work under their own guidelines and they're not used to dealing with a real structured organization. They're very free spirits.
>
> It's a luxury, but it's somewhat enjoyable to watch new people struggle with these things. It's fun to watch Debbie and watch smoke come out of her ears. It's fun to watch Scott go around in little circles and bounce into the wall. I can sit back and think, "I've been there." I've been there and I know those frustrations, but I also know these people can do it. There's nothing more true than doing it yourself and getting the answers. Perhaps I can save them some grief, per-haps I can give them some perspective, some opinion, some history that might make it easier for them. But ultimately it's up to them whether to take that advice or not.
>
> —*Tom McCabe*

⋀ ⋀

John Zell gets characteristically emotional about the future of the team. "I love being on the team and being a mountaineering guide," he says. "It's just all associated. It's just a natural thing for me to be on the team. It feels like what I'm supposed to be doing, what I want to be doing, what I should be doing. I just hope it doesn't change so drastically we can't do what we do best."

In a trend infuriating to John, the spring and summer of 1994 see increasing involvement of the valley's fire departments in rescue work. Under Steve's aegis the departments in Aspen, Basalt, and Carbondale begin to train for water rescue and high-angle rescue. Aspen firefighters hire a guide and begin to take classes in rock climbing.

"We are the most respected rescue team in the United States. We are one of the best Mountain Rescue teams in the United States," John says emphatically. "We have to listen to these rumors that are stupid, that we're being phased out by the fire departments—which to me is ridiculous because they fight fires. They're not trained to do rescues in the backcountry.

"It scares me, because Bob has more confidence in them than he does with us," John says. "It upsets me. It really upsets me that we're going to lose the respect that we have."

That respect, that goodwill, is valuable capital. It's one of the reasons the sheriff is gracious to Mountain Rescue in public. It is Mountain Rescue's ace in the hole if the team ever has to go to the mat with the sheriff. Despite the budding détente in the summer of 1994 between Mountain Rescue and the sheriff's office, team members believe that if something truly bad happens, if a victim dies because of a bad decision made by the sheriff's office, the team's good standing in the public eye will allow it to prevail in a public battle. It is a belief unproven, a belief perhaps naive, a belief only rarely spoken. It is a belief no one wants to test.

The power of the team's reputation is visible at every monthly meeting, in the new, curious faces in the back of the room. Even as the veterans bemoan the politics and consider giving up something they love, new volunteers sniff shyly around the edges, wondering whether this is for them. They are drawn for different reasons—curiosity, a penchant for action and drama, a desire to be part of something solid in a town that seems too transient.

Josh Landis began attending meetings at the end of 1993. After a summer of rescues he has a different understanding of what Mountain Rescue is about—it's not the "nonstop excitement" he expected. Like so many who come to 630 West Main and stay awhile, he has found the people to be as interesting as the work.

"There seem to be more of the longtimers here, people who care about a lot more than just making a buck," says Josh, who dropped out of the University of Colorado to move to Aspen. "They seem like a bunch of real people, they've chosen this for

their home and want to contribute to it, and they're just real un-
selfish with their time and energy."

A Colorado native, Josh is nauseated by the conspicuous consumption and big-volume tourism of Aspen. He is drawn by the
grounding the team has given him in the community, by the opportunity to learn and to contribute. Strong, fast, willing, he has
been earning the acceptance of veteran members as the months
have passed. He's not jaded by the politics. He's not worried
about whether the sheriff's office will take over the team. He's
simply trying to get his feet under him, buy his equipment, learn
his knots.

"I didn't really think about how much time I would be putting
into it," he says. "Time and money. But I figure the time and
money would pretty much balance out with the rewards of doing
something positive, the training I get through Mountain Rescue
and all of that. I was making good money when I got on the
team, and I wasn't really liking what I was doing. So I figured at
least I was putting the money into something that was worth
doing."

/\\ /\\

"I really don't know if I want to commit the time for another
year," Scott says, nursing a cup of coffee on an early September
morning, "but I feel I probably should, and I probably will."

It's been a year since Scott first got serious about the idea of
running for the post once held by Greg Mace. He's needed most
of his first term to grow comfortable in the president's job, and
he doesn't want to waste that education. He's forged fragile ties
with Steve and Bob, and in his quiet way he intends to shoulder
the burden of nurturing those ties because he doesn't want to
ask anybody else to do it. He admits the fact only grudgingly, but
he knows Steve can be good at his job. He also knows Steve is
going to be with the team for the foreseeable future. Steve has
succeeded in creating a position for himself with Bob, and that
means the team will have to live with him. Like the others, Scott
knows a trend when he sees one.

"Paid people? I hope not," he says. "You know, I see it going
that way, probably. I could see probably one person on our team

getting paid. I don't want it to be me—I don't believe in it. I believe in giving to the community, but the demands, the increasing time commitment—we can only give what we can give. There's times when you can't give it all.

"I don't want the responsibility of being on a paid team," he continues. "Then you're more committed to it, then there's more responsibility to respond and be involved. You can't make the call and say, 'No, I'm not going out.' I can see it, with the reduction of helicopter use, with the shitty rock we have on Castle and the Bells or any of those, if we ever have to deal with a technical rescue on them, there may be a point that we say no. And I think if we're paid we're going to be pushed harder.

"I want to be able to give. It's something unique about this community here—small town, six thousand, eight thousand people—and a good, hard core of forty-five people that are willing to give their time. But I think it's going to go the way of the fire department, with a paid chief."

Although he's never talked to Bob Zook about being paid, Scott echoes Bob's sentiments. Bob worked as a paid member of the Yosemite National Park rescue team, and he didn't like it.

"It's a lot harder to get out of situations you don't feel comfortable in, in a paid rescue environment," says Bob. "I like to be absolutely clear-conscienced when I do a rescue. I want to be doing it for my own reasons, and not have that money in there clouding things up."

⋀ ⋀

The American West will never be what it was. Indeed, it never was what we think it was. It has been mythologized since the first fur trappers began exploring its hidden valleys and high peaks, returning with tales of great wealth embodied in the land. The open spaces of the West have become part of the American psyche. They are the physical embodiment of the chance to start anew, to be wild and free. The realities of the West—its conflict and heartbreak, its history as a resource colony and a sponge for federal subsidy—pale in the face of the perception. Even as the Rockies shudder beneath change in the late twentieth century they are yet burdened by myth, and every season saddled with a new crop of dreamers, immigrants, and adventurers who come to Colorado to find something, to start over, to change, to explore, to challenge themselves.

There is no wilderness here anymore, no place where you can't reach a road in a day or two of walking, no place without satellites and contrails overhead. It is possible to stand on the summit of the Maroon Bells and make a call on your cell phone. Wilderness isn't a place now, it's a decision—a decision harder to enforce in the face of the crowds who take to the woods each falling season.

With the disappearance of wilderness the original ethic of Mountain Rescue-Aspen is vanishing, too. Cell phones and personal injury lawyers, risk managers, and insurance waivers are the new realities of rescue work. A good knowledge of the mountains and a strong back are no longer enough. The 1990s seem, by all accounts, to be the twilight years of the volunteer team. Such a development should come as no surprise, for the valleys of Colorado, especially those around the big resorts, are fast acquiring urban characteristics. Volunteering for the community good is a relic of small-town America, a Norman Rockwell value we praise even as we mourn its vanishing.

Aspen has grown to the point where tourists complain in letters to the editor about the noise of traffic keeping them awake, and there is no sign of this onetime mining camp shrinking back to small-town status. Mountain Rescue-Aspen, at least in its original form, likely will be a casualty of these forces that take their toll on the land, the community, and the valley's collective soul. What has mattered to this team for forty years has been its ability to work together to get the job done, to be a team. The most valuable thing Mountain Rescue-Aspen possesses is also its most ineffable: its sense of being one, of being a team of people who wanted to do the job, not people paid to do it. Given the chance to profit from their work—whether by selling movie rights or taking a little cash for finding a trio of lost dogs—team members consistently choose not to. That is what the New West, the demands of the modern world, will kill if the reality predicted by Bob Braudis comes to pass.

It won't be the sheriff's fault. He is reacting to the demands of a larger society, a world that expects its wilderness to be tame. The decades-old social compact between mountaineers and mountain towns isn't shared by new arrivals from the world's cities and suburbs. The great majority of people moving to Pitkin County, Colorado—most probably to all the Rockies—have neither the time nor the inclination to learn the ways of mountains. The same people who demand twenty-four-hour room service in Aspen's once-funky hotels expect to be helped out of the woods sooner, and more competently, than did visitors a generation ago.

"Everything we do is fodder for a lawsuit," Bob Braudis laments. "I don't like it. I don't know what went wrong with our country."

"This is no fun," says Steve Crockett of his efforts to bring Mountain Rescue-Aspen tightly under the sheriff's hand. "Doing this stuff is no fun. That institution, it has great culture over there. I hate to see it go. But professionally, it has to go."

The irony of the emerging situation is that someone may die as a result of all the sheriff's efforts to avoid being sued. What is being beaten out of the Aspen rescue team is the ability to operate, as Dick Arnold described it, with "one foot over in the shaky, crumbling rock." No longer will rescuers be able to put themselves at obvious risk to save someone else's life. Rescue work, inherently dangerous, is now to be made safer, at least in the sheriff's mind. The threat to Pitkin County's coffers and the sheriff's wallet if something goes wrong is too great not to undertake such a safety effort. Bob and Steve will try to diminish the risk of a great catastrophe. That means more hiking and less flying, which translates into longer response and evacuation times, which mean a greater risk of a victim dying on the mountain. No longer will volunteers be leaping out of hovering helicopters onto windswept ridges. Instead there will be more carryouts, more difficult technical lowerings. The chance of a fiery, catastrophic—and newsworthy—accident will be reduced. The likelihood of smaller catastrophes, of rescuers breaking legs, twisting ankles, and dislocating knees, will be much greater. That is the choice

Bob and Steve have made, and that is the one they intend to stick with—even if victims die.

"The books don't always work up here," says Scott, referring to Steve's by-the-book approach, "especially when somebody's life is at stake. He's going to make a call someday and, unfortunately, the call's going to be made 'no helicopter,' and somebody's going to die on us. Somebody's going to crunch, I'm afraid."

"Let's put it this way," Bob says. "If I'm the sheriff in ten years, hopefully everyone who is a member of Mountain Rescue-Aspen will share my values that just because you're a volunteer doesn't mean you shouldn't fly with the safest helicopter pilot. The cost may be a grand an hour as opposed to six hundred an hour, and maybe someone's going to have to die while waiting for that helicopter before I put you in a thirty-year-old Huey."

∧∧ ∧∧

Particularly the people who don't have a sense of volunteerism, they don't understand it. "Why do you do it? It's got nothing to do with your job." It's who you are. It's not a job. I don't get paid for it. It costs me a lot of time and energy. But if you don't do that, you don't understand. There are people who go through periods where getting their lawn watered is good enough reason to come in [to the office] at eleven o'clock in the morning. But God forbid you spend those same three hours doing something for somebody else.

It's just weird. People don't understand it. Fuck 'em.
—*Ray Peritz*

Julie Geng, twenty-seven years old and visiting from Boulder, is close to the summit of Castle Peak when she and Bob Weiss wander from the faint trail high above the timberline. Trying to scramble up a small rock outcropping, Julie loses her footing and tumbles down a steep scree slope. When she comes to a stop a hundred feet later she has a broken ankle, chipped teeth, cuts all over her face and head.

Ron Bracken, Judd Anders, and Van Kyzar are headed toward Moon Lake, preparing for a summit attempt on Capitol Peak, when they hear the page. They call Bob Zook, the 502, on Van's radio. "It sounds like it's pretty close to the road," Bob says. "I think we've got it covered. You guys go ahead. Have a good climb."

Chris Myers, the 501, meets Steve Crockett in the basement of the courthouse. Tom McCabe, shopping for school clothes with Merrin, hears the call but elects to spend the day with his daughter. Scott Messina, preparing for a long trip he is to begin guiding the next day, also hears the page but has work to do, and doesn't respond.

John Zell takes the wheel of Rescue 1 for the better part of an hour, slamming the truck up the tortuous, improbable track to Montezuma Basin, a rocky, twelve-thousand-foot-high bowl immediately east of Castle Peak. Coming upon a Jeep parked in the narrow road, John turns to his passengers, Ray and Vicki Chavka. "I'm pushing this fucking thing off the road!" he warns. He's wired and he wants to be there. Now.

"You can't do that," Ray says. "You can't do that."

John eventually negotiates past the Jeep to the end of the road, a flat spot amid a giant bathtub of broken rock. Kevin Hagerty arrives at the same time on his dirt bike.

The reports coming from Julie's climbing partner and other climbers descending the peak are confusing but very, very bad. Julie is said to have lost teeth. One side of her head is swelling. She's nauseous and hypothermic. Her pupils are dilated unevenly. These are the signs of a severe head injury. Worse, Julie is not near the road, as Bob had thought. She lies just off the summit at 13,900 feet. The air is cold and damp, threatening heavy rain. Julie's location cannot be seen from where the four rescuers stand.

Flint Smith, the paramedic who was with Greg Mace the day he died, is hiking in the area. John enlists his help. At one o'clock—three hours after Julie's fall—the four men start up the rocky ridge toward Castle's summit, moving as fast as they can. They leave Vicki at the truck to relay radio traffic. An hour later Debbie, Carl Ellerbrook, and Alex Irvin, having arrived in Rescue 2, follow the first team. Debbie scouts for helicopter landing zones as she goes. Thunderstorms circle the peak as the second team struggles up the south ridge toward the summit. They bear a litter, ropes, a brake system.

We need more people, Debbie radios. We need a lot more people. A second page is sent out. Van Kyzar and Ron Bracken are too deep in the West Snowmass Creek Valley to hear it. Their pagers remain silent.

When Ray and John reach Julie she is smiling. Her pupils are normal. She's not nauseous. Her situation is bad, but not as bad as John thought. He calms down a little. John and Flint examine a gash on her head. She may have a skull fracture, they agree. They can't tell. An X ray that night will prove their hunch correct.

Ray ponders how to lower her down as John and Flint bandage Julie's head and splint her ankle. Everyone tries not to slide down the loose scree that shifts and rumbles with each move. The second team arrives, and Carl sets the steel Stokes litter down. Debbie rips the wrapper off a PowerBar and begins eating. Alex unlimbers the climbing rack—fifteen pounds of rock-climbing equipment—and places a series of camming devices in the cracks of a nearby rock outcropping. These will be the anchors for the lowering system. As force is exerted on the anchor system the cams spread against the sides of the crack, gripping it. Not as good an anchor as the team would like, but the only one they've got.

The air is cold, forty-five degrees. If rain comes there is no place to hide and a serious risk of Julie becoming hypothermic. Julie's condition is stable for now, John radios to Chris. That means no helicopter, Steve says from his post next to Chris. "This is hell," Chris argues, showing Steve a photograph of the mountain's east face. "It may be only a half-mile carry, but it's hell." Steve holds firm: If she isn't likely to die on the carryout, she's going to be carried out. At three o'clock Marion leaves the cabin and drives to the trailhead with a pack full of drugs.

Several recreational climbers have stayed with Julie. Debbie wants to use them to help get her down. She'd like to have several dozen Mountain Rescue members to alternate carrying the litter, and she doesn't have nearly that many. "We need to *move* on this mission," she snaps into the radio. The sheriff's deputies in the courthouse don't like it, but they agree: Use the other climbers if you have to. Scott, who has been listening on his radio, can't stay away any longer. He comes by the cabin and prepares to haul more equipment to the staging area.

Clipping his harness and his fate into the litter, leaning down the slope, John doesn't ask Ray or Alex how solid the anchors are. The question does not arise in his mind.

It is almost five o'clock when the litter team starts down the fifty-degree slope of the couloir. Below them lie nine hundred feet of loose scree and head-size boulders. The rocks are sharp and many edged. They shift with every step. There are no other anchors on the way down the gully, only loose rocks. Underneath the plastic litter shield covering her gauze-wrapped head, Julie hums Christmas carols. As long as she hums, John, walking beside her, knows she is all right.

The litter has to be lowered the full distance off the lone anchor Alex has built. Ray must tie ropes together with a knot called a triple fishermen's and pass it through the brake. As the rope gets longer the friction of it across the rocks in the couloir grows, and the litter team strains against it, pulling the litter downhill. The rope expands and contracts like a rubber band. The jostling takes its toll on Julie. She keeps humming, but she is in a lot of pain.

"The worst part was those triple fishermen's," Ray says. "I mean, I tied them three times over, just to make sure they were right. I was going to tie that knot and hang seven people on it. My armpits were streaming."

It was a bitch—it was a bitch! We'd be going down, stretching the rope, and we felt like they weren't letting it out steady. All of a sudden we'd go flying back up the hill, and we'd fall on top of the patient. She'd be screaming. We were scrambling. The boulders were about a foot [across], and it was really, really treacherous. The guy behind me, he kept getting nailed by boulders that I'd step on and they'd fall onto his shins. It was really, really bad.

We had Carl in the back, he was pulling with all his might. He was just, "Arrgh, arrgh." You could hear him in the back. And whenever we'd spring back up, the guys at the bottom of the litter would fall on her ankle, and she'd be crying.

—*John Zell*

Two hours later the team is off the steep slope but still nearly a thousand feet above the vehicles at the end of the road. Rick Deane and Marion hike up to meet the litter team. Marion feeds morphine into Julie's veins. He wraps a blood-pressure cuff around an IV fluid bag and pumps the cuff up to force the liquid into Julie's arm.

As the gray day drifts into night the team unclips the litter from the rope and begins to carry. Time and again the volunteers fall under the litter or stumble in the sharp rock. Slowly, laboriously, as the skies spit rain, the team drags the injured climber over old snow and crumbling rock, away from the peaks that scrape the heavens, down toward the waiting ambulance and the valleys of man.

EPILOGUE

THE STORY of Mountain Rescue-Aspen is an ongoing one. In February of 1995, five months after this manuscript was completed, a young man named Doug Hamilton was killed in an avalanche in Conundrum Creek. Some Mountain Rescue-Aspen members, displeased with the way the sheriff's office managed the body recovery, criticized Steve Crockett publicly for the first time. The result was what Henry Kissinger might call a chrysalis of rapprochement: a good-faith attempt by Sheriff Braudis to listen to Mountain Rescue's concerns about Steve and the way he runs search-and-rescue missions, in exchange for a promise from Mountain Rescue to try to work with the sheriff and his staff rather than against them.

The lives of individuals have gone on, too. From late fall of 1994 to early spring of 1995, the following happened:

Pitkin County Sheriff *Bob Braudis* ran unopposed and was elected to a third four-year term.

Following the election *Steve Crockett* added several rooftop antennae and an official Pitkin County seal to his white sheriff's department Jeep Cherokee.

Tom McCabe was not hired as a sheriff's deputy. His divorce moved toward completion.

Chris Myers announced in October that he would take a two-month leave of absence from the team and probably resign in 1995. On January 1 he went to noncurrent status, remaining on the team roster but inactive as a member.

Scott Messina reluctantly ran for a second term as president, explaining he didn't want to waste the experience he had gained from his first year. He was unopposed.

Linda Koones stepped down from the board of directors.

Debbie Kelly was elected in Linda's stead as the team's treasurer. She began guiding backcountry ski trips for Scott, whose business was growing.

Dave Lofland returned to Aspen and rejoined the team's board of directors.

Mariela Zell became pregnant with her first child, which she was due to deliver in September.

John Zell began thinking about "getting a real job."

Ron Bracken moved with his girlfriend, Terri, to Fort Myers, Florida, in order to go to nursing school. He promised to return to Aspen, and to the team, in June.

Dave Brown took his first shift as a 501 in early December and directed the rescue of several lost or overdue snowmobilers.

Dr. Jon Gibans climbed the eight-thousand-meter peak Gasherbum II in Pakistan.

Dr. Marion Berg became a respectable snowboarder on the slopes and a pool shark after dark, winning cash at the local billiard tables.

Kevin Hagerty grew a thick, blond beard and spent much of his ski patrol job at Aspen Highlands ski area controlling the avalanche hazards in Highlands Bowl.

Carl Ellerbrook attended night school in order to become an Emergency Medical Technician.

Alex Irvin went mountain climbing in Peru and Ecuador. He subsequently sold some of his photographs to the *New York Times*'s travel section.

Ray Peritz changed jobs, forgoing hotel deals in favor of selling security systems.

Jace Michael spent several months traveling in Thailand.

Van Kyzar, as 501, managed the Mountain Rescue response on Doug Hamilton's body recovery.

Bob Zook traveled to Russia to work on telecommunications equipment deals.

David Swersky—along with nearly twenty rescue team members and 377 other people—completed the annual America's Uphill race *up* Aspen Mountain ski area. He continued to take his 501 shifts and said no more about leaving the team.

Rick Deane bought the Unimog from the team, which replaced it with a faster but much less distinctive—and more cramped—red Toyota 4runner.